D1611289

From Turmoil to Triumph

New Life After Mergers, Acquisitions, and Downsizing

Mitchell Lee Marks

LEXINGTON BOOKS
An Imprint of Macmillan, Inc.
NEW YORK

Maxwell Macmillan Canada
TORONTO

Maxwell Macmillan International
NEW YORK   OXFORD   SINGAPORE   SYDNEY

Library of Congress Cataloging-in-Publication Data

Marks, Mitchell Lee.
From turmoil to triumph : new life after mergers, acquisitions, and downsizing / Mitchell
Lee Marks.
p.   cm.
ISBN 0-02-920055-5
1. Organizational change—Management. 2. Personnel management.
I. Title.
HD58.8.M2653   1994   94-4758
658.4'06—dc20   CIP

Lexington Books
An Imprint of Macmillan, Inc.
866 Third Avenue, New York, N.Y. 10022

Maxwell Macmillan Canada, Inc.
1200 Eglinton Avenue East
Suite 200
Don Mills, Ontario, M3C 3N1

Macmillan, Inc. is part of the Maxwell Communication Group of Companies

Printed in the United States of America

printing number
1 2 3 4 5 6 7 8 9 10

To Mario and David,

who triumphed over their turmoil.

Contents

Preface

Just as we were getting up from the table after a lunch interview, a magazine columnist tossed out one last question to me: Did I think there had been much change in the field of organizational development over the past ten years? I thought for a while and replied that there really was very little new in the "technology" of organizational change and development. The basic approaches and values that have guided the field for several years remain as the ones underlying the strategies and tactics changing and enhancing organizations and their members today.

Then, slightly compelled to say something more substantive, I added, "If anything is different, it is the increasing recognition that people in organizations have been saturated with change and transition in the last few years and that some formal effort has to be made to help people let go of the pain of the past before they can move on to accept subsequent changes."

Leaving the restaurant, it struck me that this was no mere afterthought. Nearly every corporation has gone through a major change or transition in the 1980s and 1990s, be it a merger, acquisition, downsizing, restructuring, reengineering, leadership succession, or culture change. Most, in fact, have experienced several transitions, often overlapping one another. These events have not just changed the structure and style, policies and practices of organizations, they have had a profound impact on the people who spend their working lives in these organizations. And, it has been a mostly negative impact, as employees over the past several years have watched their co-workers get laid off, their career paths and aspirations evaporate, their cynicism increase, and their faith in their leadership diminish. The survivors of these transitions see themselves working harder for fewer rewards. Some even envy their former co-workers who lost their jobs: "At least they can get on with their lives," points out a manager from a firm engaged in four waves of downsizing in six years.

What concerns these employees most is that they see no end in sight to the parade of transitions, and they feel they have no power to avert any subsequent impact. Yet, there can be no doubt that organizations must continue to change to remain competitive. To be sure, as technological advances, global competition, and other factors conspire to turn up the pressure on profit-seeking organizations, the pace of change in the workplace is only going to increase. But, how much transition and disruption can people handle in their work lives? What are the limits of dealing with changes in ownership, structure, culture, work procedures, and reporting relationships before people throw their arms up in the air say "no more!" Or, as one manager in a company that was acquired by a foreign firm, rightsized, restructured and reengineered all in the period of three years put it, "When is our leadership going to recognize that people's bodies are showing up at work, but their minds were left at home a long time ago?"

Organizational leaders have gone through their own painful transitions along with their work forces. Yet, many senior executives have put the past behind and are looking forward to emerging business opportunities. Buoyed by improving economic conditions, they are optimistic that the worst of times are over and they have their sights set on new challenges and great opportunities. Spend time with middle managers and other employees who represent the heart and soul and the mind and muscle of work organizations, however, and you will find that they remain sore and angry over treatment they and their co-workers experienced over the past several years during turbulent times of transition. They are holding onto their experiences and perceptions of the past, and are neither ready nor willing to heed their leadership's call to charge ahead and capture new business opportunities.

This book is about the unintended impact of organizational transitions and what can be done to overcome the pain of the past so that people can give their full attention and effort to current and emerging business opportunities. It describes exactly how mergers, acquisitions, downsizings, reengineerings, and other transitions are debilitating to employees and organizations, and documents the negative psychological, behavioral, and business consequences of living through transition. Next, it shows how to help employees, teams, and business units recover from transition in a way that builds a new and better organization. This book describes how leading organizations successfully use transition as an opportunity for organizational renewal. They have transformed the turmoil of transition into the triumph of positive change by acknowledging the unintended consequences of transition, helping people let go of their attachments to and anger about the past, and, then, getting employees to understand the new realities of life after transition and align their work behaviors with the objectives of the posttransition organization. In short, this book shows how to rebuild employee spirit, team performance, and organizational systems following transition.

This book is written for a wide variety of audiences. Senior executives and middle managers who identify with one of three situations will find this book of great interest and practical assistance: those who acknowledge they have a work force bruised and battered by transition and recognize they have a job to do in rebuilding their organization and employee ranks following transition; those who see an improving business situation but have been frustrated by the disappointing results of efforts to rally employees to capitalize on opportunities in a strengthening economy; and those who are about to set out on a merger, downsizing, restructuring, reengineering or other transition and want to learn from the experiences of other executives and managers before them. This book will also be helpful to internal change agents, human resources professionals, and external consultants working in or with organizations during or following a period of transition. People who study organizations and the behavior in them will gain insight from reports of the experiences of employees and executives who have lived through turbulent times of change and disruption and of the applied efforts to help individuals, teams, and organizations recover after transition. And, this book will be of keen interest to the many managers and employees who have lived through the turmoil of transition—it will affirm that their pain and anxiety are legitimate reactions, yet offer hope by showing how to triumph over the turmoil by taking control over one's work situation and contributing to both personal and organizational success.

A substantial portion of this book was prepared while I was with William M. Mercer, Incorporated. I very much appreciate the support provided by senior management throughout my tenure there. Especially, however, I am indebted to the many consultants at Mercer who both deepened my understanding of organizational issues and were a pleasure to have as colleagues. Roger D'Aprix, Peter Lawton, Bob Dods, Marcia Inch, and Dave Kieffer are among the consultants with whom I learned about organizational transition and enjoyed working.

I am grateful for the support of David Nadler and the full team at the Delta Consulting Group. Although only at Delta for a short time, I am inspired by my colleagues' combination of keen insight into organizational life and friendliness and fun with which they approach their work.

Philip Mirvis has been a companion for several years through various journeys into corporate life. My understanding of organizations and the people who work in them is greatly enhanced by the opportunity to collaborate with such a skillful researcher. Even if I had learned nothing from working closely with Phil, which hardly is the case, it would have been time well spent for the humor and playfulness he brings to living life.

Many people contributed long, hard hours to the preparation of this manuscript. Among them are Heidi Hess, who made a tremendous contribution in many ways, and Lucy Dubin who provided significant research assistance. Debbie Schwartz and the operations staff at Delta Consulting Group, headed by Annie Matta, teamed together to assist in the final preparation. This book has benefitted greatly from the team at Lexington Books who worked with me throughout the process. I am especially obliged to Beth Anderson, who brought considerable skill and charm in her role as editor. And, I appreciate the guidance and effort of production editor Carol Mayhew and publicist Diane Wright.

Finally, this book is made possible by the hundreds of men and women from dozens of organizations who shared with me their experiences of living through and recovering from transition. They confessed their angst and described their feelings and actions as the very foundation of their work security, career aspirations, and organizational identity was dissolving beneath them. They also, however, spoke genuinely of their hopes for the future, foremost their wish to recommit their energies toward contributing to work organizations of which they once again could be proud members.

Part 1

Transition

1

Organizational MADness

I want to call your attention to the positive changes occurring in work organizations today. Boosted by a strengthening economy following the recession of the late 1980s and early 1990s, executives are optimistic about enhancing both short-term business results and long-term competitiveness. This confidence sparks, for example, increases in capital investments to take advantage of emerging business opportunities. The tangible results already realized from recent major changes in organizational architecture also buoy executives' spirits. Some firms have downsized, yielding leaner and more agile corporations, and others have restructured to shed bureaucratic layers. Still others have radically altered their business processes through reengineering studies that unleash innovation and discard nonessential work activities. In many organizations, culture change efforts have taken aim at strengthening commitment to total quality and raising standards of customer focus and service. And technological advances have made possible previously unimaginable savings in production time and costs.

Similarly exciting changes are taking hold in the environment in which corporations operate. Vast new markets are opening or becoming more accessible in areas as diverse as eastern Europe, the People's Republic of China, and Latin America. In the United States, the federal budget deficit is being attacked with unprecedented seriousness. Across national borders, trade barriers are tumbling down. Moreover, corporate alliances are accelerating at an exponential rate the research, development, and bringing to market of great new technologies, products, and services.

By all accounts we are embarking upon an economic and business recovery. But there remains a part of the recovery that is missing—the human element. Consider just a few recent cases:

> After buying Pillsbury for $5.7 billion in 1989, Britain's Grand Metropolitan embarked on a $140 million productivity drive. Profits rose 50 percent in 1990 and 30 percent in 1991, while some five hundred and fifty employees were trimmed at headquarters and work was shifted to more modern plants. Work that had been performed by twenty-year employees earning $8.10 an hour at Pillsbury's Green Giant frozen vegetable factory in Watsonville, California, for example, was shifted to the company's outpost in Irapuato, Mexico, where workers earned a *daily* wage of $7.58.

> Following years of losses, Goodyear earned $352 million in 1992 on sales of $11.8 billion. The company was producing 30% more tires than in 1988, with 24,000 fewer employees.

> In the service sector, advertising agency J. Walter Thompson boosted billings 24% to $2.1 billion between 1986 and 1993, but with 650 fewer employees.

Even for employees who have kept their jobs, economic recovery has translated into more work rather than more reward. In 1983 each package Federal Express delivered yielded $22.95 in revenues. The average ten years later was only $13.11. But in return for lower prices, customers were dialing the Federal Express number more often. Employees lugged 10 to 15 percent more packages than they were eighteen months earlier, but their real wages declined by more than 15 percent since 1988. Despite upticks in economic indicators, workers feel less secure and more burdened. Responding to a 1993 national survey, 62% of white-collar workers said they lived with the fear that a family member might lose his or her job, and 38% felt they had fallen behind since 1992. Only about one-half of employees, reports another survey, believed their company provided security to workers who perform well.

In contrast to their workers, organizational leaders see the potential for financial growth, organizational success, and personal reward. Corporate executives anticipate that after a long and difficult struggle, victory in an important battle is just at the top of the next hill. They see the goal and will confidently rally their troops on the mission at hand. Then the cry will come for the troops to charge up the hill and take the prize.

Only the troops will be neither ready nor willing to charge up the hill. Rather than focus on the opportunity ahead of them, they will be unable to let go of the pain behind them. Their vision of the target will be obscured by the emotional residue of anger, distrust, and depression built up over years of false promises and unmet expectations. Nor will the troops have the confidence that they can take the hill—their self-esteem will be battered, and their faith in their organization broken. Most significantly, the troops will not see how any personal gain will result from taking the hill. Instead they will fixate on memories of their fallen comrades: the casualties of layoffs and downsizings, and the "walking wounded" whose careers were sidetracked.

Employee Worries

Fear of job loss following a merger or acquisition was the number one worry among senior executives in the one thousand largest U.S. companies in a 1991 survey (see exhibit 1.1).[1] The timing of the survey—after merger and acquisition activity had significantly waned due to the recession, the tightening of capital by major financial institutions, and, in general, a greater sensibility in guiding corporate combinations—makes it all the more dramatic. Executives and other employees retain vivid memories of the trauma experienced when firms are merged or acquired, cultures clash, and redundant positions are eliminated. Even in organizations that have not merged or been acquired, employees have learned (from past jobs or vicariously from their neighbors, friends, or relatives) about the stress and anxiety associated with an organizational transition.

The number two fear reported by the executives surveyed was burnout. *Burnout* entered the popular vocabulary in the 1970s after studies of mental health and other social service professionals documented how large work loads and minimal resources contributed to a sense of hopelessness in aiding clients. The "system" was not working, and these professionals grew physically tired and

What are Today's Executives' Greatest Anxieties?

1. Loss of job due to a merger or acquisition — 54%
2. Burnout — 26%
3. Failure to get promoted — 8%
4. Being fired — 6%
5. Failure to get a raise — 5%
6. Insufficient income to meet living standards and financial obligations — 3%
7. Illness — 2%

EXHIBIT 1.1

psychologically alienated. They expressed anger and doubt about the worth of what they were doing along with an overall lack of job interest.

Today, *burnout* signifies feelings of physical and emotional exhaustion, alienation from others, and reduced personal accomplishment. It is equally likely to occur in big corporations, small businesses, government offices, or not-for-profit agencies. In organizations that downsize through layoffs or hiring freezes, surviving employees have to work harder to cover the tasks of others. Fewer support staff or other resources are available to help get the job done. The 1990s workplace offers scant advancement opportunities, as management levels are eliminated and career paths are obscured. The recession that began the decade has limited pay increases and bonus pools, prompting people to ask what the payoff is for working so hard. One middle manager from a high-technology firm that had gone through a merger and two subsequent waves of downsizing within a four-year period put it this way: "I get to work early, stay late, come home, throw some food down my throat, put the kids to bed, do some more work, fall asleep, and get up and do it all over again. What kind of life is this? Yeah, I've kept my job, but how could things be any worse if I lost it?"

Fears of job loss and feelings of burnout extend well beyond the executive suite. In the late 1980s professional, managerial, and other white-collar employees joined blue-collar workers (the targets of job cuts and wage freezes in past economic downturns) in suffering through layoffs, reduced benefits, and a falling standard of living. Though always painful, these conditions are more tolerable when one perceives them as being shared by others and leading to some payoff later on. In the 1980s, however, middle class workers saw the rich get richer while their own future prospects dwindled. Employees in the 1990s see organizations willing to slash payroll as deeply as necessary to satisfy short-term financial targets. For example, at McDonnell Douglas the human pain of layoffs—as the company moved from a peak employment of 53,000 down to 15,000—produced short-term increases in stock price, profitability, and cash flow, but not in the organization's long-term viability or its likelihood to provide new sources of employment. An announced plan to lay off 4,000 workers in its commercial aircraft division pumped up the company's stock price nearly 10 percent in one day, but it led analysts to wonder how much deeper McDonnell Douglas could cut before it could no longer compete with Boeing and Airbus.

People are not unwilling to work hard or to commit to the business objectives of their workplace. Instead, they have become paralyzed by fear and suspicious of management declarations that "everything is under control" and "business as usual" will be maintained despite obvious evidence to the contrary. In many organizations, employees have grown cynical following successive introduction of programs under the rubric of "total quality management," "rightsizing," "reengineering," and "value-added work analysis" that produce little in the way of real positive change. As employees feel they are receiving less from their organization, they give less in return. As a manager from a large health care organization explained:

> It's like each side takes something away, so the other reciprocates. First, the company took away our security when they downsized; there went our loyalty. Then they stopped merit pay raises when they introduced the new compensation plan, and we took away our commitment to doing creative and high quality work. Next, career options went out the window with the delayering; so people stopped working hard because there was no payoff for it. I used to love coming to work at this place; now I show up, and it's simply a matter of them paying me for my time.

The word around corporations today is that at the first sign of stability in the economic recovery, people will jump ship. The best and the brightest—those with the most marketable skills—will lead the way. Others, the dazed and disillusioned among them, will stay and work in an unimpassioned and indiscriminate manner. They will rely on obsolete skills, information, and practices that poorly equip them for the challenges at hand. A work force without top-level talent, a commitment to excellence, and the necessary tools for success will severely hinder any organization's ability to "charge and take the hill" in an economic recovery.

Organizational MADness

The development of a fearful, suspicious, and cynical work force in many organizations is in large part due to what I refer to as organizational MADness—the impact of Mergers, Acquisitions, and Downsizings on short-term employee well-being and long-term organizational effectiveness. During the 1980s and the first half of the 1990s, work organizations have been taken over by this MADness. Nearly 35,000 combinations of publicly traded firms occurred worldwide between 1983 and 1993, and many more deals involved privately owned companies. More than two thirds of the eight hundred largest U.S. companies reorganized, with Fortune 500 companies employing 3.7 million fewer workers in 1991 than in 1981. More than 1.5 million people in the European Community lost their jobs in 1992 alone, pushing the unemployment rate there past 11 percent. And in the land of traditional lifetime employment and seniority systems, more than 60 percent of Japan's top 100 companies have cut jobs or encouraged staff to take early retirement.

A 1993 survey of three thousand wage and salaried workers revealed that 42 percent have been through a downsizing. Unlike past reductions in force, white-collar workers were hit hard in the most recent wave of downsizing. Middle managers, who make up 6 percent of the total work force, accounted for 22% of all layoffs.

Two timely studies add more detail into the scope and impact of downsizing and restructuring activity in U.S. business:

Laborforce 2000. A 1992 study of 406 randomly selected Conference Board member companies illustrated how common job elimination had been in the last few years and how likely it was to continue.[2] Five out of every six companies in the study had restructured and downsized in the preceding five years, eliminating an average of 12 percent of all jobs in the company. In one out of seven companies, at least 20 percent of all jobs were eliminated. Almost three-quarters of the companies planned to cut more jobs in the next five years, and fully one-half of the human resources executives interviewed believed that periodic downsizing was essential to competitiveness. It is safe to conclude, then, that downsizing and restructuring will continue into the late 1990s.

AMA Survey on Downsizing. Since 1987 the American Management Association has surveyed its corporate membership annually on work force reductions. Of 910 firms responding in 1992 (a sample tilted toward large companies and the manufacturing sector), almost half reported work force reductions during the past year.[3] On average, 9.3 percent of the work force was eliminated. The AMA study also gives testimony to the recurring nature of downsizings. More companies (43 percent) had downsized in two or more of the previous six calendar years than once (23 percent) or not at all (35 percent). Year-to-year analysis of the AMA data offers more dramatic evidence: on average, over the six-year period, nearly two-thirds of the firms that downsized in a given year repeated the exercise in the following year.

Workplace stability has almost disappeared. Fully half of the 1980 Fortune 500 companies were absent from the 1990 list. These blue-chip corporations, once synonymous with employment security, fell by the wayside as a result of mergers, restructurings, and bankruptcies. The people who self-selected into large organizations—choosing a workplace expected to offer long-term job security and a buffer from the jarring roller-coaster rides of less established firms—never bargained for the change and disruption they have experienced since the 1980s.

This is not to suggest that organizational transition and transformations are without value. Organizations have to change to achieve, maintain, or enhance competitiveness. Some Fortune 500 organizations should fall from the list as the technology upon which their products are based becomes obsolete, as marketplace dynamics change, or as the price that has to be paid for poor management decisions regarding strategy, organization, and finance. Organizations, like organisms, must some day degenerate and die.

The point here is that the rapid pace and massive scope of organizational change in recent years has taken a psychological toll on people in organizations. This is an inevitable by-product of life in today's workplace. Moreover, the shock waves felt in large organizations reverberate into smaller firms, as well as public-sector and other not-for-profit organizations. When jobs are lost in large corporations, they are also lost in suppliers and other firms in the communities where plants are closed or offices shut down. In the 1990s, everyone, it seems, has a friend or relative who lost their job in a downsizing or "got the shaft" in a merger. And media reports often focus on the sensational and unsavory cases of organizational transition. Though hearing others's stories has no bearing upon employees' own vulnerability to organizational MADness, it can color their views of their own situation. During trying times, people are especially attentive to hints of bad news.

Even more debilitating to people is the prolonged confusion brought on by the ongoing changes in the workplace. Organizational MADness often means multiple waves of change and transition—a merger may lead to a restructuring and then two or three rounds of downsizing, along with changes in policies and procedures. Even the most dire form of organizational change, the death of an entity, is not always as straightforward as it once was. Employees may be strung along a sequence of cost-containment maneuvers, bankruptcy, and reorganization before the eventual end of operations.

Dynamics Driving Organizational MADness

The frequency of mergers, acquisitions, and downsizings in business is being driven by a broad set of dynamics in the business environment and within organizations.

Global Competition. The marketplace for many organizations has expanded from within a region to within a nation to the entire globe. In some industries, it is expected that only a few Asian, European, and North American competitors will survive consolidations to emerge as global gladiators for market share.

The attitude that strength comes with size is fueling the current merger mania in key U.S. industries. For instance, U.S. bankers argue that consolidation is essential for improving their competitiveness on a global basis. They note that in 1991, for the first time in fifty years, no U.S. bank ranked among the top twenty in *American Banker*'s annual ranking of the world's largest banks. In the United States, 251 million people are served by 12,600 commercial banks, 2,000 savings and loans, and almost 16,000 credit unions. In contrast, fewer than 3,000 commercial banking companies and savings and mutual banks serve the entire European Community's 320 million consumers. In Japan, no more than 170 commercial banks serve a population of 125 million. As U.S. banks grow larger, redundant positions—and career opportunities—will be eliminated.

Government deregulation. The impact of deregulation during the Reagan and Bush administrations endures in the United States in industries like air transportation, where corporate leaders responded quickly and aggressively by combining companies and reducing head count. The airlines have consolidated into a few megacarriers, with hungry acquirers gobbling up Piedmont, Pacific Southwest, Republic, Air California, Ozark, Western Airlines, and others. In addition to corporate identities being tossed aside, thousands of jobs were eliminated through postmerger downsizings. Carriers less active in the consolidation crunch—including Pan Am, Midway, and Eastern—went the way of bankruptcy and eradicated still more jobs.

Worldwide, deregulation and privatization are having tremendous social and emotional impact in many countries. The 1993 announcement of plans to take Air France private, for example, resulted in a strike and civil unrest by workers to the point of shutting down the airline for several days.

Technological change. Technology continues to become increasingly more sophisticated and effective in enhancing quality and efficiency in the workplace. Firms are taking advantage of new technologies, from factory automation to computers and communications gear, to reorganize work and make it more efficient. Often, though, this comes with a tremendous human price tag. The steel industry, for example, produced 100 million tons with 577,100 workers in the 1960s. Three decades later it produces just as much tonnage with 207,700. At the GE Fanuc Automation plant in Charlottesville, Virginia, state-of-the-art wizardry places electronic components onto circuitboards in half the time of older technology. The beauty of the machine—and the bane of the unemployed—is that GE has doubled capacity without a proportionate increase in headcount. Service industries (banks, insurers, and retailers, among others), which employ 75 percent of the work force, are automating jobs and displacing lower-skilled workers. Between 1990 and 1993 Sears eliminated 21,000 positions this way.

Even as the economy recovers, technological advances allowing greater production by fewer people are resulting in the never-before-seen phenomenon of "jobless growth." Historically the positions of lower-level employees were those put at risk by robotics and other forms of automation, but information technology is also having a tremendous impact on middle management ranks. A desktop computer using decision-support software can do the job of gathering, analyzing, and disbursing information more quickly and, arguably, with more cost-effectiveness than a middle manager. And as technology advances, the skills needed to keep pace with the machines change. For employees at any rank, the shock of job displacement is compounded by the realization that no employer wants the skills they have developed over the years.

The Total Quality and Reengineering Movements. Broad movements toward total quality management (TQM) and reengineering of business processes have taken hold in U.S. organizations. The TQM concept swept through manufacturers in the late 1970s and 1980s and is now landing in service industries. Business reengineering (the making over of entire work processes) struck organizations in the 1990s with the promise for quantum-leap enhancements in organizational performance, but not without a human toll. The flattening of hierarchies, the downsizing of management, and the contracting out of key support services are harbingers of more transformations to come.

Worldwide standards of quality, coupled with advances in information and communications technology, will lead to a dramatic increase in service productivity into the twenty-first century. Like the agricultural revolution of the seventeenth and eighteenth centuries and the industrial revolution of the nineteenth and twentieth centuries, the quality revolution will be accompanied by a reevaluation of work methods. Although they increase customer service and productivity, enhancements to work processes inevitably imply disruptions to individual tasks, work team procedures, and entire organizational processes. People will continue to be rocked by the elimination of positions, dead ends to career paths, and radical changes in corporate culture.

Delayering. The 1980s produced a drive to strip away the layers of bureaucracy and managerial excess built up during the go-go growth years that stretched from the close of the World War II into the 1970s. As long as markets and revenues grew, corporations erected hierarchies to support managers who managed other managers. When growth rates leveled in the 1980s, top-heavy corporations lost their stability. In an effort to save money and get decision makers "close to the customer," many of these firms cut middle management ranks.

Working life was once characterized in terms of the career ladder. People slowly climbed through the organization; few reached the top, but most made steady progress until they settled on a plateau, where they remained until retirement. Now that the career ladder has lost many of its rungs in today's delayered organizations, climbing it requires greater leaps of skill and experience and takes substantially more time. Managers must expect to be in the same job longer. Once they could deal with job dissatisfaction by thinking, "Well, this is only temporary. I'll soon be promoted." Today they need to find ways to make their current positions more enjoyable and rewarding.

Economic conditions. The sluggish economy of the late 1980s and early 1990s was a prime contributor to organizational MADness. It turned executives' attention to managing costs rather than garnering elusive revenues.

The Bureau of Labor Statistics estimates that some 2.3 million workers are displaced every year in the U.S. because of the changing financial conditions of their businesses. More specifically, pressures to increase earnings and control costs are constant for many companies, leading some—ranging from giant IBM to smaller Silicon Valley high-tech firms—to turn to periodic downsizing. When revenues decline, the expense side of the balance sheet is attacked by reducing head count. In addition to jobs eliminated by automation, Sears announced it would dump 50,000 jobs related to its catalog operations in 1993, the deepest in a series of cuts made during a four-year overhaul of its merchandising group to combat declining sales and market share.

Corporate Rationalization. Aggressive cost cutting often accompanies a major corporate restructuring where plants and positions are "rationalized" for a better match between supply and demand. Responding to the dismal economy and a continuing loss of market share, General Motors in late 1991 announced plans to eliminate 54,000 of 304,000 U.S. blue-collar jobs by 1995 through early retirement, attrition, and perhaps layoffs. Also at risk were 11,000 white-collar jobs, on top of 15,000 already slated for elimination. More broadly, as restructuring becomes common, shuffling people has gotten as routine as shuffling paper assets. Waves of downsizings and rehirings may enable a firm to adjust to short-term market fluctuations and to appear more dynamic. But as Secretary of Labor Robert Reich notes, "It also serves as a deceptive palliative. It allows the firm to avoid undertaking more basic change. And, it demoralizes everyone involved."[4]

The Healthy Side of MADness

Certainly organizations need to "rightsize" by eliminating unnecessary work and responding to economic, legal, technological, and consumer changes. If organizations did not change, they would not remain competitive. Organizational leaders, however, must come to terms with the fact that the *way* in which organizations transformed themselves during the economic recession of the early 1990s has stifled personal motivation, hindered team performance, and damaged organizational effectiveness.

MADness does not imply that organizations are malevolent in their actions. In many cases mergers, acquisitions, and downsizings are prudent business moves that enhance competitiveness and survivability in the ever-changing business environment. Molson

Breweries' merger with Carling O'Keefe was an essential strategic move in a quickly consolidating business. AT & T's acquisition of NCR was the kind of dramatic step the company had to take to wake up its sleepy computer business. General Motors' repeated waves of downsizing have enhanced the likelihood that the firm, and its many remaining employees, will endure over the long haul.

A transition can be beneficial for organizations and their people. There is fat to be cut and waste to be eliminated from many corporations, even profitable ones. Companies wallowing in red ink are wise to eliminate a portion—be it 5, 10, or even 20 percent—of the work force to strengthen the survivability of the vast majority of employees. And a serious assessment of work force apportionment is an integral component of the organizational introspection needed to rebalance a firm and its resources to take better advantage of emerging market trends or technological advances.

Transitions can also spark organizational regeneration. A CEO with the right mix of visionary and charismatic leadership skills can rally employees around the notion that the transition is not only a necessary response to business realities, but a proactive opportunity to improve how work is approached and conducted in the organization. A transition holds the potential to "unfreeze" the organization and its people, providing a rare chance to change corporate culture dramatically and reinforce a new way of doing things. A middle manager or supervisor can use the unfrozen state as an opportunity to enhance teamwork, increase effectiveness, and identify and correct impediments to productivity in his or her work group. The results can include the adoption of new behaviors and attitudes in work teams to support innovative work enhancements and a sincere commitment to quality.

And individuals can experience a personal form of renewal as a result of company transitions. Although many employees stay mired in maladaptive responses to the stress and uncertainty of a transition, others come to recognize that in crisis there is opportunity. Searching out ways to gain from the transition, they share three key characteristics. First, they feel in control of things that matter to them. They recognize that they cannot manage what is beyond their control and do not try; instead, they assess the situation and act in the areas they can influence. Second, they feel involved in what they are doing. They see themselves as architects of change rather than as victims of it. Third, they seek challenges, take risks, and look upon their work with a fresh perspective. These employees recognize that the rules of the game have changed, that there is no "business as usual." They see the company's transition as an opportunity to learn new skills, to test their ability to cope with stress and uncertainty, and to find creative ways to meet work requirements.

Unfortunately, however, using transitions as an opportunity for personal growth, team development, or organizational renewal is very much the exception, not the rule. Reports of downsizing experiences rarely describe productive, regenerating, or even rebalancing outcomes. In contrast, they depict downsizings as painful, wrenching, and bloody. Worse yet, many downsizings fail to achieve desired results, despite the pain organizations and their people are put through. In a cover story on the "morale crisis" in U.S. business, *Fortune* magazine reported that half the senior managers surveyed in 275 major companies (representing 26 percent of the U.S. gross national product) felt their cost-cutting programs and restructurings had not achieved their objectives. In another study of 1,005 corporations where restructurings had occurred, *Fortune* reported that

> Most senior executives admitted their companies had missed the mark in one way or another. Fewer than half met their cost-reduction targets, despite much bloodletting. This, they reported, was often because they had cut people without reducing workload, so that pricey outside contractors, and sometimes new full-time hires, had to be called in to take up the slack. Only 32% raised their profits to a level they thought acceptable, and just 21% improved return on investment to any appreciable degree.[5]

From Turmoil to Triumph

A growing number of leaders of organizations are learning from the turmoil of organizational MADness. They are "rightsizing" their organizations rather than "downsizing" their head counts. That is, these chief executives and business unit heads are pressing for efforts to reformulate how work is approached rather than merely to cut out jobs without eliminating work. Senior executives are increasingly focusing their attention on corporate combinations and alliances that add strategic value, and away from mergers and acquisitions based solely on financial motives. And leaders are embracing the more complex—yet potentially more fruitful—work of discontinuous change over incremental change.

Still, organizational leaders must accept that most transitions in the 1980s and early 1990s were poorly managed and that they have to contend with the consequences today. No executives intended to anger or alienate their work force, yet these conditions inhibit any subsequent efforts for positive organizational change. Just like parents who accept only after the fact how their behavior influenced their child's development, organizational leaders must acknowledge the imprint left on people following transitions. And just as a stepparent inherits the psychological makeup of a stepchild, executives who take over operations must accept the psychological baggage people carry with them to work.

Fortunately, adults are more psychologically adaptive than children. They can rebound from even the most painful of situations. That is what this book is about: how to help employees let go of the unintended pain and consequences they experience during and after transitions, and how to help organizations use such transitions as an opportunity to build a new and better workplace. It tells about taking shell-shocked troops, rebuilding their confidence in themselves and their leaders, and preparing them to triumph in their charge up the hill, enthused and committed to achieving desired goals. By integrating human recovery into the economic recovery, corporations and their people can be ready to take advantage of emerging business opportunities.

Organizational Transition

This book describes how corporations and their employees recover from organizational transition. Transition is distinct from change. A change is a path to a known state: something discrete, with orderly, incremental, and continuous steps. Moving the start of the weekly staff meeting from 9:00 A.M.to 8:00 A.M. is an example of a change. It may cause some disruptiveness and require some adaptation, but its discrete nature allows people to know exactly what to expect and lets them get on with their lives inside and outside the organization.

A transition, by comparison, is a path to an unknown state: something discontinuous that involves many simultaneous and interactive changes and the selection of "breakthrough" ways of thinking, organizing, and doing business. Transition poses a break from the past. It involves death and rebirth; existing practices and routines must be abandoned and new ones discovered and developed. Adapting to transition is much more psychologically taxing than is adapting to change.

Transition Types

Two general types of transition are relevant here—*event-driven* and *large-scale* organizational transformation. The first type of transition coincides with a major event in the organization's history. The triggering event could be a combination (a merger with a similar-sized partner or being acquired by another firm), a change in organizational design (like an internal restructuring or delayering), or a change in head count (as with a downsizing). Other event-driven transitions include the arrival of new leadership (say, when a new CEO comes on board or a shake-up occurs elsewhere in the senior ranks), the adoption of new technology (perhaps concurrent with a reengineering effort), and the rapid growth experienced when markets are expanded or a large number of new employees are added.

The second type of transition is associated with a planned transformation. This is the type of transition that occurs through large-scale culture change, for example, an effort to get employees "close to the customer" or the adoption of a total quality management philosophy. Or a cumulative series of changes may signal to employees that their company is moving from an old to a new way of operating. Occasionally, this type of transition is aligned with changes in corporate strategy, as has been occurring at J. P. Morgan & Company for the past several years. A decade ago, Morgan was in the business of lending money to corporate clients. Then, in the mid-1980s, a revolution took hold in finance as corporations, including Morgan's traditional clients, found it cheaper to get funds through newly emerging sources like junk bonds. Unable to take care of its clients' full set of needs, yet still wanting to increase revenues and profits, Morgan faced a core business strategy decision:

add new customers or add new businesses. In choosing to the enter the investment banking business, Morgan's leadership presaged movement away from its identity as a traditional commercial bank.

The change in business strategy implied a change in corporate culture. Morgan's leadership set forth to proactively examine business practices, in areas such as increased attention to expenses as the company moved into more competitive businesses. It also assessed the predominating values guiding the corporation's operations. As a result, transition in Morgan has meant replacing a historically paternalistic culture with one in which more obligation is entrusted to employees. Through a variety of methods—ranging from explicit communiques to implicit, but nonetheless dramatic, actions—Morgan is conditioning its work force to the realities of a new employment relationship. When Morgan displaced two hundred people through the move of its domestic custody business from New York City to Delaware in 1993, for the first time ever it was unable to find jobs elsewhere in the organization for all affected employees. Changes in the company's benefits program (in which employees now share responsibility for managing their profit sharing funds) and in career development (whereby employees rely less on the organization to map out their careers) are also signaling a transition in the company's culture.

Transition as a Way of Life

At a recent workshop on "Organizational Recovery After Transition" attended by managers from major organizations, I asked participants to introduce themselves and indicate why they had come. "I'm from Sears," offered the first woman, "and we've had five restructurings in five years." Almost as if to one-up her, the next participant reported, "I'm from Nynex, and we've had nine restructurings in four years." "Well," said the next, "I'm from Citibank, and I've had seven bosses in four years."

Increasingly, people in organizations are being exposed to multiple waves of transition, often with one transition overlapping another. Take the case of Majestic Manufacturing (a fictionalized name, but a real situation). At its peak in the mid-1980s, Majestic boasted revenues of $9 billion, employed 16,000 people, and was recognized as a stable, well-managed, blue-chip company. It also was regarded as an excellent place to work. People took jobs there because they wanted a place of employment with stability, predictability, and growth. The typical Majestic employee had long tenure, high loyalty, and expectations of life-long employment.

In 1985 Majestic made an opportunistic acquisition of a competitor's operations. In announcing the acquisition to employees, Majestic CEO Justin Jordan (again, a fictional name) acknowledged that it would result in some redundancy in positions and promised to take care of this through attrition, assuring his troops there would be no layoffs. As tough economic times set in during the latter half of the 1980s, however, Majestic's debt obligation loomed larger and larger. Revenues remained flat, expenses increased, and margins eroded. Within three years Jordan ordered two major restructurings, the first to streamline decision making in general and the second to eliminate bureaucratic hurdles slowing the introduction of new products to market.

The restructurings changed the organization's design and reporting relationships, but produced few cost savings. Still confronted by debt and flat growth, the company had to cut expenses dramatically. In 1990 Jordan announced the first reduction-in-force program in Majestic's history. It was voluntary, providing enhanced early retirement benefits for employees over 55 and severance pay incentives for all other employees. Despite its voluntary nature, the program sent shock waves through the ranks of Majestic managers and employees.

A few months after the reduction-in-force announcement, Jordan proclaimed a new vision for Majestic: it would become the "premier" company in its industry segment. Soon Jordan initiated two projects to achieve this vision. First, he engaged McKinsey & Company to conduct a value-added work analysis. Shortly thereafter, Jordan returned from a conference on total quality management to announce that he had commissioned a training company to deliver a "continuous improvement process" program to all Majestic managers.

As the dismal economy continued throughout 1990 and into 1991, Majestic managed a small operating profit but could not reduce its heavy debt load. Long-term prospects for revenue growth were diminished by the lack of a general economic recovery, and Jordan concluded that severe cost cutting was necessary for his company's survival. In March 1991 he announced that Majestic would have to implement an involuntary downsizing program.

The Mind-Set of Employees

The 1985 acquisition was a turning point in the stable psychological work contract between Majestic and its employees. The merger and two subsequent restructurings in the late 1980s produced more change and disruption than Majestic employees had ever experienced or bargained for. After three major reorganizations in four years, employees were worn out from the scope and pace of change in the company. Because Jordan had promised there would be no layoffs after the 1985 acquisition, employees felt he had betrayed them when he announced the 1990 reduction-in-force program. Even though the layoffs were voluntary, employee perceptions of management credibility hit rock bottom.

Jordan's premier-company initiatives were intended to pump up employee morale and organizational effectiveness, but they backfired. The successive introduction of *premier company*, *value-added work analysis*, and *continuous improvement* into the corporate language confused employees. Cynicism grew. Employees began to look out for management's "flavor of the month." They strongly criticized leadership for bringing in consultants and programs that never changed anything. The McKinsey value-added work analysis lingered on and on, but no apparent changes were made. Managers went through a weeklong continuous improvement process training, but once back in their work areas were never pressed to use what they learned. "We didn't walk the talk," confessed one senior vice president, referring to leadership's failure to reinforce words with actions.

The most dramatic influence on the mind-set of Majestic employees was the 1991 involuntary downsizing. The program hit workers hard. They were stunned that their company's leadership would betray them with such a clear break in the historic ties between employer and employee.

Recovery and Revitalization

The Majestic case highlights how organizational transitions produce inadvertent effects. Like thousands of other companies, Majestic must focus its energies on enhancing business processes, organizational effectiveness, and employee productivity to meet ongoing competitive pressures. This implies more transition, but, first the organization and its people must recover from their history of past, poorly managed transitions. By *recover*, I mean addressing both the emotional realities and the business imperatives associated with regrouping after a transition or a series of transitions.

Recovery focuses on those who remain with the firm. It recognizes the need to drive business success by minimizing the unintended effects of transition, gearing people up for their new roles and responsibilities, and renewing motivation for making a run at business challenges. Recovery requires that all members of an organization have a shared direction of where they are headed and are tolerant of the pain involved in getting from the old way of doing things to the new. It involves managers in helping their work team members rebound from the psychological trauma of transition, clarify new work roles and responsibilities, and secure the organizational capability and individual motivation needed for success. And it engages people in understanding how and why their workplace is changing and how and where they can exert control during and after the transition.

These benefits revive organizations and their people by instilling new life and energy after the turmoil of transition and preparing them to triumph in their quest for new success. *Revitalization* sustains positive changes in perceptions, practices, policies, and processes. Together these changes resuscitate individual employee spirit, work team performance, and organizational systems and direct them toward a desired new order in the organization.

The Need to Recover After Transition

Some skeptics might ask why it is necessary to help organizations and their members recover from transition. These individuals either have not experienced the human pain and organizational inefficiencies that accompany transitions, or have refused to acknowledge these side effects. These skeptics might question the need to attend to recovery in the following ways:

It's a lousy economy out there; aren't people glad to have a job? People certainly appreciate having a steady job during difficult times. But employment that merely provides for security needs is not enough for intelligent, well-educated workers, who want psychological along with financial rewards. The real question to ask is this: once the economy recovers, will the best and brightest people be psychologically committed to realizing an organization's new business opportunities, or will they defect to another team?

But if these people jump ship, aren't there others waiting in line for their jobs? Studies show that even short periods of unemployment produce drastic changes in how executives view themselves and the world around them. Most regain their self-esteem soon after they find jobs, but their alienation and cynicism about employers remain. An organization needs people's hearts and minds, not just their bones and muscle, to pull away from the pack and capitalize on emerging business opportunities. Organizations looking for human resources from the outside will not find a talent pool immune from organizational MADness. They cannot escape the job of healing the psychological wounds caused by mismanaged transitions, generating excitement about the current opportunities, and recommitting people to organizational goals.

People are resilient, aren't they? Yes, people are resilient; they can bounce back from debilitating circumstances to become productive. The extent and speed of bouncing back, however, can be influenced. An internal study at Honeywell found that, on average, employees spent two hours per day distracted from work obsessing over how they would be affected by a restructuring. Imagine how much time and money would be saved if that could be reduced to one hour per day per employee! Why wait months or years for a work force to recover from a transition when it could only take weeks or months?

Don't people want to look to the future rather than dwell on the past? Psychological research is clear that people must first actively let go of the old before they can accept the new. An organizational recovery program accelerates both parts of this process.

Haven't people always dealt with change and transition in organizations? Employees have always had to contend with disruptions to their accustomed working situation. But prior to the MADness begun in the 1980s, the relatively relaxed pace of organizational life in general—and of change in particular—provided a conducive setting for gradual adaptation to change. Employees could deal with the effects of coping with changes without significantly burdening organizational results. Steady increases in consumption during the 1950s, 60s and 70s meant that practically all a company had to do to see revenues grow was put an "open for business" sign in the window. Distractions from productivity and profitability caused by personal reactions to transition were offset by the momentum of increasing revenues. Moreover, the wide spacing between waves of transition ensured that people could regain their footing and composure before being upended by another swell.

Even the types of changes confronting people were different. People faced modifications in aspects of their working life, not radical makeovers of the overall approach to doing a job. A clerk may have had to deal with incremental changes when word processors replaced typewriters, or when the deductible rates for the company health care plan were adjusted. Today the clerk has to contend with such discontinuous transformational changes as reengineering work flow processes or reformulating the psychological relationship between employer and employee. Yesterday's changes in specific pieces of the work situation left a mostly stable and secure foundation upon which to move forward. Today whole worlds break up, producing a dizzying and disarming specter of change with which to contend. This intensifies forces for holding on to the known and, as a result, interferes with the need to let go of the familiar and accept new organizational realities.

Recovery and Competitiveness

The objective of organizational revitalization is not merely to recover from transition, but to rebound with a work force that has an enhanced capacity to operate competitively. Perhaps the greatest recovery of all time is the turnaround of Japanese manufacturing quality and economic growth after World War II. Modern Japan rose phoenix-like from the ashes of its defeat because the country's leadership created an environment within which organizations and ideas could blossom. Yet producing a wave of innovative products and manufacturing techniques will not alone sustain Japan's eminent position. Rather, it must find the resources to contend with newly emerging challenges from within (such as the growing discontent among Japan's youth) and without (like threats from Third World countries with lower cost structures).

Approaching and entering the twenty-first century, organizational efforts to achieve, maintain, or enhance competitiveness will be influenced by the availability of a well-trained and highly motivated work force to help achieve desired organizational outcomes (productivity, quality, and profitability). In addition to globalization, technical advancements, and other changes in the business environment, organizations must contend with a human resources pool that is in flux. Some particular characteristics of the modern work force will make the job of revitalizing after transition both more essential and more exacting.

High Demand, Low Supply. A simple look at the number of jobs lost through downsizings and the unemployment figures suggests that there is a cornucopia of human talent ready to replace any current people who leave the organization. These statistics are deceiving. Just because there are a lot of people out of work does not mean there is a healthy pool of qualified candidates. To the contrary, the requirements of jobs are changing faster than the capacity of workers. Restructured organizations and reengineered work processes that squeeze organization charts vertically force the horizontal expansion of jobs that remain. Redesigned positions demand different skills, more intelligence, and extended competencies. The choices to meet these needs are simple: retrain current employees, or recruit new ones. The problem is that the supply just is not there. Organizations have not been investing in retraining and retooling their human resources. And the talent available on the open market is limited by low quality (poor training) and low quantity (post–baby boom reductions in population).

Jumping Fences. To recruit new talent, then, employers will look more intently at luring people from other organizations. There they will find a work force ready and willing to jump ship to retaliate for how they have been treated during years of MADness. A substantial number of employees today are staying at jobs they do not like: they don't like the work, they don't like the way the boss is treating them, they don't like the way they are communicated with, they don't see opportunities to advance, and they don't feel part of an inspired team. Much of the loyalty in organizations in the 1990s is fragile, although some employers take it for granted. Thousands of good people are waiting for the economy to show tangible signs of improvement. Then they will look for greener grass and eagerly jump the fence to another pasture.

Two-Income Households. Fence jumping will be aided by the radical rise in the number of two-income households. With well over half of married-couple households now having two incomes and more than one-third of all households having two adult earners, for the first time in history tens of millions of workers are able to set aside several months of income. With that amount of money in purse or pocket, these workers can afford to be more independent when reviewing their employment situation. With a financial safety net below them, workers will be less apt to put up with insipid work, insensitive managers, and inefficient organizations. Workers increasingly will either insist on more intelligent work situations or set their sites on alternative places of employment.

Psychological Fulfillment. Good people will not jump fences for money alone. Compensation is important (especially benefits in this age of high health care costs and important dependent care responsibilities) but people will seek other ways to fulfill their needs from the workplace. Organizational values, ethics, culture, and physical working conditions are important to today's socially conscious employee. The capacity to act and acknowledgment of a job well done are important, too. A source of frustration for many people following transition is the lack of support in getting tasks accomplished. Things like having the right tools, equipment, information, scheduling, supplies, and coordination of effort are important. People want to go home after work with a sense of accomplishment. They want to achieve, and they value opportunities for professional growth and advancement. In today's delayered organizations, this does not necessarily mean promotion but job enrichment, skills enhancement, and knowledge acquisition.

If good people leave, and it is more difficult to attract and hold qualified replacements, what is left? The mediocre talent that stays behind and the newcomers struggling up the learning curve may upset standards of productivity, quality, and customer satisfaction. The human resources dilemma will be felt right at the bottom line.

Revitalizing Organizations and People After MADness

Revitalizing the corporation is not only important for healing a battered and burnt-out work force, it is a requirement for rebuilding America's productive capability. Any breakthroughs in workplace productivity or gains in organizational competitiveness will come only from a group of people who share a sense of where they are headed and who commit themselves psychologically to getting there. People want meaning in their work lives, including the ability to express themselves creatively. But they also crave a sense of direction from their leaders, especially after living through the turmoil of misguided organizational transitions. People want the security that comes from knowing they are headed toward a specific goal rather than wandering aimlessly. They also seek the excitement that comes from triumphing at something special—like when NASA put a man on the moon, when Sperry rolled out Univac One (the world's first commercial computer), or even when any office of any company surpasses its sales target.

People are capable of rebounding psychologically to charge up what had been perceived as unattainable or undesirable hills. A prime example occurred during the 1992 presidential election in the United States, in which Ross Perot rallied thousands of previously apathetic citizens around his vision of a government that served the people and focused on attacking the national debt. In short order an organization sprang up that placed Perot's name on the ballot in all fifty states; he eventually captured nearly 20 percent of the vote. The Perot example, however, also shows the human toll when people are let down by their leaders. Perot's announcement midway through the campaign that he was withdrawing prompted intensely emotional reactions from his supporters, including anger at Perot, disillusionment and cynicism toward the political system, and reinforced feelings of futility in being able to make a difference. Though some supporters returned to Perot's camp when he reentered the race, others remained angry and suspicious and could not muster the commitment to come back into the fold.

This is the same set of reactions experienced by employees who faithfully follow their leaders only to be disappointed when a merger, downsizing, or other transition erodes executive credibility and hinders the achievement of expected results. People can say no to voting, but they have to earn a living. They continue to come to work, but—consciously or unconsciously—they withdraw their psychological or physical effort. Or, like the flight attendants at American Airlines who went on strike in November 1993, they fight back. While company press releases described a dire financial situation and accused the strikers of not grasping the economic imperative to cut costs in a competitive industry, it was senior management who did not grasp the real issue. Instead of working with the unions to construct an enterprise that could triumph in a better business environment, American Airlines CEO Robert Crandall drove a wedge between management and his workers by treating the latter as disposable numbers and blaming them for the airline's frail economic health. After years of MADness marked by acquisition, consolidation, and contentious labor-management relations, American's flight attendants went out on strike to win back their self-respect.

The turmoil of years of organizational MADness requires that new life be breathed into the work force to make it a competitive asset. Organizations that historically contributed to increased quality of life for workers have become disabling and disenchanting. An effort to revitalize the organization can be more than a reactive response to overcoming the unintended human and business consequences of a transition. It can be a proactive opportunity to rebuild the organization, work teams, and individual contributors in a way that results in greater efficiency, desired cultural norms, and renewed zeal. Organizational recovery and revitalization can be a platform for clarifying organizational vision, work team missions, and individual responsibilities, as well as for unifying these forces into a coordinated effort to achieve desired business goals.

2

The Opportunity and The Challenge

After the organizational MADness of the 1980s and 1990s, employees know that turbulence and change are ingrained aspects of contemporary working life. Increasingly, people accept that "business as usual" means "business as unusual." While employees understand that transitions are essential to survival in an increasingly competitive environment, however, in most organizations they remain cynical about the payoff for going through the pain of such changes. They do not see how transitions lead to organizational enhancements.

But the posttransition period can be an opportunity to build a new and better organization. Living through a transition shakes people up; over time, they eventually will settle down. If nothing is done to manage this process, odds are that people will return to their old ways of doing things, hold onto their old perceptions, and retain their old expectations. Alternatively, if the posttransition period is managed to take advantage of this opportunity, then people will settle into new behaviors, perceptions, and expectations that are more in line with the new desires of senior executives and with the realities of the organization.

Transition as an Unfreezing Event

One of the most helpful models of change management is the simplest: the three steps of *unfreezing*, *changing*, and *refreezing* introduced by social psychologist Kurt Lewin (see Exhibit 2.1).[1] Suppose that your target for change is not an organization, or an individual for that matter, but an ice cube. If you want to convert its shape from a cube to a cylinder, you can proceed in one of two ways. The first is to take out a hammer and chisel; with the right skill, you could transform the ice cube into the shape of a cylinder. There is a clear cost to this approach, however: you will lose a good amount of the volume of the ice cube as it is chiseled off. The alternative course of action is to unfreeze the ice cube, change its mold to that of a cylinder, and refreeze it. Unless you are clumsy in pouring the unfrozen water from one mold to the other or the new mold has an unacknowledged hole, you have the desired cylinder shape without the loss of volume in the ice cube.

Moving back from ice cubes to organizations, the first step in the process of change is to unfreeze present behaviors or perceptions. For organizational change, the unfreezing event might be senior executives attending a conference that opens their eyes to the need to enhance service or product quality or data from an employee attitude survey that reveal serious problems in teamwork across departments. The second step is changing the organization from its original behavior or perception to a new one. This could involve, for example, the introduction of total quality management training to enhance work behaviors or the implementation of a series of team building interventions. The refreezing step is to establish processes that reinforce the desired behaviors or perceptions and lock them into the organization. In the quality case, this may mean providing financial incentives for documented enhancements in service or product quality derived from implementing the TQM approach. In

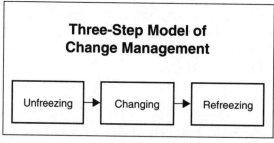

EXHIBIT 2.1

the case of teamwork, this might be a modification of the organizational structure to provide for easier interaction across groups or the broader sharing of information between departments.

These three steps are simpler to state than they are to implement. Their implementation becomes even more difficult when the context is moved from a discrete case of change to a more discontinuous case of transition (and yet again more difficult when dealing within a context of multiple waves of transitions). The desired mold, for instance, may be a moving target as concurrent changes and transitions try both executive patience and employee confidence. Also, some portions of the target of transition may be more or less unfrozen at any given time. Senior management may be ready to charge ahead with a TQM program after hearing a quality guru speak at a conference, but rank-and-file employees may remain rigidly resistant to the program even after thorough training if they sense signals from their immediate supervisors not to bother with using the technique on the job.

In the turbulent business world of the 1990s, transition could be seen as bleeding across both the change and refreezing steps. Consider Bank of America's acquisition of Security Pacific Bank in California. Motivated—that is, unfrozen—by a host of factors (including changes in interstate banking laws, visions of synergistic gains through economies of scale, and competitive pressures exerted by large foreign banks and the growing frequency of mergers involving other major U.S. banks), Bank of America's leadership felt a need to make a big move. The change step was to move beyond its incumbent strategy of growth through small acquisitions and merge with a large competitor. The acquisition of Security Pacific, truly a transition in its own right, was the action taken to change Bank of America from its original state to a new state. Refreezing the desired change—securing the financial benefits of economies of scale—occurred through such other transitions as alterations in the corporate structure and repeated waves of reductions in force affecting nearly 10,000 employees.

The most productive way to view transition, however, is not as a change or refreezing mechanism, but as an unfreezing step (see Exhibit 2.2). Transition disturbs the status quo: it jars people, changes relationships, redefines work team composition and goals, and disrupts behavioral norms and accustomed ways of doing things. It

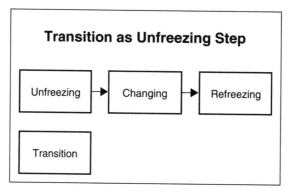

EXHIBIT 2.2

also opens the door to think in a proactive manner about what life after the transition could be like.

A fine example of this comes from New York based Manufacturers Hanover Bank. In the 1970s and early 1980s, "Manny Hanny" was plagued by flat revenue growth, problem loans to developing countries, and expense account abuses. Senior management's response was to strengthen corporate staff control over line managers. This was an appropriate reaction in light of the financial problems at hand. Ultimately, however, it resulted in a bureaucratic organization whose control mechanisms slowed decision making and diverted managerial time and attention away from business innovation.

Eventually CEO John McGillicuddy and his senior team dealt with the financial problems that had necessitated the tight control. The bureaucracy, however, was frozen in place through the policies, procedures, and staff positions that remained, along with an acquiescent mind-set. Operations executives were quite unhappy with this aspect of the company culture, yet senior management never countered the high levels of bureaucracy and inflexible staff control that had become a way of life in the bank.

In 1992 Manufacturers Hanover merged with Chemical Bank. While the Chemical name was retained, McGillicuddy became CEO of the combined bank. This "merger of equals" ultimately had an unfreezing effect. (Although *merger of equals* is rarely an accurate term, the Chemical Bank–Manufacturers Hanover combination could well be described this way: it was a very friendly deal; the two banks were of approximately equal size; both CEOs remained on board; and staffing was coordinated with an eye toward balance between the two sides.) To identify opportunities for integration, but also to symbolize the mutuality between the sides in merger planning, teams of managers from the two banks were assigned to integration planning teams. Inevitably issues of culture edged into discussions of business strategy and operating procedures for the new bank. Unlike in typical merger planning negotiations, in which managers tend to view their culture as superior to the other side's and defend their way of doing things, planners from Manufacturers Hanover wanted a less bureaucratic postmerger organization. They saw the merger as an opportunity to rid their workplace of bureaucratic excess.

In other firms, the way employees describe the transition experience gives testimony to its capacity to unfreeze organizations and people:

- "Everything's up for grabs," exclaimed a marketing manager after her first merger transition planning meeting.
- "Leave no stone unturned," a CEO instructed his staff as he ordered a serious cost containment program.
- "Things aren't like they used to be," bemoaned a staff accountant from a firm that announced its first ever involuntary reduction in force.

What makes a transition so stressful for people—its ability to separate them from their favorite projects, tasks, mentors, coworkers, perks, and ways of doing things—concurrently provides the benefit of unfreezing people. A transition also has the potential to put organizational structures, systems, strategies, programs, and processes "into play." Hiring guidelines, reward systems, decision-making approaches, job designs, reporting relationships, and all other aspects of the organization are temporarily pliable and ready to be set in a new mold.

The Cognitive Basis of Change

For change to occur at the organizational level, however, it must occur at the individual level and, in particular, in the ways people interpret the environment in which they operate. Individuals have limited data processing capabilities that must be used to evaluate vast amounts of ambiguous information. To make sense of their world, people rely on simplified representations, or *mental models*, consisting of concepts and cause-effect relationships used to understand various situations. These models are shortcuts that help people select and interpret data from the universe of information bombarding them. They also act as filters that reject information, interpretations, or actions that do not conform to an individual's ideas about his or her environment. Thus, efforts to respond to a changing situation may be hampered by unconsciously selecting and interpreting responses based on a mental model that blocks out some of the realities of environmental change.

Certainly mental models may be updated, adapted, and improved as events occur in the environment and provide information that modifies erroneous beliefs, but this seldom happens in a timely manner. Lessened responsiveness to customer needs and greater confusion about what it takes for a person to get ahead in an organization are among the inevitable results when significant changes in the environment either go unnoticed, are improperly interpreted, or are addressed through inappropriate actions.

Organizational recovery after transition hinges on changing the beliefs held by members. Changing beliefs, in turn, requires unlearning familiar concepts or assumed cause-effect relationships and replacing them with new concepts and associations. Mental models that can no longer reliably explain occurrences in the environment must be altered and updated with new understandings. This learning occurs in a manner akin to the unfreezing, changing, and refreezing process. During unfreezing, old beliefs are discarded as inappropriate or useless. Once old beliefs are unlearned, new understandings about the environment can be achieved, often via experimentation. In the final step, new belief structures ultimately become solidified (or frozen) as they are supported by anticipated events. Of course, in today's ever-changing business environment, "frozen" takes on a relative meaning.

Change by Design or by Default

As the shock waves of a transition subside, people settle into patterns of thinking and acting in their organization. One of three scenarios will prevail:

- The transition experience will *not* significantly alter people's mental models, and they will retain the assumptions, perceptions, and behaviors that served them in the pretransition organization.
- The transition experience will alter people's mental models, and they will settle into and rely upon assumptions, perceptions, and behaviors that were reinforced *inadvertently* during the transition.
- The transition experience will alter people's mental models, and they will settle into and rely upon assumptions, perceptions, and behaviors that were reinforced by senior management's *design* during the transition.

Amidst transition there is tremendous pressure upon employees, especially those in busy middle management positions, to "go with what they know." There is so much turmoil and disruption, and so much up for grabs, that people look for stability and consistency wherever they can find it. Customary habits and beliefs, as discussed above, will influence what people notice as they experience transition. If there has been no modification of people's mental models, they will revert back to accustomed ways of conceptualizing and doing things. The transition may have temporarily unfrozen these people, but the mold and mechanisms for refreezing did not change.

The problem with this scenario is that the assumptions, perceptions, and behaviors that served people well in the pretransition organization may not be appropriate after the transition. This could be costly to the organization, as in the case of a reengineering effort and subsequent restructuring that misses its target of facilitating the exchange of pertinent information across work teams because department managers continue to restrict the sharing of information even after the changes. Or it may be costly to employees who, for example, deny their vulnerability and fail to adapt when their employer abandons a no-layoff policy, eliminates tuition reimbursement programs, or replaces traditional promote-from-within practices with aggressive recruiting and hiring from outside the company.

Alternatively, the transition period may be so dramatic and intense that it challenges employees' existing mental models. The experience of living through a transition (including both perceived and real dynamics) may obliterate concepts or assumed cause-effect relationships that predominated prior to the transition, replacing them with new concepts and associations. Depending on how the transition is managed, this unlearning, changing, and relearning follows one of two patterns: new mental models emerge by default as the result of inadvertent management actions or they emerge by design as the result of proactive management efforts to cast a new mold.

A case of change by default is seen in the acquisition of a small manufacturing company by a much larger conglomerate. The lead company knew it was buying into an industry in which it had no expertise. Its intentions were to keep the target company's top management in place; with the exception of changes in accounting practices to conform to its own standards, the conglomerate mandated no changes in operations. Leaders from the acquired company, however, lurched into a crisis management mode as they experienced remorse for having sold their company, became overburdened by the joint responsibilities of running their operations and preparing mountains of financial reports for staffers from the conglomerate, and frequently met among themselves to strategize how to fend off any additional overtures for change. Senior management, which had maintained close informal relations with rank-and-file employees suddenly became invisible. Employees felt abandoned by and out of touch with their leaders. In an attitude survey conducted a year after the takeover, employees expressed how their trust toward management had plummeted, and they conveyed feelings that leadership was not concerned about the welfare of employees. Interviews with senior executives revealed that they were no less concerned about employees than before the transition. Their behavior had inadvertently sent a different message, however, and the damage was done: a union drive was initiated shortly thereafter. Although the drive was defeated, fighting it required the expenditure of tremendous resources.

In contrast is the case of the merger by design of two hospitals of equal size. The senior administrator, who came from one of the two hospitals, wanted to use the merger as an opportunity to revisit all facets of organizational life, from standard operating procedures to core competencies for managers. Her initial communications of this desire were met with great cynicism from the two management teams: managers from her hospital assumed they would have an edge in gaining positions in the merged operation, while those from the other side suspected they would be at a disadvantage. Both sides were startled when they saw the chief administrator's words backed up by actions—every manager and supervisor would have to apply for jobs in the postmerger hospital and compete against counterparts from the other side and, perhaps, outside applicants. This approach had some short-term costs, like a prevailing sense of abandonment by the administrator's former team and some interpersonal conflict among individuals vying for jobs, but, in the long run, it had the intended effect of breaking down old expectations and setting the stage for the design and implementation of a truly new organization.

The New Organizational Order

An organization's leadership can influence employees' new mental models and behaviors to coincide with the kind of organization desired by that leadership. This opportunity could be realized by accident. Doing this by design, though, requires that senior leadership articulate a *new organizational order* in which people can settle after being uprooted by transition. This new organizational order is the mold that defines the change in the middle step of the unfreezing-changing-refreezing model (see Exhibit 2.3). A new organizational order articulates the following:

Direction—where the organization is headed

Mission—the organization's purpose for being, including what distinguishes it from competitors

Culture—the ways things are done in an organization, and the values, attitudes, and beliefs that underlie more readily observable behaviors and practices

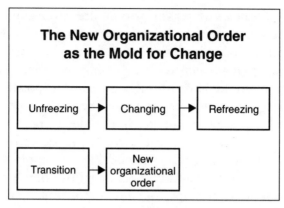

EXHIBIT 2.3

Psychological contract—the explicit delineation of what both employer and employee bring to their relationship, and what they can expect in return for their contribution

Core competencies—the traits, skills, knowledge, and related attributes that an organization values and needs for success in a particular position

Architecture—the design of the social and work systems that make up a complex organization (including formal structure, work practices, informal organization or operating style, and processes for selecting, socializing, and developing people)[2]

The new organizational order is like a vision—it paints a vivid picture of where the organization is headed. Statements of vision are important in recovering from organizational transition. They inspire confidence among an anxious work force that the organization is on the path to becoming new and better. But a vision is beyond the reach of what realistically can be attained. People who already feel beat up from the bumps and bruises of a transition do not need to be confronted by something beyond their grasp. Rather, they need help in understanding how *today's* behaviors and expectations can best be positioned to provide for both short-term survival and long-term revival. Thus the articulation of a new organizational order must be more than a vision.

CEO Garland Cook of Pittsburgh-bed Integra Bank used a new organizational order to revitalize his firm after transitions. Integra emerged from a series of acquisitions as one of the fastest-growing financial institutions in the country. The acquisitions were extremely friendly, but they brought together a mix of corporate cultures and diverse operating styles from banks that previously had focused on serving the specific needs of rural, suburban, or urban customers. Although postmerger integration moved forward relatively well, the formerly independent banks were not leveraging their respective strengths. Moreover, employees were torn between conflicting management approaches and what standards were being used to judge performance on the job. Cook quickly saw the inertia that was setting in among his managers and employees as competitors began to bite into market share by introducing new products and services. While intending to continue Integra's growth by acquisition, Cook recognized that the greatest flurry of activity was behind and set his attention on articulating and building a new order for the bank (see Exhibit 2.4). At a meeting of his senior management team, Cook described the changes he wanted to see:

The Old and New Organizational Orders at Integra Bank

Old Organizational Order	New Organizational Order
Jobs	Careers
Clutter	Continuous improvement
Open 9 to 5	Saturday and evening service
Tin man	"Heart" recaptured
Constant change	Stable state
Eye on the next shoe dropping	Eye on the ball

EXHIBIT 2.4

- In contrast to the situation at most contemporary organizations, Cook wanted employees to feel that they could develop careers at Integra. He wanted to replace the predominating expectation of "having a job" with one of "building" a career."
- There was, in Cook's words, "considerable clutter" in the old bank—inefficient operations, unnecessary procedures, and enormous waste of money, time, and resources. He envisioned a continuous improvement orientation in the new organizational

order in which people and teams would analyze their actions and carry forward only those that truly added value to the accomplishment of work.

- A banker's-hours mentality of nine-to-five service predominated in the bank. Cook preferred that employees embrace higher levels of customer service, including availability on Saturdays and in evenings.
- Cook spoke passionately about his desire to recapture the "heart" of his organization. He felt some of the fun and the humanism of the institution had been lost as its size increased over the years. He believed his staff members were basically good people who, like the Tin Man in *The Wizard of Oz*, did not need to be given anything they did not already have. Rather, he needed to guide them in calling upon the resources already within themselves.
- Anticipating a lull in acquisition and postmerger integration activity, Cook saw a new organizational order of relative stability in structure and size.
- Particularly because of this upcoming lull, Cook wanted people in the new organizational order to keep their eye on the ball and focus their attention on business results. In the old organizational order, most were waiting for the next shoe to drop.

The Integra case shows how the new organizational order need not be communicated as a concrete document. Rather, it is more a fluid working draft intended to help senior executives define what they want their posttransition organization to be like. From it may come well communicated statements of direction and mission, clear cultural norms, shared expectations of the psychological contract, common understanding of core competencies, and implementation of the desired organizational architecture.

Articulating a new organizational order helped the administrator of the two merging hospitals convey her expectations and dreams to her subordinates. Soon after the merger announcement, she sent a letter to all employees from both institutions describing her view of what the merged hospitals could and should be. It was a fairly typical statement of direction ("Be the hospital of choice for residents of our community"), greeted by employees in a fairly typical manner ("That's nice, but will I have a job?"). Meanwhile, as she developed her architecture for the postmerger organization, the administrator's thinking focused on the teamwork necessary to achieve the new direction. She acknowledged the extensive use of teams in all hospitals, but she saw them as confined in the old order to single functions or routine tasks. She found little use of teamwork in such other contexts as resolving difficulties and exploring new ways of providing better service to patients.

The administrator conceived of a culture promoting and reinforcing teamwork. She began to articulate this to people from the two hospitals in her formal communications—memos and newsletters—and in informal visits with groups of employees. She modeled teamwork by using groups of managers from the two institutions to make decisions she previously had handled on her own. She also spoke of a psychological relationship between employer and employee that went beyond pay and benefits in exchange for high-quality work: only those people who wanted to work collaboratively with employees from different departments and levels, she said, need apply for positions in the new hospital. This was reinforced through the development of job descriptions that specified, in addition to technical and professional competencies, the ability to function in a team orientation.

All of this was done *before* any decisions were made regarding the structure or staffing of the new institution. The theme of teamwork became a focal point to help the postmerger hospital staff recover from the draining work of merging operations while maintaining patient care, dealing with culture clash during integration, and overcoming anger and conflicts that spilled over from before the combination.

The metamorphosis of General Electric during Jack Welch's tenure as chairman shows a sharp contrast between an old organizational order and a new one. Prior to Welch's appointment in 1981, GE's business diversification was as wild as its bureaucracy was untamed. GE was in forty-three businesses, ranging from medicine to mining and from credit to construction, with various degrees of success. Its hierarchy was hefty, and the chain of command well respected—corporate communication was purely from the top down.

Welch asserted that all GE business units not placing either first or second in terms of market share in their industry would be sold, combined, or closed. He broke down the old conglomerate GE and replaced it with a new organization concentrating in three basic areas: electrical core products, high-technology businesses, and services. Welsh also made over the corporate culture from a stodgy bureaucracy to a lean and agile operation. Architectural changes brought the number of strategic business units down from 250 to 43. The salaried work force was reduced by 13 percent and the hourly work force by 18 percent.

The pressure to be lean has had an effect on the way businesses operate in GE. They have reorganized and become more functionally aligned. The functional organization allows consolidation and fewer people. As a result, there is a greater orientation in the new order toward product management and matrix organization in order to focus more on customer needs and other key business factors.

The new organizational order in GE reflects a strong respect for people and investment in training and development. Before managers had moved often and across businesses, but Welch championed longer stays in a job and in the same business. GE's Crotonville training center became renowned for its leading-edge curriculum and teaching methods. Work-through sessions, in which employees could speak up, out, and at their superiors typified the respect for upward communication and experimentation in the new organizational order.

At GE, the ascendancy to the chairman's position of a man who foresaw a new order was the transition that broke down the old organization. By articulating his view of the new way of doing things, taking time to explain where the organization was headed and why, and backing up those words with actions (like selling businesses, flattening structures, and revamping rewards), Welch breathed life into his desired new organizational order,

Transition survivors typically are receptive to statements describing the new organizational order. Their world has been shaken up, and they engage in a vigilant search to learn what is expected of them, what they can expect, and how they can protect themselves against future fallout (or, more positively, contribute to desired business goals). Yet management often fails to provide a clear picture of what the posttransition organization will be like. This disappoints and frequently angers employers, who assume some master plan must be lying in wait behind closed doors. In reality, few executives have thought through their desired posttransition end state.

Precisely how people respond to the statement of a new organizational order depends on their experiences and perceptions molded during the transition. If management failed to "walk the talk" after announcing a commitment to quality, or if its promises of enhanced organizational life rang hollow, then people will see the statement of the new organizational order as nothing more than management's latest fad. Conversely, if management leveled with people about the pain of transition but provided little in the way of a new vision for the organization, then surviving employees will eagerly receive a statement that fleshes out where their organization—and they—are headed. But receptivity to hearing a statement of a new organizational order is one thing; agreement with its components is another. Employees may not be fond of what the new organizational order represents, even though they find some solace in seeing that the uncertainty of the transition period replaced by something tangible.

For the mold of the new organizational order to take hold, it must be refrozen (see Exhibit 2.5). This occurs in the establishment of the various systems, structures, strategies, management processes, technologies, and relationships that follow after the transition. Refreezing the new organizational order ultimately means reinforcing the desired change through actions that help people learn newly relevant concepts and cause-effect relationships and result in new mental models consistent with the new situation. If the desired organizational order is reinforced, then employee spirit and the motivation to act are revitalized along with

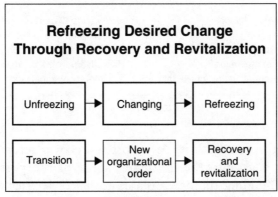

**Refreezing Desired Change
Through Recovery and Revitalization**

Unfreezing → Changing → Refreezing

Transition → New organizational order → Recovery and revitalization

EXHIBIT 2.5

the work team performance required to make a successful run at business opportunities.

Opportunities in the New Organizational Order

The opportunities in a new organizational order are almost limitless. If the new organizational order calls for and reinforces increased teamwork, greater attention to internal or external customer service, or more sharing of responsibility in the psychological work contract bonding the organization and its people, then these are among the potential gains of the new way of doing things. In addition to its content, the *process* of defining and achieving the new organizational order after transition can result in a number of important benefits (see Exhibit 2.6):

Some Opportunities in the New Organizational Order

Resuscitating Human Spirit
Reenergize burned-out employees
Create a high level of aspiration
Focus people on future possibilities
Increase capacity to act

Living the Vision
Rally people around a vision
Clarify their mission
Determine operating guidelines
Focus people on what matters
Prioritize competing demands

Renewing Human Resources
Strengthen pay-for-performance link
Enhance selection systems
Invest in training and development

Helping Middle Managers
Understand the madness
Define their role
Regain their footing

Enhancing Work Methods
Enhance creativity
Provide problem-solving skills
Embrace experimentation
Increase appropriate levels of risk taking

Promoting Organizational Learning
Imbed double-loop learning
Create diagnostic opportunities
Increase upward, downward, and
    lateral communication

EXHIBIT 2.6

Resuscitating Human Spirit. An effort to recover after transition breathes life back into the moribund spirit of the posttransition work force. Building the new organizational order revitalizes employees physically and emotionally exhausted by organizational transition by inspiring them to high levels of individual, team, and organization achievement. This can-do attitude—and the tremendous energy that comes with it—overcomes the cynicism and depression that bring down people and their perceptions of what can be accomplished. The new organizational order also focuses people on the future rather than the painful past. This helps to loosen the grip of those holding on tightly to the past; for those ready to let go, it offers something new and relatively secure to grasp onto. Recovery and revitalization after transition energize people further by increasing their self-confidence and capacity to act. Individual initiative is encouraged and supported in the pursuit of the new order. Evidence from attitude surveys used to track employee reactions to transitions in two companies (one a manufacturer and the other in financial services) show significant rebounds in morale, job satisfaction, and the ability to complete work requirements as the new order develops.

Living the Vision. Recovery channels individual motivation toward the needs of the company by rallying people around a blueprint for a new and better organization. A shared sense of where the organization is headed and well-communicated mission statements that clarify the direction and purpose of business units or departments dissipate much of the ambiguity that settles in the posttransition organization. Employees translate the direction and mission into operating principles, policies, and procedures that guide their individual behavior on the job. This occurred in an electronics company where the earnest but seemingly vague vision of "being the best in customer service" was brought to life by order takers who committed to a procedural guideline of answering all phone calls by the fifth ring. In an insurance company that once had bought business at any price, managers executed the new order by writing policies that promoted profit generation over revenue generation. These examples show how people come to understand and accept the *new* organization's priorities. Employees, work teams, and functional units are then able to concentrate on bringing life to the new vision.

Enhancing Work Methods. With clear direction and priorities, employees can actually "work smarter" following transition—an often stated but rarely realized goal. Leadership's rhetoric is converted into action by providing employees the time and resources to revisit and revise their approaches to work, to maneuver them in line with the twin goals of enhancing work methods and enacting the new organizational order. This cultivates an environment that nurtures creativity and embraces experimentation, which together enhance organizational learning. It also develops problem-solving repertoires and promotes a level of risk taking appropriate to the organization's need to change its way of doing things. In the electronics firm, order takers proposed scaling back nonessential paperwork to free themselves up to answer customer calls by the fifth ring. Similarly, sales managers in a pharmaceuticals firm eliminated preparation of reports detailing activity with small accounts that did not warrant the time investment.

Renewing Human Resources. In addition to enhancing work methods, recovery allows an organization to make over its human resources practices and programs. Several organizations have acted to strengthen the pay-for-performance link in their compensation plans as part of building a new organizational order. Revised human resources systems also identify and bring on board people with the skills or competencies that fit the new order. The technical abilities and leadership qualities that reinforce the new way of doing things may need to be found outside the organization (requiring revisions in selection systems) or nurtured within the current employee population (where employees may be "retooled" to fit the mold of the new order). Training and development programs utilizing advances in adult learning technology will prepare people to make their best possible contribution to organizational objectives.

Helping Middle Managers. While recovery after transition aids members at all levels of the organization, it particularly addresses the many issues confronting middle managers who are frightened by the disproportionate layoffs in their ranks and frustrated by the paucity of information available to help them address employees' concerns. First, it helps these managers understand the madness that is going on within their organization and in the business environment. This increases their ability to communicate the whys and wherefores of transition and recovery to their team members. Second, the articulation of a new organizational order gives clarity to the roles and responsibilities of middle managers, in terms of both managing core business activities and contributing to a successful recovery. This may be especially important in cases where the new order alters traditional hierarchical relationships. Third, recovery helps middle managers regain their footing following the wrenching transition period. Part of recovering from a transition is reestablishing middle managers' self-confidence that they can lead their teams through turbulent times.

Promoting Organizational Learning. Organizational recovery promotes double-loop learning in organizations. The process of articulating a new organizational order counters the habits that interfere with learning during times of rapid change and transition. People look for—rather than filter out—data that do not confirm their mental models, and they interpret those data in the context of the new organizational order. This new context may allow them to see and solve long-standing problems that they never before recognized.

A high technology firm beset by a series of new product failures downsized dramatically to maintain economic viability. Following a restructuring that brought functional specialists together in product teams, the president announced his commitment to building a new organization characterized by discipline and self-scrutiny. To nurture these qualities, he set up regular "presidential reviews" of products that did not fare well in the marketplace. The reviews ascertained what objectively occurred, what the original intentions were, what unintended consequences resulted, and what could be learned as a result of the failure. After the first few reviews, the president and his top team noticed a recurring pattern: product design teams were thinking about technology-laden "boxes" and not about users. This learning at the organizational level contributed to another component of the new order—integrating a regard for user needs at each step of the new product development process.

Learning while building a new organizational order is also promoted through increases in upward, downward, and lateral communication. As trust is rebuilt and experimentation embraced, employees overcome their fears about speaking out. Managers and other leaders become more proficient at listening. Downward communication increases through the delivery of information about the new order, including what to expect of it, which actions can and cannot be taken and why, action plans and progress toward realizing the new order, and reward system alignment. Coordination across groups increases along with the flow of communication. Success stories confirming the building of the new order in one area are grist for the organization-wide communication mill. The enhanced information flow and other features of recovery after transition build a learning and adaptive capacity within individuals and teams; this learning encompasses new skills, new data bases, new technologies, and new systems, all of which are required to live the new organizational order.

Challenges to the New Organizational Order

A wide range of challenges confront effective organizational recovery following transition. Three particular sources—the mind-set of employees, prevailing organizational dynamics, and the manner in which the transition is managed—throw up roadblocks along the path to the new organizational order (see Exhibit 2.7).

Employee Mind-Set

Transitions affect people in different ways. Some feel like winners—they emerge with the position, project, or budget they sought. Others feel like losers—they lost something or someone important to them as the winds of transition blew through. Still others, in most cases the majority of people, have a mixed set of feelings based on their personal cost/benefit assessment of how the

---

Challenges to the New Organizational Order

Employee Mind-Set	Organizational Dynamics	Transition Management
Resistance to change	Crisis management	Lack of consensus
Regression to primitive behaviors	Constricted communication	Programmatic change
Powerlessness	Outmoded systems	Lack of resources
Demotivation		

EXHIBIT 2.7

transition affects them, their immediate work team, and the overall organization. Thus people's responses to the notion and the content of a new organizational order should not be overgeneralized. Experience, however, points to some common challenges to building the desired organization.

Resistance to Change. Employee resistance takes many forms and can sidetrack any change effort. On the heels of a transition, people need a certain degree of stability or security, and movement to a new organizational order presents yet another round of anxiety-producing unknowns. Locked-in mental models prevent employees from perceiving a need for change or understanding the business or personal benefits of the new way. Old expectations and habits are difficult to give up, especially when they led to success before the transition. For example, building up a large staff may have been a source of high power and compensation in the old organizational order, but may not continue to serve a manager whose superiors are looking toward a lean and mean operation.

People's resistance to change may be rooted in fear, but it also may come from a need to defend the old way of doing things. Discussion of a new organizational order that appears to criticize the way things were done in the past will produce defensiveness. Usually the people who have created the past practices and policies are still in the organization, and it is difficult for them to separate criticism of their systems from criticism of themselves. If they feel attacked, then they are likely to spend considerable energy defending why things were done the old way rather than contributing to building the new order.

Regression to Primitive Behaviors. Many people respond to organizational transition by regressing to primitive behaviors. They restrict communication or take actions that seem decisive, yet are not well thought out. During and following a transition, people at all levels experience an urge to hold on tightly to information and feelings. For executives, this means putting on a tough facade to give the impression that all is under control. For the rank-and-file employee, this includes repressing emotion to not show any sign of vulnerability—in case there is another wave of layoffs down the road, no one wants to be tagged as a weakling who cannot take the heat. Managers of work teams regress by taking back any decision-making discretion given to employees through participative management and empowerment programs. In general, "hard-nosed" management dominates over "humanistic" management. Consultant Harry Levinson labeled the economic recession "a blow to psychological management."[3]

Powerlessness. Most people experience a perceived loss of control during transition, as dynamics beyond their influence dominate the action. The sense of powerlessness yields individual inaction and managerial paralysis. Characteristics of the posttransition organization, such as unclear reporting relationships or accountability, may exacerbate this sense of powerlessness. This is particularly pertinent in cases where work has been reengineered to cut across different business units.

Demotivation. People behave in ways that get them the things they want, provided they have the ability to get the job done and expect to be rewarded for doing so. The expectancy theory of motivation expresses this as a function of a multiplicative relationship among three factors: instrumentality (I), a person's perceived relationship between how hard they work and how well they do ("How well can I complete this task?"); valence (V), the employee's feelings about how attractive the rewards are ("How much do I like/need this reward?"), and expectancy (E), the employees' expectations that effort will indeed be rewarded (How likely is it that I will receive the reward?").[4] The employee assigns a probability between 0 (no likelihood of occurring) and 1 (total likelihood of occurring) to each factor; being a multiplicative relationship, a low probability rating on any of the factors results in low motivation (see Exhibit 2.8).

Expectancy Theory of Motivation

$$\text{Motivation} = \underset{(0-1)}{E} \times \underset{(0-1)}{V} \times \underset{(0-1)}{I}$$

EXHIBIT 2.8

Thus any of three cognitive conditions present after a transition may demotivate an employee. First, an employee might feel unable to complete a task even when giving his or her best effort ("How can I get everything done well and on time when there is so much work being thrown at me and I do not have the information or other resources I need?"). Second, the employee may not find current rewards attractive ("Why should I work so hard if all I am going to get is a merit increase of a measly few percentage points or the `privilege' of keeping my job here, where there is more competition for fewer promotions?"). Third, the employee might conclude that promised rewards are not delivered by the company ("Why should I bother when they reneged on giving me that promotion?").

Organizational Dynamics

Challenges to achieving the new organizational order may also come from organizational dynamics that work against the desired end state. These dynamics include management behaviors that interfere with the exchange of valid information and organizational systems that fit the old mold rather than the new one.

Crisis Management. The uncertainty of transition, coupled with the potential for high-stakes loss and gain, leads to a crisis management orientation. Regressing to primitive management behaviors and anxious about working in an uncharted context with new political gamesmanship, top executives scurry to act decisively in commanding their situation. They focus on strategy and tactics, and their troops are supposed to fall in line like loyal foot soldiers. But the troops do not fall in line; instead, they are worried and unsure how to behave.

Research on the handling of crises shows some predictable reactions for organizations contending with high levels of uncertainty and challenge. Organizations facing a crisis centralize decision-making in an authoritative mode. Much as stress leads executives to tighten up and turn inward, crisis leads an executive team in the same direction. Centralization serves many useful functions to an executive team facing a transition. It ensures that information flows to the top and executives are able, in concert with trusted associates, to sort out possible losses and gains and map strategy for moves and countermoves. In an authoritative decision-making mode, executives only have to answer to themselves. They are not bothered by irrelevant data and do not have to explain themselves to subordinates favoring other decisions. This mode of decision-making proves heady to many executives and accentuates their beliefs that they are masters of their organizations.

But this crisis orientation can have its costs. For example, centralized decision-making can shut the top team off from important information that may be developed in open exchange with subordinates or, in the case of a merger, with executives from the combining organization. It also can insulate the top leaders and promote a "groupthink" mentality as strategies are considered. A crisis management mode hinders recovery when these reactions reduce decision quality during transition planning and implementation, thus reducing organizational effectiveness after the transition, or are carried into the posttransition period.

Constricted Communication. When employees hear the announcement of a transition, they assume that senior leadership has a plan. This is, after all, a "business move." What employees do not understand is that in most acquisitions, senior management is not entirely sure of what it has bought and must take time to study integration options. In the case of a downsizing, senior management is likely to announce a reduction in force to realize cost savings before any thought has been given to where the company is headed. In the case of a cultural transformation, executives may purposely avoid committing to a definite plan of action so as to remain open to midcourse corrections. Yet employees interpret silence to mean that the plan is being withheld from them.

Even in the best of times, there is static on the communication lines in most organizations. This situation gets worse during times of change and crisis. Employees do not trust the messages they hear and are cynical about management's intentions. Ironically, these same employees crave information—they want proof that the transition makes sense for the company and its future, signs that it will be well managed, signals that people will matter, and answers as to what the change means for them personally.

Senior managers, in turn, are wary of saying too much to employees when so little is known. They are legitimately afraid of say-ing something that later could be proven wrong or be used against the company in a wrongful discharge suit. Some executives feel they have to have a tangible plan before communicating with their people. Others say they are too busy to communicate. Still others fantasize that by not communicating about the transition they are "buffering" employees from stress. It is as if they have a picture of employees blissfully whistling while they work and acting as if no news is good news. If you ask employees, of course, they will tell you that no news is bad news.

Constricted communication during transition is the basis for anger, distrust, and cynicism that linger afterward. It creates a precedent and becomes ingrained in the organizational culture to the extent that upward and downward channels of communication are shut off. Most importantly, it is difficult for top executives to create a new organizational order when they are out of touch with employees' current perceptions of everything from how to improve operations to what motivates them. A recent survey conducted by William M. Mercer, Incorporated found that only about half of all employees feel it is safe to say what they truly think, or that man-agers seek out or listen to their opinions (see Exhibit 2.9). Just one-third of employees say their ideas are acted on or that they are given the reason why their ideas are not used. And only one in four employees reports that management takes employee interests into consideration when making important decisions.

Employees' Views on Opportunities to Participate

Question	% Agreeing
Is it safe to say what you think around here?	49%
Do managers seek out your opinions and ideas?	48%
Do managers listen well to your suggestions?	48%
Are your ideas and opinions acted on?	33%
When your ideas and opinions aren't used, are you told the reasons why?	31%
Does management take employee interests into consideration when making important decisions?	24%
Source: William M. Mercer, Inc.	

EXHIBIT 2.9

Outmoded systems. Their complex environments do not prevent most organizations from attempting to create stability and predictability in their management control systems. Transition adds an internal layer of turbulence that disrupts the normal course of events. It thus disturbs and undermines existing systems, making them irrelevant and/or inappropriate. As a result, the organization may lose the capacity to coordinate the work being done, monitor performance, and make corrections as in normal control processes.

Most organizations have not designed themselves for ongoing changes of strategy and structure. Systems designed for the pretransition state may not be appropriate for the posttransition state. And, in the case of multiple waves of change, even a new system designed with a particular vision or end state in mind may soon lose its relevance and efficacy for management practice.

An organization's reward system is a key example of how an outmoded system can interfere with building a new order. When the new order heralds enhanced teamwork but the reward system continues to reinforce individualism, employees will be confused and in conflict. Eventually, if not immediately, people's behavior will gravitate toward what is rewarded.

Unless people are moved to act in new ways, to go beyond the old organizational order, there can be no new order. Senior managers often are too quick to separate vision from implementation and, as a result, to leave organizational details out of their thinking. This short-circuits the process and leaves people unclear about and uncommitted to the new organizational order. Cynicism about the difference between what top management says and what the system rewards may be the single largest blockage on the road to recovery.

Transition Management

A final set of challenges to organizational recovery emanates from how the transition itself was managed. The process of moving through the transition can leave management and employees scrambling in directions in conflict with the desired end state. This results from some key deficiencies: a lack of true management consensus regarding where the organization is headed, a lack of innovation in implementing change, and a lack of resources in building the new organizational order.

Lack of Management Consensus. The failure to convey a clear sense of the new organizational order may be due to managers who do not share a common perception of it and who therefore pull in different directions. Often this occurs even when managers think they agree. For example, managers accede relatively easily to such broad objectives as "pushing decision-making authority down the hierarchy." But hiding underneath this goal are as many interpretations about how to implement it as there are managers. One manager in a communications conglomerate gave employees discretion to make decisions on routine business activities not requiring capital expenditures above $250. Another solicited employee input for decision alternatives but ultimately made the decision herself, and still another announced his decisions a day before they were to be implemented just in case any employee had an objection. Shared understanding of the new organizational order needs to be probed at a deep and specific level to determine whether managerial thinking is truly in sync.

Programmed Change Versus Self-Invention. Additionally, unless people feel some degree of ownership over the new organizational order, their actions in reinforcing it are halfhearted. In general, commitment to the new organizational order depends on how it fits with a person's perception of the interest of the organization and of his or her personal interests. In authoritarian, one-size-fits-all prescriptions for change, senior leadership knows in advance (or thinks it knows) what will be required to effect the change, and success is believed to depend on following the program. The opportunity to engage people in bringing the new organizational order to life is reduced to having them "stick with the process"—the former requiring action and innovation, the latter resulting in passivity and obedience. It is the difference between creating a work of art and coloring by numbers. Change strategies are constantly being derailed by individuals and groups who, having no personal investment, refuse to "get with the program."

A number of arguments can be made in favor of prepackaged approaches to organizational change. There is clearly a great deal of efficiency in capitalizing on what has been learned in other organizations and in implementing well-developed change programs. The problem is that standardized tools allow little room for invention and reinvention. Programmatic change runs the risk of remaining a program rather than becoming part of the fabric of the organization.

Invention and reinvention are especially critical when values congruent with employee involvement are part of the new organizational order. Implementation of a new order often demands an emotional and value-oriented commitment to change. If managers simply go through the motions of establishing a more participative management style, employees quickly recognize that the managers' behavior is insincere. When stress or controversy develops in the organization, the program is easily abandoned and managers revert back to their traditional way of operating.[5] The new organizational order, then, must be more of a blueprint to guide the local efforts of teams and their leaders than a rigid program or mandate.

Lack of Resources. The most precious resource in recovering from an organizational transition is time. There never is enough of it to accommodate both the tasks of transition management and the demands of running the organization. Inevitably, the pressures of managing a transition cut into the resources available to run day-to-day business operations. Business momentum gets lost, projects are derailed, and staffing is thrown off balance.

The development of a new organizational order takes time—time to conceive, communicate, test, revise, and implement. Following a transition, managers want to get out of the blocks fast and show they can produce results. If there is even the slightest cynicism about leadership's intentions for a new organizational order, time spent on innovation and experimentation will be viewed as a wasteful distraction from core business activities. Downsized teams will be racing harder to get the same amount of work accomplished. People pumped up by promises of organizational enhancement will look around for signs that the transition has lived up to its billing, but they will be discouraged by the lack of time made available to design ways to work smarter or think creatively.

Other resources—people, information, tools, and equipment among them—also may be less accessible following transition. Cost-cutting measures often eliminate research assistants, librarians, clerical help, and other staffers who provide information and other resources to managers. Regional research centers were closed in favor of one national center during a downsizing in a large public relations firm. While the latest technology (fax machines and electronic mail on a computer network) helped, the slowed-down turnaround time became a hindrance to serving clients and preparing proposals in a timely manner. Sometimes even the most mundane of resources may be missing. After a defense contractor based in southern California completed waves of downsizing, one vice president wanted to remove the scores of empty desks that remained in his department's work area. His telephone calls to maintenance, however, were unsuccessful. The person responsible for moving furniture was a victim of the downsizing, and no one knew who was responsible now for that duty.

Transition as a Steady State

Transitions can be so rapid and repetitive today that organizations need to build a work force that can change several times. The work of establishing a new organizational order, then, includes getting and keeping people in a relatively pliable state. That is, part of refreezing a new mental model is keeping the expectations that unfreezing and remolding may—and likely will—be needed at any time.

There is no indication that the pace of organizational change is slowing. A new economic world order is emerging: national economies and financial markets are becoming more closely linked into a global economy, Third World nations are emerging as significant competitors, the United States is no longer the single dominant economy of the world, the life cycle of products is declining, significant political challenges to the free market are demanding new ways of doing business, and workers' technical skills are lagging further behind technical advances.

It is a cruel irony that the stress and sense of urgency that unfreeze an organization during transition also prompt a crisis management orientation that detracts from executive efficacy in managing recovery. Scarce resources, unclear end states, and predispositions toward burnout, cynicism, and anger are among the conditions that can be improved by a recovery program, but that also hinder creativity, innovation, and risk taking at a time when they are needed most. These conditions—and others—must be managed if recovery is to succeed at revitalizing individuals, teams, and entire organizations.

Unintended Consequences

At the annual party celebrating the conclusion of our softball season, I asked Albert, a teammate, if I could get him a beer while I was at the bar. "No thanks," came his reply, "my doctor ordered me off all alcohol until he does some tests on my liver." Surprised at this response from a seemingly healthy man in his mid-twenties, I asked Albert if everything was okay with his health. He began to tell me about his job as a staff accountant in a medium-sized manufacturing firm:

> The stress on my job has just been unbearable. We've had a hiring freeze for over a year now. Only a few people are left in our department, and management expects us to pick up the slack. Its really not that much more work, but the pressure to get things done is intense. There is no room for slippage. Everybody wants their reports done first, and if we mess up in even the slightest way we get screamed at. We live in fear of being laid off. And no one is helping me prioritize my work or the work I'm doing that used to be done by others. I don't mind pitching in during tough times, but I don't think management understands what they are putting us through and how tense and stressful things are in our department.

George, a thirty-one-year old marketing executive, sacrificed his love of music to study engineering in college. To make himself even more employable, he earned a master's degree in marketing. Since then he had found himself bobbing on a stormy sea of corporate restructuring:

> I lost my first job in Kentucky at a failed savings and loan in 1987. About two months later, I found a job developing and marketing new products in Ohio. I moved our family to Dayton and fell in love with the city and the company. I felt I could spend my whole career there. I received two promotions and a series of excellent reviews. Then, the company restructured and I was out of a job. After about six months, I heard of a company in Pennsylvania looking for marketing and product development skills. That job lasted nearly two years until the company was acquired. I landed my next job in the same city and was as enthusiastic and confident as I was in my first job out of college. The company was new-product and marketing driven—my specialties. The job lasted seven months until the recession hit the company's sales. I've lost four jobs in five years, despite personally performing very well. The American dream just isn't coming to me. My dream isn't to do better than my parents—it's to have security and build self-esteem for myself and my family.

On a trip to the Bay Area, I visited former clients at a professional services firm that had acquired a similar-sized competitor two years earlier and recently had gone through a downsizing to "rationalize" staffing levels. By all accounts, the merger went swimmingly; it was regarded in the business press as a rare successful combination in a business plagued by big egos. While visiting I ran into Nancy, the head of the administrative services group, and asked how she was doing:

> We have just gone through a small downsizing; about four of our thirty administrative people were let go. But I have been going nonstop ever since the cuts. I feel like I am treading water and juggling balls at the same time. I haven't taken a lunch break in four days. I don't mind the hard work, but I don't see any relief in sight. I don't know how much longer I can go on before something gives—either me or the work.

Physical illness and disease, emotional despair and alienation, intellectual stagnation, and the acceptance that running harder only results in falling further behind—these are the experiences of the survivors of organizational transitions, the people who retain their jobs following mergers, acquisitions, and downsizings. It is on the minds and muscles of these survivors that a firm's future depends. These distressed and depressed employees are expected to help their organization triumph over difficult times brought on by economic recession, a loss of market share or profitability, a brush with bankruptcy, or a wrenching corporate transformation.

An organizational triumph cannot occur without the concurrent triumph of the people who constitute the organization, and vice versa: individual triumph cannot occur outside a context of sound strategy, prudent financial management, effective structure, and efficient and high-quality work processes. Yet executive attention must expand beyond strategic planning, research and development, and financial accounting to the human side of recovery. As has been said for many years now, a human problem requires a human solution. And the impact of transitions clearly has resulted in a human problem for organizations and their leaders.

Unintended Human Consequences

In principle, a transition should enable an organization to improve its competitiveness without impairing its ability to execute its strategy. In practice, however, a transition can exact a heavy toll on organizational effectiveness and employee well-being.

Wrenching Experience for All Involved

A transition that involves the displacement of people is a wrenching experience for all involved, and the norm in most organizations is to get it over with as quickly and quietly as possible. Terminations are painful to execute, and no one wants to stretch out the dirty work.

Even the toughest, most bottom-line-oriented executives find it difficult to make cuts. It is one thing to speak abstractly of the need to reduce costs and another to make decisions that affect people's lives. Intellectually, senior executives may rationalize that a reduction in force is necessary to regain or sustain profitability. Emotionally, however, they dread making the cuts. Few CEOs themselves actually let senior staff members go, instead passing the burden on to subordinates.

Middle managers are truly that—managers caught in the middle between the conflicting agendas, perspectives, and demands of those at the top and bottom. They feel squeezed. Top-level executives are distant and remote, talking about strategy, planning, and other matters less tangible than middle managers' needs to get products out the door or to keep service quality up amid the turmoil of transition. Meanwhile lower-level employees are looking for concrete direction and support, but middle managers do not have the direction and support to give.

Research shows that managers and supervisors have the most impact on making or breaking employees' reactions to a transition. Yet they are poorly prepared for their role in making a transition successful. When an organization offers a voluntary approach to downsizing, for example, managers and supervisors find themselves in the awkward position of counseling employees on whether to stay or go. No one wants to tell an employee his or her services are no longer needed, even if it is the most humane thing to do when a subsequent wave of involuntary cuts looms on the horizon. This is especially difficult for managers in large organizations engaged in multiple waves of downsizing. The obvious low performers have already been removed, leaving only good contributors who have to be shown the door.

After the cuts are made, work team leaders have to accomplish more with fewer resources. Supervisors and managers struggle to maintain productivity with fewer bodies at a time when people are emotionally distraught. Lip service may have been given to how the downsizing will result in a leaner, meaner, smarter, and, generally better organization. But now no one has the time to think of smarter or better ways of doing things.

Support staff find themselves overwhelmed by the multiple demands placed on them during a transition. Human resources professionals, for example, are staggered by the work load involved in processing terminations and scheduling outplacement services, preoccupied by knowing their own area—a non-revenue-producing staff function—is likely to be one of the hardest hit, and burdened by the line of employees outside the door waiting for a shoulder to cry on.

Finally, a transition threatens the self-esteem and sense of fairness of all employees. People can rationalize layoffs based on performance, say, when an employee is repeatedly late to work or fails to meet production standards. But people cannot rationalize the fact that hardworking fellow employees have lost their jobs because of an economic downturn. Downsizing victims blame themselves for not seeing it coming, or not doing something to protect themselves. For victims and survivors, a reduction in force eats away at the assumption of fairness in the work place as they wonder why leadership could not stave off the dreaded event or identify some alternative course of action. Survivors see the human carnage of lost jobs and destroyed careers, and wonder, "How could an organization I want to dedicate my life's work to do this to people?"

Some executives like to believe that downsizing survivors, grateful just to have a job, are ready to roll up their sleeves and get down to work. The real consequences, however, are very different. Survivors of organizational transitions experience a broad range of psychological and behavioral reactions that begin with rumors of impending change, continue through the weeks and months of transition planning and implementation, and linger long after the dust settles. They have a lasting impact on employees' perceptions of the current organization and expectations for its future. The work of rebuilding after a transition must begin with *accepting* that there is unintended human and organizational fallout from transition, *understanding* these consequences, and *acting* as proactively as possible to recover from them.

Psychological Reactions to Transition

Survivor Syndrome. Symptoms of the "transition survivor syndrome" have been well documented during the years of organizational MADness.[1] Often people feel guilty for having been spared, similar to the psychological reaction of children who lose a playmate or sibling in a fatal accident. The survivor responds to the tragedy with extreme guilt and asks, "Why couldn't it have been me?" Survivors also may become depressed at their inability to avert future layoffs or disruptions to their work routine. In the short run, they become distracted from their work responsibilities. Over the long haul, employees who have been through a transition have considerably less confidence and trust in their employers.

Despite paring down the payroll, leaders of downsized companies find it difficult to realize the increases in productivity and cost savings they had hoped the layoffs would produce. As *U.S. News and World Report* reported, "The survivors of corporate downsizing are like recovering casualties of a lost war—grateful to be alive, but uncertain of what they are living for. Some have found opportunity amid the carnage of fallen colleagues, but others have become deeply distrustful and fearful they may be next."

Loss of Confidence in Management. One of the most enduring symptoms of transition survivor syndrome is the erosion of employee confidence in their management. Several factors contribute to this. First, many employees wonder why their leaders did not take proactive action to prevent layoffs or avoid the ugliness of a postmerger culture clash. Second, employees do not see how transitions have added any value to the workplace. Outplacement specialists Right Associates surveyed 909 firms that downsized in 1991 and found that 72 percent of employees still on the job did not think the newly revamped company was a better place to work and 70 percent felt insecure about their future with the firm. Third, there is a growing sense that management is motivated by greed rather than by concern for customers or employees.

The irony here is that mergers, acquisitions, and downsizings can be productive tools to enhance organizational effectiveness and profitability and, as a result, job security and quality of work life. The way transitions are implemented and managed, however, often destroys workers' regard and respect for their organizations and leaders. In one national survey, nearly three-quarters of employees whose companies were *not* involved in a merger or layoff in the past year reported being confident in the long-term future of their company. In contrast, only about one-half of employees whose firms had been involved in a merger or layoff were confident about their company's future.[2]

Cynicism and Distrust. A major unintended consequence of organizational transitions has been the growing cynicism of the U.S. work force. People do not mind enduring some pain if they see a payoff for it, but this has not been the case in most organizational transitions. Promises that nothing will change during the transition, and of enhanced effectiveness following it, are rarely fulfilled. In many organizations people see few benefits—for the business or for themselves—resulting from the ordeal.

Poorly managed transitions have had a *negative* not merely a *neutral* effect on the mind set of employees. In mergers, employees see how senior executives who leave the company land on their feet with generous golden parachutes, and how those who stay often have well-endowed employment contracts. In downsizings, employees in the middle and lower ranks rarely witness the pain being shared by those at the top. People have grown distrustful of their leadership and cynical of opportunities to succeed in their companies. A national study found that 43 percent of working Americans doubt the truth of what management tells them and believe that their companies, given a chance, will take advantage of them.[3] In recent strikes at Caterpillar and American Airlines, an intangible issue—suspicion of senior management—aroused workers more than anything that could be written into a contract.

Decreased Morale. The Laborforce 2000 study of downsizing and restructuring found that morale dropped among surviving employees in six of every ten companies engaged in a downsizing. Interestingly, the drop in morale was the same whether companies downsized for strategic reasons or to contain or control costs. The American Management Association survey on downsizing yielded even more depressing results: 77 percent of reporting companies experienced a decline in morale after a downsizing, and the more frequently a company downsized, the worse the consequences (see Exhibit 3.1). In contrast, a 1991 survey of chief executive officers showed that 91 percent believed morale in their companies was just fine.[4]

Survivors are angry, both at themselves for not seeing trouble before it arrived and at their leaders for exposing people to such stressful treatment. They hurt because the sight of coworkers being dismissed is painful, as is accepting that one's own career dreams have been derailed by a merger or reorganization. And they are frustrated because their ability to get the job done is hampered by the confusion of the posttransition organization, and because they see few signs that things are going to get better soon.

Reduced Loyalty. During transitions that involve a reduction in force, organizations often inadvertently hurt most the employees

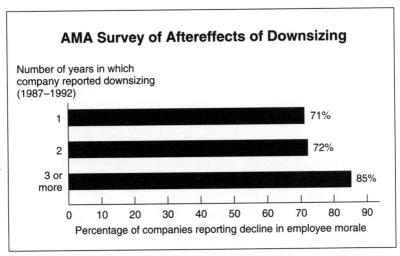

AMA Survey of Aftereffects of Downsizing

Number of years in which
company reported downsizing
(1987–1992)

1	71%
2	72%
3 or more	85%

Percentage of companies reporting decline in employee morale

EXHIBIT 3.1

they least wish to alienate: those who are very loyal to the organization at the onset. Most people who join organizations need to feel that they are a part of, and are contributing to, a larger collective. One outgrowth of people's need for group membership is that they expect and want to be treated fairly by the groups to which they belong. Research conducted by a team from Columbia University suggests that if loyal employees believe that layoffs were unfair, their loyalty drops sharply; even more so than that of survivors who are less committed at the outset.[5]

Dismal Outlook. Even for those who breath a momentary sigh of relief for having retained a job, dismal signs predominate in the posttransition organization. Survivors feel sad about the past and anxious about the future. People miss their former mentors, coworkers, and other colleagues who may have exited in a downsizing. They also miss their former political connections to the powerful decision makers in the organization.

When they set their sites on the future, people become further dismayed. All signals point to fewer opportunities for advancement when delayerings eliminate traditional career paths and mergers bring on board more competitors for fewer slots at the higher rungs of the corporate ladder. People even see themselves having to work harder just to stay in the same place.

Finally, there is less fun on the job. The rhetoric of cost reduction puts a damper on the informal perks and playfulness that many people enjoy at work.

Loss of Control. What really concerns survivors is the sense that they have lost control over their work lives. No matter how well they do their jobs, they could be hit in the next wave of layoffs.

The rapid pace of change in today's business world means that one's position, pet project, or potential for advancement could be eliminated at a moment's notice, with nothing one can do to counteract it. A middle-level marketing manager from an acquired consumer products company exemplified the control issue during an interview a year after the merger announcement:

> I used to think that if I did my job well, completed my projects on time and in fine manner, I would be able to control my fate. That's no longer true. This merger is bigger than I am. I've seen other managers from our side—people who clearly were good, if not excellent, performers—get the shaft. I didn't ask to be acquired, but now my track record doesn't count for anything. I'm at the mercy of some bureaucrat at headquarters. I'm no longer the master of my own fate.

While senior executives have the most at stake in a transition in terms of position, power, pay, and perks, they also have the most control over their situation. They design the combinations, fight the takeover battles, conceive the restructurings, anticipate the downsizings, and arrange for their financial security. Other employees cannot exert control over whether their workplace is being merged, downsized, rightsized, or restructured, and their sense of lost mastery over their fate extends well into the posttransition period.

For some people, walking away from their current organization is their only perceived opportunity to take control over their work life. A research chemist whose firm had just gone through a major restructuring, was clear on her plans: "What is hard work going to get me here? All I've been hearing from this organization is hard work is going to help me keep my job. Well, that's not good enough for me. I was raised in a time when good work was rewarded with an occasional promotion. There was a career path. Now with this delayering, there is nowhere to go. Why should I stay here?" Another manager, from a financial institution, had his plan set for taking back control: "Senior management must think they have us by the balls right now because the job market in banking is so poor. But I can tell you this, at the sight of the first ray of light of an upturn in the economy, I'm walking out of here and not looking back."

When remaining employees see the best and brightest performers jumping ship, it reinforces negative feelings and cynical attitudes. And, importantly, it is these highly skilled and creative individuals that an organization must hold onto to rebound effectively following a transition.

Changing Psychological Work Contract. As Denise Rousseau of Northwestern University's Kellogg Graduate School of Management points out, long-term employees come to believe that there is "more to their job than just the money they make, just as a spouse might think there is more to a marriage than the obligation of financial support." This psychological contract commits both sides to maintaining the relationship, with the employees supplying loyalty and the company steady employment.[6]

The traditional expectation that if you work hard, if you are skilled, and if you are devoted, you will be rewarded with money, benefits, promotion, and a secure retirement is no longer valid. The psychological contract between employer and employee now contains more caveats: if the company remains profitable, if it does not get acquired, if the overall economy does not get too bad, if the marketplace does not change, and if technology does not advance. In other words, there are no guarantees.

The old psychological work contract, spelling out a paternalistic relationship between employer and employee, has evolved into a new one stressing self-sufficiency (see Exhibit 3.2). As long as both sides consent, there is no problem in changing the rules of the game. Employers seemed to be ahead of employees, however, in recognizing that the contract was changing. Through communications programs and training seminars, some organizations attempted to convey to their work force that their psychological bond was changing. But, it was not until employees learned the hard way—through the merger mania of the 1980s and the rightsizing rage of the 1990s—that they found out just how the rules had changed.

Psychological Contracts, Then and Now

Organizational psychologist Walter Tornow has seen the changes in psychological work contracts from his vantage point as vice president of human resources research and planning for Control Data Corporation. He describes the history behind the turnabout in these terms:

Then, there was stability, predictability and growth. Firms expected to increase steadily in revenue and number of employees.

Now, there is change, uncertainty and personnel cuts. Reorganization, cutbacks, mergers and acquisitions threaten job security and career paths.

Then, companies saw their work force as permanent, tried to "build" employees through training and by providing steady employment, and valued loyalty.

Now, the work force is flexible, companies "buy" workers for their particular skills over the short run and care most about immediate performance.

Then, employees were committed to the company and expected steady advancement up the corporate ladder. Compensation was based on the philosophy of rewarding hard work and loyalty over the long term. Pensions, life insurance and health care plans that addressed long-term needs were decided on and funded by the company.

Now, opportunities for advancement are limited by slower growth and leaner organizational structures with fewer levels of management. Employee commitment is shifting from loyalty to company to loyalty to self. Employees are asked to contribute to flexible "cafeteria-style" pension and health plans that permit them to choose the benefits most useful to them.

Then, career paths were linear and job preparation generally meant one-time learning. Education and professional training were usually job specific.

Now, employees can expect multiple careers and there is greater need for lifelong learning to avoid obsolescence of job skills.

Source: Mitchell Lee Marks, "The Disappearing Company Man," *Psychology Today,* September 1988, p. 38.

EXHIBIT 3.2

Locking In. An increasing number of people are "locked" into their jobs for security reasons and not because they like the work they are doing or the place they are employed. Many people do not feel they can afford to jump ship amid the rough seas of difficult economic times. Replacement jobs offering similar pay and benefits are hard to find. In addition to the nation's roughly 14 million jobless, as many as 10 to 15 million people who lost their jobs between January 1990 and August 1992 regained employment only at lower wages.[7] And holes are appearing in traditional social safety nets as some states cut back unemployment payments to cope with their own financial crises.

Behavioral Reactions to Transition

Working Harder, Not Smarter. Employees in posttransition organizations often liken their situation to that of a chicken with its head cut off—frantically moving about without any sense of direction, or hope for survival. Or they talk about struggling to keep their heads above water: they know what they have to do, but they are weighed down by the burden of a heavy work load with competing demands. Others, meanwhile, keep their heads in the sand like ostriches, hoping that the winds of change will blow by them.

The work load rarely gets smaller when the work force does. Survivors who return to work following cuts face the dismal prospect of being part of that 80 percent of the people who now have to do 100 percent of the work. Everyone is working harder but feeling as though they are accomplishing less. Inevitably, work falls through the cracks.

The situation is exacerbated by a likely backlog in the work load carried over from the transition planning and implementation periods. One of the basic tenets of effective transition management is to involve people in planning and implementation activities. In a merger, for example, some employees may participate in fact-finding or decision-making task forces to aid integration planning. In one consumer products company, the CEO announced a major reengineering initiative and told managers assigned to internal design teams to allocate three days a week on the effort. Involvement comes with a cost, however, as managers get distracted from core business operations. Ultimately it adds to the burden of employees who still have to get product out the door or services delivered to clients.

Firms that have not experienced a downsizing are likely to have severely limited hiring or frozen it entirely to stave off the likelihood of painful terminations. In these companies, too, people find themselves working harder. The average American in the 1990s puts in

140 more hours on the job annually than two decades ago, according to a study by the Economics Policy Institute. The Bureau of Labor Statistics reported in 1992 that nearly 25 percent of the 88 million full-time workers in the United States spent 49 or more hours on the job each week, up from 18 percent just ten years earlier.

What about the promise of enhanced organizational effectiveness that accompanies the announcements of many organizational transitions? The reality is that no one has time to stop and think of creative ways to approach work. Work teams or task forces may be convened to identify ways to eliminate non-value-added work. Typically, however, these groups are insufficiently prepared to overcome the group dynamics and individual power plays that can sidetrack team creativity and decision-making. When these groups fail to produce enhancements to the workplace, people become more dismayed toward their situation and cynical about the future.

Meanwhile, there are demands from all directions—superiors, peers, and subordinates—that increase the pressure on transition survivors. "Everybody here is so worried about looking good and wants their work to take top priority," noted a staff analyst in a consumer products company. "My boss says to ask my internal customers if what they need in a week can instead be delivered in ten days. But I'm afraid to do that—it may cost me by being labeled as someone who can't cut it around here."

Lack of direction. Compounding the sheer volume of work confronting people who survive a transition is a lack of direction in prioritizing which tasks to tackle first. After the merger of two health maintenance organizations, the leadership was indecisive regarding the relative merits of either aggressively pursuing increases in membership roles or conservatively maintaining levels of profitability. Middle managers were paralyzed by this lack of direction, waiting to see which way they should lead their groups. The director of operations expressed the frustration: "Does senior management want us to go out and run up the membership roles, or are they interested in protecting the margin? Either one is fine by me, but someone has got to let me know which way we are going, because I do not want to build an organization that is headed one way and then get chastised because I was supposed to go the other way."

Risk Avoidance. Why wouldn't the operations manager and his peers just step up to the plate and make a decision on their own? Because risk taking plummets following a transition. Employees are so scared that there is a self-imposed pressure not to make waves or take risks, just at the time when innovation is needed. Further cuts may be in the offing, and no one wants a blemish on their record that may be used against them when the next list of victims is drawn up. Instead, managers and employees go with what they know, relying on what has worked for them in the past. These are just the behaviors that have gotten the organization in trouble! At the very least, what may have worked in the past is unlikely to work within a new context of changed market, workplace, and social demands.

New company initiatives like total quality or reengineering programs may offer promise when they are rolled out by senior executives or consultants. But unless there is hands-on follow-up by leadership, major new programs or processes are unlikely to be embraced by operating managers. The latter will resist experimenting with new concepts or processes during a stressful time when they see so much is at stake.

Political Behavior. Political game playing increases sharply in organizations following transition. One way people shore up their sense of control is to lobby for themselves, both inside and outside the organization. Employees spend time promoting their value to executives and managers, as well as reminding them of any outstanding favors that may be owed. They network with friends and associates from outside the organization—a distraction from getting their work done but an important protective action to take in the event of future layoffs. Coworker relations may become strained as individuals explicitly or implicitly put down their colleagues in an effort to make themselves look better in the eyes of superiors.

Politics prevail also at the group level as work teams "look out for number one." Managers erect barriers between teams, focusing on group results rather than the big picture: in the short run, what is best for the team is seen as more important than what is best for the organization.

Role Ambiguity. A constant problem interfering with organizational effectiveness in the posttransition organization is role ambiguity. Survivors wonder who is responsible for what and who to go to for what decisions. A lot of time is spent wondering how to prioritize work and how to operate in an environment in which direction is not forthcoming. This is especially frustrating for achievement-oriented people who want to start building a good track record in the posttransition environment. They hope to make a positive first impression on new superiors, peers, and subordinates, yet they do not always know who to go to or work with to get the job done right and on time.

Withdrawal. According to Herman Maynard, a former senior manager at DuPont who took early retirement, these psychological and behavioral reactions to transition have prompted many employees "to withdraw their personal and professional power from their jobs, while making it look like they're still working."[8] People's bodies show up to work, but not their hearts and souls. As executives exhort their employees to boost productivity, improve quality, and be more globally competitive, more workers are simply responding with a shrug.

Stress and Performance

Stress is a necessary and life-sustaining function. Consider a caveman walking with a club dangling over his shoulder. He sees a saber-toothed tiger across the field. By nature, that caveman is thrust into a stress reaction with the singular objective of identifying the threat and eliminating it through either fight or flight. Chemicals produced in his body prompt physiological reactions, like increases in hearing and sight acuity, to assess the threat better. Blood rushes into his legs and arms to fight the threat or flee from it. If it was not for the stress reaction, the caveman would likely—and literally—be consumed by the threat.

Stress performs a similar function in modern organizations. If an employee senses a threat to his or her well-being, it is perfectly normal that a stress reaction will ensue. The reason why stress has a bad reputation in our society is that our bodies can only handle small doses of the chemicals produced in the stress reaction. When they are exposed to multiple and continuing sources of stress, people develop the illnesses associated with stress. Furthermore, stress reactions are influenced by the amount of perceived control people have over the source of stress in their environment. Unlike the caveman, who has total power to decide how to contend with the saber-toothed tiger, employees have few choices in facing organizational transitions.

A classic inverted-U-shaped relationship exists between stress and performance (see Exhibit 3.3). Performance is at its peak when a moderate amount of stress exists. Too little stress translates into too little motivation to produce; too much stress (a much more likely occurrence in organizations in transition) taxes mental and physical responses and detracts from performance. While stress increases people's vigilance in gathering information, too much of it can lead them to simplify and distort what they hear. Leaders of posttransition organizations must contend not only with expected levels of anxiety and inevitable rumors but also with people's perceptions of what might happen, based upon horror stories from other situations.

High levels of stress have a detrimental effect on performance both quantitatively and qualitatively. During and after a transition,

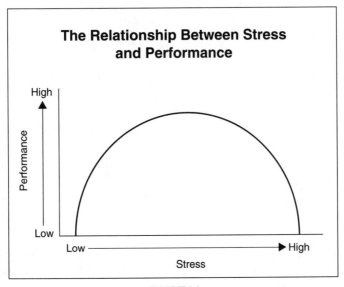

EXHIBIT 3.3

people become distracted from doing their jobs. They huddle around coffee machines and water coolers, exchanging the latest rumors. Some also are at the copying and fax machines, preparing and sending out their resumés. High levels of stress also interfere with cognitive processes in intellectual tasks and with the quality of work produced in manual tasks. People respond in robotlike ways instead of thinking creatively or strategically about the situation at hand. One vice president of quality control at an aerospace firm involved in repeated waves of downsizing and restructuring described it as "like waiting for an earthquake—you do not know when the next shocks will be felt, but you know they will be coming. And you do not know if this will be the big one or not."

Sources of Stress. Organizational transition prompts stress reactions in employees in a variety of ways. The *loss* of someone or something to which people are attached is painful, and it necessitates a period of mourning or depression while they make adjustments in their lives. The potential for loss abounds in a transition—people may lose their job, coworkers, title, status, or perks. They also may lose the opportunity to realize their career aspirations, achievement of their ego ideal, and their sense of personal competence.

One key to understanding the consequences of transition is to realize that the *threat* of loss is as debilitating as an actual loss. Whether the threat is to a person's self-esteem or to his or her physical person, the resulting stress response is the same. Job insecurity is experienced like job loss. Worrying about not fitting into the postmerger culture, lamenting about one's track record accounting for nothing and having to prove one's worth to new superiors, or agonizing over what might happen to one's career all produce stress. Stress is based upon subjective perceptions, not objective reality. It matters not what senior management intends to do, but what people fear their leaders may do.

Next, the *frustration* experienced when anyone or anything even potentially prevents a person from meeting basic needs or getting what they want is another source of stress. People incur added stress they feel helpless to do anything about their situation. This is why long hours of work during and following transition do not necessarily create higher levels of stress, but a high degree of pressure coupled with a lack of control will. Frustration is at its worst when a person has little perceived discretion to negotiate deadlines and manage work load.

Finally, the critical mass of *uncertainty* in a transition is a source of stress. The announcement of a merger, acquisition, downsizing, or large-scale organizational change initiative usually creates more questions than answers. People do not know what to expect and, in today's environment, generally anticipate the worst. Some may have new duties to master, a new superior and peers to adjust to, and new policies and procedures that alter established ways of working. For others, there is the more palpable uncertainty about job security and company identity.

Cumulative Effects. The stress of an event is determined by the amount of change it implies, not necessarily whether the change will be beneficial or detrimental. Stress research shows that marriages and births can be just as stressful as divorces and deaths. Both disrupt the status quo, entangle family and friends, and require that people adapt to new circumstances. Most transitions are seen by employees as a mixed bag of costs and benefits. A downsizing may be painful but also lay the foundation for enhanced business results. A culture change in a historically paternalistic organization may distort people's hopes for security but encourage them to take responsibility for their own career development. The arrival of a new CEO may inject enthusiasm and inspire greatness in an underperforming organization but also produce many changes in protocol and processes.

Thus even positive changes induce stress. This is important to consider because the effects of stress are cumulative. A series of small, seemingly innocuous changes can add up to a large and significant change in the eyes of people. Multiple waves of transition—merger followed by downsizing, restructuring, and changes in everything from benefits to culture—overwhelm people's capacity to cope with stress.

All of this becomes stress inducing when it taxes a person's ability to cope effectively. Unsure of why change is occurring and how it may affect them, and unable to voice their concerns or control their fate, employees' accustomed ways of coping with stress are exaggerated. It is commonplace in organizations engaged in transition to see people handle stress through the "fight or flight" reaction. Anger and aggression are prominent in takeover targets, but they also can be found in friendly acquisitions and in internal reorganizations. Interviews conducted with employees during or soon after transitions are laced with seething indictments of managerial ineptness and examples of strained working relations across groups. By contrast, lethargy, detachment, and other signs of escapism can be found among acquired and reorganized white-collar professionals whose work keeps them out of political power circuits.

Fight or flight reactions should be expected during and after a transition, but they can be costly. Angry managers cannot work for the common good because they are spoiling for a fight and will poison the attitudes of their subordinates. Professionals who remain in body but not spirit after the transition cannot be counted on to contribute fully to fact finding or decision making, but they will surely gripe openly about the resulting decisions.

Stress also takes a toll on people's well-being. Increased drug and alcohol abuse is common among workers surviving a transition. Calls to employee assistance programs skyrocket, and it is common to hear reports of a variety of psychosomatic reactions to stress: trouble falling asleep at night, headaches and back pain, smoking again after having kicked the habit, and increased tension and conflict at home and on the job.

Rates of illness and absenteeism swell at workplaces in transition, and there are plenty of numbers to document the human and financial cost of organizational MADness. At an acquired Fortune 500 manufacturing firm I studied, incidents of high blood pressure among employees rose from 11 percent in the year preceding the merger to 22 percent in the year following its announcement. In a study conducted by Northwestern National Life Insurance, 65 percent of employees surveyed reported that they suffered from exhaustion, insomnia, or other stress-related problems; one-third said they were close to burnout. Stress saps between $100 and $300 billion annually from the U.S. economy in the form of lost workdays and health care costs related to illnesses like exhaustion, depression, and heart attacks.[9] Dr. Reed Moskowitz, director of the stress disorders clinic at New York University Hospital Medical Center reported a 50 percent increase in requests for help from bankers, brokers, and others in the financial services industry in 1991 and

1992, a period marked by vast consolidation and internal reorganization among banks, securities firms, and insurance companies.

The Saturation Effect

Organizations may operate within a context of ongoing radical changes, but people can only handle so much disruption. Over time their threshold for dealing with stress, uncertainty, and disorientation is met. Their ability to cope with all the changes is impaired, resulting in detrimental attitudes, maladaptive behaviors, disappointing performances, and the many other unintended consequences of organizational transition.

Think back to the case of Majestic Manufacturing. Employees there encountered a series of transitions and changes between 1985 and 1991. As characterized in Exhibit 3.4, each of these events resulted in the experience of cumulative stress. After rumors of impending change and vicarious experiences of events occurring at other companies in their industry, Majestic workers were subjected to the acquisition, poor economy, restructuring, voluntary reduction in force, programs like value-added work analysis and TQM, and finally the involuntary reduction-in-force. By the time the last

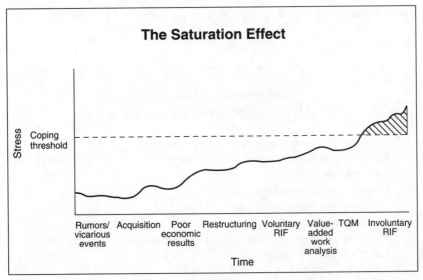

EXHIBIT 3.4

event was announced, many Majestic employees had become numbed by the dizzying course of events.

In many organizations the work force has suffered an intellectual and emotional paralysis brought on by their saturated coping capacity. They are psychologically worn out, unable to take on the responsibilities involved in meeting new challenges. As economic recovery—and its potential for business opportunity—arrives, people are not ready to take advantage of the situation and give a good fight.

Unintended Business Consequences

The cost of mergers, acquisitions, downsizings, and other transitions have been measured in financial as well as human terms. It is common knowledge that many mergers and acquisitions fail to achieve desired financial results. What is less well known is how few do: only about one in five mergers or acquisitions are considered to be successful, whether in terms of return on investment, postmerger share price, or subsequent divestiture.[10]

The Laborforce 2000 study of downsizing and restructuring found that four out of ten companies surveyed experienced undesirable business consequences (see Exhibit 3.5). Many companies were not prepared to handle the work that remained after downsizing and underestimated the costs required to cover tasks that had been performed by former employees. Some 41 percent of the

---

Unintended Consequences
Experienced After Downsizing

Increased need for retraining the remaining work force	41%
Increased use of temporary workers or consultants	36%
Increased use of overtime	35%
Increased retiree health care costs	30%
Contracted out entire functions	26%
Lost the wrong people	20%
Absorbed severance costs that were greater than anticipated	16%
Lost too many people overall	6%

EXHIBIT 3.5

companies that downsized reported a greater need to retrain remaining workers. This implies a double whammy: costs were experienced as a result of both taking people off their regular jobs and training them to do additional jobs. One-third of the companies increased use of temporary workers and consultants, often at a cost higher than the expense of previous employees, and a similar number increased use of overtime. One in every four companies contracted out an entire function.

As to direct financial impact, three in ten companies said that retiree health care costs increased following downsizing, and 16 percent found they had to absorb severance costs greater than anticipated. Another criticism of poorly planned downsizings is that people with critical skills or needed talents take advantage of incentives to leave the company. In the Laborforce 2000 study, one out of every five companies reported losing the wrong people as a consequence of downsizing.

Health care costs incurred by organizations rise for both victims and survivors of downsizings. It is easy to see how health care costs can increase for transition casualties. The psychological trauma of losing one's position, or of unceremoniously being invited to leave through early retirement, triggers psychosomatic ailments. Moreover, early retirees have more time on their hands and, as a result, more time to visit a health care provider and ring up expenses. Not so obvious—but equally costly—are increased health care costs for survivors, who also are subjected to the psychosomatic effects of intense stress on the job. A study of Boeing employees found that those who experienced a high degree of emotional stress on the job were more than twice as likely to file back injury claims than other employees.[11] Working harder to cover the work of others also results in a higher accident rate. Especially problematic is the case of a delayering or other restructuring in which older employees return to jobs involving physical labor after being in less strenuous supervisory jobs. A study by William M. Mercer, Inc. found that although 37 percent of 177 companies surveyed cut their work force by an average of 13 percent over a fifteenth-month period, nearly one-third (32 percent) reported an increase in workers' compensation claims.[12] Overall, one in five companies said their workers compensation costs increased between 50 and 100 percent.

The 1992 American Management Association survey on downsizing also documented how the business goals of organizational transition prove elusive. As Exhibit 3.6 shows, companies that had downsized since January 1987 were nearly as likely to report a decline in productivity as an increase. Fewer than half of the downsized firms increased profits after the cuts were made, and a quarter of them said operating profits went down. In testimony before the Joint Economic Committee of Congress, Eric Rolfe Greenberg, director of the AMA study, concluded that "the after-effects of downsizing are problematic at best and raise the question as to whether the cure is worse than the disease."

Future Consequences

The unintended human and business consequences of organizational transitions are potent enough to not only erode employee well-being and organizational quality and productivity today, but also to derail hopes of restoring their confidence, capabilities, and competitiveness. If left unchecked, the repercussions of organizational MADness can contribute to a dire scenario:

- Inadequate training and skill enhancement of human resources
- Widespread alienation
- Social distress and turbulence

AMA Survey of Aftereffects of Downsizing on Productivity and Profits

	Percentage of Companies That Downsized, 1987–1992	
	Worker Productivity	*Operating Profits*
Declined	28%	24%
Remained constant	36%	23%
Increased	31%	44%

(Note: Column totals do not add to 100% because not all companies responded in every year.)

EXHIBIT 3.6

The tremendous promise of the information age, technological advances, and creative approaches to reengineering organizations will never be harnessed if the work force is not adequately trained to take advantage of changes and compete on a global basis, if individuals become further alienated from their places of employment, or if the failure to identify opportunities for personal and organizational development amid change and transition contribute to angst and conflict in our society.

Training

In addition to psychological problems like increasing cynicism and decreasing loyalty, organizational MADness is deteriorating organizations' ability to take advantage of economic recovery in a very practical way. As part of cost containment programs, corporate training budgets are being pared. The dollar amount spent by U.S. businesses on training in 1991 decreased 5 percent from 1990 and was even below the 1989 total (see Exhibit 3.7).[13] Training budgets were cut in 59 percent of the organizations that reduced costs as a result of the recession. Especially hard hit were training programs in management development and supervisory skills areas critical to organizational recovery.

These cutbacks have occurred at a time when a host of pressures are increasing the burden on organizations to educate their employees. First, economic and social forces have hindered the ability of public schools to turn out graduates who are well prepared to enter the work force. Everything from basics skills like reading, writing, and arithmetic to creative problem-solving or conflict-res-

---

**Dollar Amount Spent by
U.S. Companies on Training**

1991	$43.2 billion
1990	$45.5 billion
1989	$44.4 billion

EXHIBIT 3.7

olution capabilities are sorely lacking in the job applicant pool. Second, those members of the work force who have been relatively decently trained in business concepts were educated with now-outdated models of management and organization. Business school curricula and in-house corporate training programs have been based on theories and research generated within a context of rapid organizational growth and personal advancement that dominated from the 1950s to the early 1980s. This has not prepared executives and employees to work within an environment of organizational retrenchment with flat or declining revenues, cost containment pressures, and restricted advancement opportunities. Moreover, while some managers may have learned rules for managing change, most have not been equipped with the strategic and tactical training required for managing multiple waves of transition. Third, sources of informal training are decaying. Mentors and other role models for leadership are being eliminated through downsizings. Chances for personal and organizational learning are blocked by heavy work loads—spontaneous opportunities for personal reflection or analyzing and learning from situations with coworkers are seldom realized. Learning one's next job easily by being alert and watchful is a luxury no longer found in organizations.

The American Society for Training and Development said in 1993 that training expenditures averaged just 1.4 percent of payroll and that only 10 percent of the nation's workers receive formal training. This puts U.S.-owned organizations at a competitive disadvantage relative to foreign concerns. New employees at American-owned manufacturing companies receive an average of 46 hours of training, compared with 380 hours of training for new hires of manufacturers in Japan and 370 hours for new employees in Japanese-owned manufacturing sites in North America.[14]

Many of the structural, technological, and process changes taking place in organizations today through reengineering programs have the potential to enhance workplace productivity and quality significantly. But if workers are not equipped with the training to make use of these changes—that is, unless people are changed along with structures, technologies, and processes—then these efforts will fall far short of their promise. Take a look at an excerpt from a management consulting firm's promotional essay on "Reengineering the Line/Staff Relationship":

> The old paradigm of the hierarchical, centrally controlled organization—in which decisions are made exclusively in corporate boardrooms and filter down to the line—is crumbling. In its place has emerged a new paradigm: a leaner, more horizontal, performance-oriented structure that can audit its own performance and refine its processes and functions continuously as it adapts to changing corporate and competitive circumstances.

Without imparting new skills and knowledge to the people whose work lives make up that structure, it is doubtful that they will be able to take advantage of opportunities for self-assessment, refinement, and adaptation.

Alienation

Overall life satisfaction is closely linked with satisfaction at work. The onslaught of organizational transitions in the last several years has not only whittled away at employee satisfaction with particular facets of working life (such as communication, opportunities for advancement, and amount of work) but also driven a wedge of estrangement between the employee and the workplace. Lack of control over one's work situation, the feeling of being locked into a job for security reasons, and burnout amid conditions of high stress and uncertainty are ingredients for alienation from the workplace. This psychological withdrawal of the person from his or her work and work setting is primed to interfere further with both personal well-being and the attainment of organizational goals at a critical time in modern economic history.

The detachment of the worker from the workplace is similar to the detachment in the schizoid condition described by psychologist R. D. Laing. The individual who is subjected to the stress of a "threatening experience from which there is no physical escape" develops an elaborate protective mechanism: "He becomes a mental observer, who looks on, detached and impassive at what his body is doing or what is being done to his body."[15] A senior vice president at a financial services firm described this phenomenon more colorfully after being acquired and restructured by a European conglomerate, "They are relying on the poor job market in (our geographic area) to keep people here. They are going to end up with a brain-dead group of slugs."

The unintended consequences of MADness—including the powerlessness derived from a perceived lack of personal control and the meaninglessness born of the dizzying array of rapidly moving events that are incongruent with the worker's concept of how things should happen in the organization—have the potential to produce a great degree of alienation from the organization, as well as from employees' own expectations of achievement and satisfaction at the workplace. Other senior executives at the acquired and restructured financial services firm mentioned above described their employees as "lifeless," "spiritless," "apathetic," and "disinterested." These are not characteristics of a work force ready to charge up any symbolic hill. To the contrary, they are attributes of a work force that performs at very low levels and hinders the attainment of organizational goals.

Social Distress

In nations that do not make a purposeful commitment to upgrade their human resources and redesign management systems to make more effective use of those resources, productivity will continue to stagnate, and prosperity relative to other nations will decline. In Germany, Chancellor Helmut Kohl signaled this message in a nationally televised speech in late 1993, adding that "we need an enterprising spirit, vision, and courage, because our competitors are undertaking stronger efforts to increase their own performance and competitiveness."

The economic and sociopolitical consequences of declining productivity and prosperity in the United States will be disastrous. In order to remain competitive without improving productivity, American firms will have to either shift more production operations abroad or coerce more wage and benefit concessions from U.S. labor, either of which would further reduce domestic well-being. A shrinking revenue base at home will force further cutbacks in the nation's social safety net and lead to fractious political debates over health care rationing, protective tariffs, more restrictive immigration quotas, and welfare payments. Simultaneously, business will seek relief from worker and environmental protection regulations to reduce operating costs, and public-sector austerity will further accelerate infrastructure decay and failures. Worst of all, the continued deterioration of our general economic performance will inevitably lead to greater social distress and political turbulence—especially in our decaying inner cities.

Creating Meaningful Workplaces

Is this prediction too dire? Perhaps so; I hope so. Nonetheless, it highlights the job ahead in recovering our nation's competitive advantage, our organizations' ability to provide meaningful and enriching work, and our work force's perceptions that hard work and fair play can and will be rewarded in these organizations, both psychologically and financially.

People are not just angry at management for putting them through organizational MADness. They also are fearful of the next shoe dropping—things have been dropping and dropping for years now and people do not know when it is going to stop, and they do not believe organizational communications that say it will stop. They need something to help relieve their angst and guide them to a deeper meaning of their experience at work. Accepting that things will never be the same again is not enough—people have to be revitalized following years of MADness.

The potential upside here is not merely to recover from the pain and hampered productivity of recent years, but to learn from that experience. The factors that have created organizational MADness are only going to intensify, further driving organizations and their people mad: the pace of technological advances will become even more mind-boggling, globalization will increase as trade barriers come down and advances occur in transportation and telecommunications, consolidation will rewrite the lineup of companies in industries like financial services and high technology, and so on. We must learn from today's MADness to prevent tomorrow's.

Accepting, understanding, and responding to the unintended consequences of necessary organizational transitions can lead to the development of more effective and more rewarding workplaces, to a work force better prepared and more confident of its ability to succeed, and to a clearer, sounder, and more mutually enriching psychological relationship between them. The yield can be organizations whose employees feel that they have found their life's work, that their jobs have dignity and integrity, that their own creativity is enlivened, and that they experience the tremendous sense of accomplishment that comes when people work together to achieve goals that no one individual could attain on his or her own. And for those managers more focused on bottom line results than on lofty possibilities, the payoff can be workers who are more productive and successful at meeting organizational objectives.

4

Transition Management

Mazda Motor Company saw 1992 as a banner year. Perceived as just another Japanese car manufacturer, the automaker introduced five new models with the explicit intention of changing consumers' view of the company. Mazda sought to create for itself a reputation as a producer of high-quality, costlier cars, a strategy that would allow for larger profit margins. Engineering design for the new models began in 1987, just as status-oriented big spending peaked in the U.S. As large sums of money were sunk into retooling manufacturing operations, the recession hit full stride. Mazda leadership in both the U.S. and Japan grew nervous.

Committed to a line of more expensive cars in a recessionary environment, Mazda looked to its marketing professionals to create an image for the company that would counter the prevailing economic trends. It was 1990, two years before the new models would arrive on the market. "Everyone hunkered down," recalled David, a mid-level marketing manager at Mazda's U.S. headquarters in California. "We came in on the weekends and stayed late most every night. It was real backbreaking work, but we had a real opportunity to change what people thought of Mazda."

While the marketing team worked, the recession sailed across the Pacific and docked in Japan. Reacting to financial pressures at home and abroad, Mazda's leadership in Tokyo attempted three reorganizations of U.S. operations between 1988 and 1992. Each time, efforts were made to restructure business units, shift responsibilities, and cut costs through increased centralization.

Finally the make-or-break 1993 model year arrived. Sales were good, but not great. Nevertheless, the marketing campaign was very well received. Studies conducted by independent market research firms showed that Mazda's image and consumer awareness had gone way up. The hard work of the marketing professionals had paid off. Or had it?

The lukewarm sales results could not support the expectations of optimistic planning forecasts, and the Mazda organization buckled. Six months into the campaign launching the new models, heads rolled in Japan. Rumblings about another round of structural changes in U.S. operations soon followed. "The bottom was pulled out from under us," said David. "The only thing we heard from Japan was 'we don't know what we want to do, but we know we are going to change.' Then, word was out that a package was being offered to people who would voluntarily leave the company. You had to call human resources to find out about it. They wouldn't put anything in writing, but they told us they were keeping a list of who called."

With the economy in California ailing, few people volunteered to leave the company. As a result, just before for the Thanksgiving holiday, Mazda announced an involuntary reduction in force. No mention was made of who would go or how people were being selected. Employees became paralyzed, work stopped, and everyone waited to see what would happen. Then, as David recalled, the cuts came:

> Around 3:30 or 4:00 every day some one from HR would come up, talk to the department manager, and then the manager would walk up to that day's victim and hand them an envelope. In front of everybody, the manager told the person they had a half hour to clear out. Armed guards were posted all over the place, in case anyone stayed more than their thirty minutes.
>
> Each day, right around 3:00 P.M., the tension of people waiting for the HR person to come up and deliver the envelope was so thick you could cut it with a knife. No work got done; everyone just waited for the inevitable. Then we got a clue about how to know what your fate would be that day. Targeted people's personal computers would be shut down at 1:00 P.M. They got a message that the system

was down or that log-on access was denied. The company did not want these people on the computer.

The worst of it was when the company turned off the wrong machines—people who were supposed to be staying assumed they were being booted out. Then there was the day that the entire system went down by accident . . .

This went on for more than a week. No explanation for why the cuts were being made ever was given. Rumors began to circulate of yet another reorganization. David survived the Thanksgiving wave of downsizing, but well into 1993 he did not know what his fate would be in the reorganization.

The company has told us nothing. People are learning what they know from industry magazines. Everyone is paralyzed again. And there is incredible anger at Japan and at our local leadership.

There is no loyalty here; no one is going to go the extra mile after this. Two years ago we worked sixty-five-hour weeks. People were willing to do it, because this was a great place to work and we were doing something that mattered. Personally, I am devastated. From here on in, its just a job for me. I'll put in my forty hours and that's it. I'm looking elsewhere, even though rumor has it that I might get a promotion as part of the reorganization.

What really concerns me is I have to do this for 35 more years— put myself at the mercy of a corporation. I don't think I can do this.

Mismanaged Transitions and Missed Opportunities

There is a classic pattern of mistakes made by many organizations as they respond to bad economic news. As their profits erode and they lose market share, employers frequently worry first about the investment community and focus their communication efforts externally rather than internally. Likewise, when executives search for creative solutions to company business problems, they too often decline to discuss options with workers or offer any kind of outlook for the future. Instead, company leaders lower their profile with their own employees as they grope for the right strategy or combination of actions. The result is nervous employees who believe that management is either insensitive to their plight or fresh out of ideas. When the leadership is finally ready to talk about recovery and revitalization, their past behavior has earned them an insecure work force more inclined to look for another job than to stay around and help.

By all accounts, Mazda introduced a fine line of automobiles in the 1993 model year. With the outstanding work of its marketing professionals, consumers came to recognize the quality and value of these cars. An uptick in the U.S. economy could pave the way for outstanding sales and higher margins. Inevitably, though, environmental pressures will heat up as competitors roll out their own improved models and government regulations mandate product changes (ranging from new safety features to enhanced fuel efficiency). Mazda's leaders will call upon their troops to respond to these challenges, much they did in 1987 when they rallied the work force around the concept of producing and selling a new breed of Mazda product. This time, however, the troops may not be so obedient, committed, or productive.

The way in which Mazda handled its various transitions—including a series of reorganizations, leadership changes, and the makeover of its lackluster image—left the company in a position where it needed to recover from management missteps. David and his colleagues succeeded glowingly at changing Mazda's image. But rather than experiencing personal pride and enhanced organizational loyalty, their hard work left them feeling taken advantage of and eroded their commitment to their company. These people will not readily pull all-nighters and work through the weekend in the future. As the economy picks up and jobs become more available, they may even jump ship and move to a competitor. The outcome would be a double whammy for Mazda—losing excellent performers with a proven track record for getting the job done and facing competition with stronger human resources.

Certainly Mazda's financial results were not at risk solely because of poor transition management. Consider, however, that if the economy in general, and Mazda's financial fortunes in particular, are swept up by a tremendous swell of consumer spending, how much greater the results would be with a committed and focused work force who approached the upswing with the right skills and a heightened self-confidence. And consider how much will be missed if the need to revive the veteran work force, and to recruit and train new hires, distracts managers' attention until the wave crests and breaks.

Transition Mismanagement

Many factors account for the mismanagement of organizational transitions and the associated insensitivity to the resulting human fallout. Some have to do with styles of organizational leaders, the assumptions they hold about human behavior, or simply the fact that they are immersed in denial about the human problem at hand. Other reasons have to do with the events themselves—the crisis mode that surrounds the deluge of information requests and decision making responsibilities in a merger, the basic unpleasantness of a downsizing, and the limited amount of time available to manage culture change when core business demands compete for executive attention. Still other reasons are rooted in prevailing organizational characteristics. The trust and teamwork required for effective transition management may be overshadowed by the counterproductive power plays of entrenched individuals or interest groups. The checks and balances that once helped the organization run smoothly now prevent necessary changes.

Frequently when an executive becomes aware of the unintended human and business consequences of organizational transition, he or she attempts to heal the wounds with a Band-Aid. Executives reach for the latest fad or attempt to copy what has worked effectively elsewhere. This quick-fix approach to managing organizational change and transition has been discounted for years by scholars, consultants, and savvy business leaders who have learned from past mistakes. A survey of 584 companies in the U.S., Canada, Germany, and Japan found that many businesses waste millions of dollars each year on trendy programs like total quality management, empowerment, self-managed work teams, and benchmarking that do not improve their operations.[1] Performance may even be hampered when these programs are implemented without considering how they apply to differing business conditions.

Recognizing the human and organizational toll of transition and the need for recovery is an important first step. A misplaced or misused solution, however, will only make matters worse as employees perceive that leadership is out of touch with the real issues of the transition. In addition, hoping to cover the problems created though transition mismanagement with a program like TQM or "business process reengineering" is akin to hoping that an infection will be treated by an application of gauze. The adoption of a trendy program raises employee cynicism about management jumping on the latest bandwagon. It fails to help people either cope with today's perils or feel better about tomorrow's prospects. Instead, leaders need to size up the injury, look beneath the symptoms to understand the underlying causes, and think through an appropriate course of treatment. This takes time, effort, skill, and money.

Explaining the proper management of mergers, downsizings, culture changes, and other transitions is not the mission of this book. Other resources are available that provide excellent guidance in managing these complex events.[2] The work of revitalizing after a transition, however, is so greatly influenced by how the transition itself is managed that a brief review of critical aspects is valuable. Moreover, given that transition is an ongoing process at many organizations, a company set on recovering from one transition is very likely to experience another before recovery is initiated. In this case, of course, how the subsequent transition is managed foretells the task ahead in revitalizing people, teams, and organizations.

Preemptive Management

The ideal way to manage organizational recovery and revitalization is to preempt its need. If a transition could be managed so that it does not break human spirit, team performance, or organizational effectiveness, then there would be no need to repair these qualities. But even in the best of transitions—those that are strategically sound, are managed carefully and offer tremendous promise for both the organization and its members—there is going to be some human and organizational fallout. Unintended attitudinal and behavioral consequences of transition are inevitable by-products of a phenomenon that produces massive amounts of uncertainty, perceived loss, crisis management, and threats to people's accustomed ways of doing and thinking about things.

The way a transition is managed influences the subsequent job of organizational recovery. Cases such as Mazda's lend credence to this supposition, but there also is empirical evidence to support the relationship. In a study spanning six years, organizational psychologist Philip Mirvis and I investigated the aftermath of an unfriendly takeover attempt, subsequent "white knight" acquisition, and eventual organizational changes in a manufacturing firm.[3] One facet of this study was the analysis of personal and situational factors that influenced changes in employees' perceptions of the workplace during the acquisition by a much larger conglomerate. We considered everything from personal demographics (age, gender, education level, tenure in the company, and so forth) to situational factors like the presence of social support in the workplace and the perceived availability of job alternatives. The factor exerting the greatest influence was the company's history of change management—the extent to which employees were kept informed of prior changes in the company, had a say in those changes, and understood the company's goals (see Exhibit 4.1). Employees who held favorable views of how the company managed change in the past reacted less negatively to the acquisition. Perceptions of how the acquisition itself was managed and the extent to which employees were psychologically involved in their organization were also strongly linked to changes in employee reactions after the acquisition.

Factors Influencing Transition Survivors

Colombia University professor Joel Brockner has studied the effects of layoffs on the productivity and morale of employees who

Relative Influence of Factors Affecting Employee Reactions to Acquisition	
High influence	History of change management Acquisition process Organizational involvement
Moderate influence	Hierarchical level Tenure
Little or no influence	Department affiliation Social support Age Gender Education level Alternate job availability

EXHIBIT 4.1

remain after the cuts. He finds that survivors' perceptions of the fairness of the layoff are determined by their beliefs about *why* the layoff occurred as well as *how* it was implemented.[4]

Legitimacy of Layoffs. Survivors assess whether the layoffs were truly necessary or caused by managerial greed or incompetence. They look around to see what other companies in their industry and community are doing. If similar organizations are downsizing, then employees are more likely to believe that the move in their own firm was justified. Survivors also judge whether management could have achieved the cost savings objectives of a downsizing through less severe methods, like attrition or wage and benefit freezes.

Amount of Forewarning. Survivors weigh the advanced notice given to victims when determining their own reaction to a layoff. The more survivors feel that adequate warning was provided, the more likely they are to conclude that the layoffs were handled in a fair manner. The issue of how early to announce the layoff decision, however, is among the most difficult in a downsizing—executives who want to be fair with all involved and demonstrate concern for people may also fear decreased work productivity or even sabotage. While vandalism or violence rarely occur following a layoff announcement (especially when the latter is handled carefully and considerately), distraction from performance is inevitable. Yet in cases where rumors are running rampant through the workplace, the announcement may actually get some workers—especially those in departments or locations unaffected by the cuts—redirected toward their job duties. And it is not unusual for work groups to accelerate their productivity after a layoff announcement. Some people throw themselves into their work as a way to cope with the news of impending doom. Others hope that management will see their increased productivity and revise the layoff plans.

Frequency and Content of Communication. Survivors want substantive information about the layoffs and life afterward, but they also want some symbolic indication that the leadership is concerned enough to keep in touch with people at lower levels. When the organization takes time to provide adequate reasons for the lay-offs, survivors judge the process as more fair. Employees also re-spond to the compassion and dignity signaled by a thorough com-munication program. As Brockner reports, however, cases of how not to communicate a layoff are easier to find than those of effec-tive communication:

> A petroleum company brought employees together for a meeting. Each employee was given an envelope with a letter A or B on it. The A's were told to stay put, while the B's were ushered into an adja-cent room. Then, en masse, the B's were told that they were being laid off. Another example of how *not* to do it was the experience of employees at a communications company, in which the word of lay-offs was leaked to the press *before* the people to be laid off were told. As a result, some people learned that they were about to lose their jobs over the radio while driving home from work.[5]

One of the most astounding examples of how not to communicate in a layoff comes from the West Coast office of a human resources consulting firm, of all places. Employees there learned of being laid off through a voice mail message! Imagine how petrified surviving employees were about checking their messages afterward.

Cutbacks Shared at Higher Management Levels. Survivors look to see if the pain of the layoffs is being shared at the top of the organi-zation. Are any executives counted among the victims, are the bud-gets and perks of surviving senior managers being shaved along with positions, and are executive compensation packages being subjected to scrutiny? Early in his administration, President Bill Clinton cut back the White House staff to symbolize his participa-tion in the sacrifices required to combat the federal budget deficit. Unfortunately, few other chief executives follow suit. Rarely do se-nior vice presidents get eliminated in a downsizing; the cuts tend to be pushed down to middle and lower levels. As part of a cost con-tainment program in 1993, Bank of America cut many full-time tellers down to nineteen-hour workweeks so they would not be eli-gible for fringe benefits—in a year when it earned 1.5 billion dol-lars and its shareholders and senior executives reaped substantial rewards. (The large California bank eventually offered programs to mitigate the burden for some affected employees.)

Criteria for Cuts. When it comes to survivor reactions, the specific criteria for cuts (seniority, merit, or function) tend to be less important than whether those criteria are administered accurately and consistently. If an organization says that layoffs are to be determined on the basis of each person's performance and contribution but superiors are allowed to retain their favored employees, then employee cynicism and distrust grow as quickly as faith in the future declines. Certainly exceptions to any rule must be allowed, but the reasons need to be explained. Also, if merit is measured through an a pediculous performance appraisal system, a well-intentioned program may be viewed as unfair.

Treatment of Victims. Policies toward layoff victims must be developed with an eye toward how survivors will respond. Outplacement counseling, severance pay, extension of health insurance and other benefits, job location assistance, and stress management workshops are among the services that directly assist victims but also send a message to survivors that the company cares and is ready to devote resources to soften people's landing. Being too generous to layoff victims, however, can backfire. In the merger of Canada's Molson Breweries and Australian-controlled Carling O'Keefe, management sought to appease government and union officials through a "model merger adjustment program" (that is, a postmerger layoff). Generous severance arrangements prompted many surviving employees to feel like they were the losers. As one manager commented, "Give me one of those fat severance checks, and I'll take my chances out on the street!"

Proactive Transition Management

There are two basic tasks in managing the human side of organizational transitions. One is to minimize the downside of transition by reducing the stress experienced by employees and helping them cope with its effects. The second is to maximize the upside by building employee understanding of and commitment to the transition, the rationale underlying it, and the opportunity promised by it. As depicted in Exhibit 4.2, stress among employees rises dramatically before and during a transition, then decreases only gradually. Commitment to the new organization builds slowly. While these

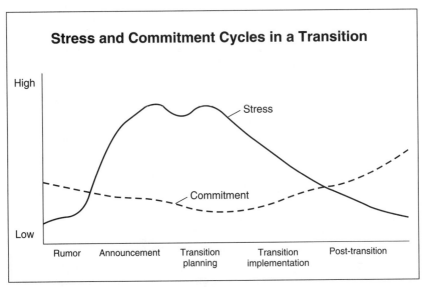

EXHIBIT 4.2

patterns are inevitable, it is possible to decrease stress and increase commitment—and, as a result, to improve productivity, quality, organizational effectiveness, and employee well-being—through careful management of the transition process. The acronym PROACTIVE helps executives understand the duties of successful transition management (see Exhibit 4.3).

Proactive Transition Management

P	Prepare for a high level of activity.
R	Rally people with a vision of a better organization.
O	Offer transition management training.
A	Acknowledge uncertainty and concerns.
C	Communicate plans and actions.
T	Tell all you can and tell the truth.
I	Involve people in managing the transition.
V	Visit with people and be visible.
E	Establish a safety net for transition victims.

EXHIBIT 4.3

Prepare for a High Level of Activity. In a study conducted at the Yale University medical school, two groups of patients were prepared for major surgery in different ways.[6] One group was given traditional platitudes: "Everything is going to be all right, the surgeon has done this procedure many times, and you'll be up and about in no time." The other group was warned truthfully of the seriousness of the surgery and the discomfort of the postoperative recuperation period. The two groups showed marked differences in how they recovered from surgery. The patients given a realistic preview of their surgery experience healed more quickly, had fewer side effects, and subjectively reported less pain than the group that was told not to worry.

Just like patients approaching major surgery, employees anticipating a major organizational transition need to be prepared for the pain, anxiety, and decreased productivity that lie ahead. They need to see the confusion and concerns they will experience not as signs of personal weakness, but as natural consequences of living through a transition. The emotions they will feel—anger at themselves or their leaders, despair over gloomy prospects for the future, guilt about being spared in a layoff—are legitimate reactions to the stress and uncertainty of a transition. Painful emotional states are more likely to become destructive (to both the individual and the organization) when they are denied or derogated as not making sense. The key is get people to accept and control their emotional reactions to transition, instead of letting their emotions control them.

Self-confidence is bolstered by learning that others have made the treacherous transition journey and emerged, though sometimes bruised and battered, as stronger and sturdier survivors of the corporate jungles. The path, however, is littered with traps like reduced efficiency and fewer resources. Thus employees also need to be readied for the work-related challenges of a transition. Some may be in store for long hours of information gathering and task force meetings to assist in transition planning or implementation. Others may encounter less cooperation from peers or support staff. All will be torn by the competing demands of keeping the business running while dealing with the transition.

Preparing supervisors and managers for the transition means

alerting them to the various ways in which their team members may respond. Superiors who anticipate subordinates' emotional pain are more likely to give them the space to work through those feelings and thereby keep such emotions from resulting in harmful effects. Team leaders who anticipate roadblocks to productivity can work with employees to assess work loads, review procedures, and prioritize competing demands. Although the pain and frustration will still be there, and will still affect individual well-being and team performance, it will be acknowledged and addressed.

Organizations prepare their people for transitions in a variety of ways. Some offer seminars that educate employees on patterns of human response to organizational transition and provide guidelines for managing oneself and others during this stressful time. Others circulate books, articles, and videos that alert people to the demands and consequences of transitions. A few firms sponsor experiential learning programs to prepare their employees further for the trials and tasks ahead. When computer distributor ValCom acquired InaComp Computer Centers, managers from the lead company spent two days in role-play exercises simulating what it is like to be acquired. This raised their sensitivity to the reactions they would encounter when working with new colleagues from the target company.

In an experiment reminiscent of the Yale medical school study, professor David Schweiger of the University of South Carolina researched the impact of a realistic merger preview in two manufacturing plants following the combination of two Fortune 500 firms. Employees in one plant received a full preview of the psychological and operational aspects of the merger. By contrast, employees at the other plant were given only rudimentary information. Employee questionnaires showed that ratings of commitment and job satisfaction dropped at both plants in the first month as some layoffs and job changes occurred. Ratings of management's trustworthiness, honesty, and concern for employees also dropped; self-reports of stress and intentions to seek work elsewhere increased. Within a few months, however, the realistically prepared employees regained their prior ratings of job satisfaction and saw the company as being far more trustworthy, honest, and caring than did those in the other plant. Eventually, performance at the realistically prepared plant improved over premerger levels. At the other plant (subject to "normal" preparation), attitudes grew worse in almost every area measured as time went on.

Rally People With a Vision of a Better Organization. People are more likely to endure the pain of a transition if they see some gain resulting from it. Ideally, this gain should be expressed in both human and business terms. When MCA was acquired by the Japanese conglomerate Matsushita, leaders countered employees' worries of new ownership by speaking of the competitive advantage to be achieved through the combination of MCA's software (the creativity of its people and stories from its productions) and Matsushita's hardware (its high technology know-how and manufacturing capability). They also cited personal benefits, ranging from the enhanced career opportunities resulting from the combination to employee discounts on Matsushita's Panasonic line of consumer electronics.

In a transition, a vision of a new and better organization helps people turn their attention away from what might be lost. It has the ability to breed confidence (if not a sense of relief) that management is thinking through where the organization is headed. As will be discussed in Chapter 8, a vision is also a template for organizing team action and guiding individual contributions toward the attainment of organizational goals. To ensure these benefits, the process through which the vision is rolled out becomes as important as the vision itself. A vision may be unveiled with some pomp and circumstance, but a more substantive value is derived by using it to build a sense of community in moving through the transition period and beyond. The vision offers something for people to look forward to achieving collectively, and it provides material for discussion as the transition is implemented. In the merger of Chemical Bank and Manufacturers Hanover, short-term employee concerns about the growing scarcity of banking jobs in New York City were offset by a long-term picture of a large and powerful new organization.

Offer Transition Management Training. While senior leaders can rally people with a vision of a better organization, the actions of immediate superiors influence employees' reactions to a transition on a daily basis. If the boss conveys an upbeat message about the possibilities inherent in a transition, then subordinates tend to feel good about the potential for positive change. Alternatively, if the superior gives off signals that the transition is something to fear or be cynical about, then similar reactions are likely from workers in his or her group.

The massive scope of change in organizations today makes transition management an important competency. Yet few people are placed into supervisory or managerial positions because of their ability to lead teams through transitions and therefore most do a poor job of guiding people through them. Most managers and supervisors dread delivering bad news in a downsizing or facing the troops in a merger without a precise and clear message to deliver. They do not have the information or insight from above to respond to the questions and anxieties from below. In a cultural transformation, managers and supervisors are on the front lines in a conflict between forces for change (like the new expectations verbalized by leaders) and forces for the status quo (like reward systems that maintain old expectations).

Workshops that develop transition management skills can ready managers for their part in a successful transition. Two broad objectives guide the design and implementation of these programs: first, alerting managers to their roles and responsibilities, and second, providing opportunities to learn and practice specific tactics. These twin objectives were used at CCH Computax, a computerized tax return processor as revenues plunged in 1990 as the company's clients—accountants and other professional tax preparers—began purchasing their own tax processing software. New products in development held the potential to regain some of the lost revenues, but they would not come to market for at least a year. President Tom Rolfe prepared to cut costs through a series of head-count reductions. His job was made more difficult, however, by the need to retain enough employees to support current customers during the peak tax season.

Rolfe commissioned a program to help managers guide their teams through change. The morning of this one-day program began with a review of how transitions were prevalent throughout U.S. businesses and were not merely an issue at Computax. Next, models of organizational and individual transition were presented, to provide insight into typical patterns of reaction, and illustrated with examples of problems confronted by managers in other companies. This was intended to show the Computax managers that others had overcome such issues as having no clear vision for the future, needing to maintain productivity and customer service standards amid turmoil, and retaining top talent being wooed by competitors. The morning concluded with an exercise in which Computax employees identified the critical issues for their particular transition.

In the afternoon, managers learned specific tactics for leading people through change. Computax's downsizing plan called for an initial voluntary reduction-in-force program to be followed by an involuntary layoff with less generous payments. Thus the training reviewed practices for counseling employees on whether to take the voluntary package or wait and accept their fate, ranking employee performance and matching skills to future job demands, delivering bad news to laid-off employees, reassuring survivors and "re-recruiting" top workers who might be looking at opportunities elsewhere. Managers outside of corporate headquarters, where the corporate communications function was housed, also were trained in how to talk to reporters who called with questions about the downsizing. Ample time was provided for managers to role-play such scenarios as telling a good performer that his or her services were no longer needed, or advising a veteran team member to sign up for the voluntary program.

During the training, Computax managers openly discussed their worst-case fears about managing during a downsizing. Many spoke of a laid-off employee in a nearby city who had returned to his place of employment and fatally shot his former supervisor and another employee. Others simply bemoaned having to deliver bad news to veteran employees who had always delivered decent performance.

At a debriefing session a week after the layoffs, managers praised the training program and cited specific ways in which it bolstered their self-confidence during the downsizing. Some benefitted from anticipating employee responses to the layoff. Others appreciated the role-play exercises, because they provided specific scripts to use and helped reduce nervousness through practice. Many confirmed that their expectations were much worse than their experiences. As one manager commented, "Some of my people who were going to lose their jobs actually felt sorry for me having to tell them the news."

A final note on transition management skills training: the intended audience must see a high degree of "face validity" in these programs. Managers want to know how to survive their merger, downsizing, or other transition. They do not want seemingly generic programs on "Thriving During Change" or "The Ten Steps of Successful Change Management." Managers are extremely busy during transitions, and they will resist attending a program unless they believe it addresses their specific needs.

Acknowledge Uncertainty and Concerns. A sure way to lose people's commitment to an organization in transition is to deny or otherwise ignore their feelings and experiences. Executives who ask "what do these people have to worry about?" or claim "If anyone is concerned about their job security, they probably are not the kind of person we want around here anyway" detract from a successful transition in two ways. First, they fail to help people understand that their concerns are legitimate and second, they fail to demonstrate the company's sensitivity to what its employees are experiencing. And managers who remain passive miss the opportunity to bolster employee support by showing that they care about (and perhaps even understand) how people feel.

Early in a transition, when managers typically have little information to impart to employees, they can meet with individuals or groups to solicit their concerns. Employees will understand if their leaders acknowledge the issues, explain why no answer is yet available, and accept the responsibility of getting back to people when one is available. At the very least, employees will leave the sessions knowing that their superiors have heard their agenda and will keep their concerns in mind as transition planning moves forward.

As transition planning and implementation occur, more formal methods for acknowledging employee concerns can be undertaken. Many companies engage in "employee sensing" or "transition tracking" programs. During the merger of Chemical Bank and Manufacturers Hanover, a quarterly survey solicited employee input and demonstrated leadership's awareness of employee uncertainties and concerns during the many months of the transition. In another merger, interviews with members of integration task forces determined their concerns about the progress and process of planning activities. Some interviewees spoke of outright conflict interfering with creative problem solving ("All we do is beat up each other's way of doing things. Nobody wants to listen to what the other side brings to the table.") Others indicated their task force process was being brought down by too little conflict ("It's like ballroom dancing, very polite and formal. We show how we do things, and they say, 'Oh, isn't that very nice.' Then they show us their way, and we respond with 'Oh, those are very nice, too.' Nothing is being accomplished in these groups."). After the findings were fed back to senior management, outside facilitators helped the task forces complete their work in a timely and creative manner.

Communicate Plans and Actions. Every book, article, and seminar on transition management extols the virtues of communication during trying times. Still, good communication efforts are very much the exception rather than the rule. At a time when up-front communication is needed most, managers have the hardest time delivering it. Some are consumed by other transition management responsibilities like serving on planning teams; others do not know what to say; and still others are absorbed by their own anxiety and fail to consider the needs of others. Whether managers own up to it or not, employees worry about the transition and ascertain, errantly, that the paucity of information means management is hiding something awful.

Silence does not have a benign impact during transition; rather, it breeds distrust and anger. It also distracts people from their work responsibilities as they huddle around the water cooler or coffee machine to pick up on the latest gossip. If the organization does not manage the communication flow, it will be managed for them through the rumor mill—a very active source of information during a transition and, inevitably, a purveyor of information far more damaging to the organization than the truth.

In a speech to the Executives' Club of Chicago, Xerox Corporation's chairman and CEO, Paul Allaire, recounted a story that demonstrates a benefit of communication beyond imparting information—that of displaying a respect for all parties and operating in a way that says "we are in this together":

> We wanted to enlist the support of our people—including our union people—but we were concerned about how much to tell them. We did not want to frighten them or demotivate them. After a lot of debate, we held a series of meetings and outlined the nature and extent of our problems. The reaction was summed up in a letter from one union worker who spoke for many. He wrote: *"Thank God you understand the problem. Those of us on the line have known it for years. You've been acting like you did not even know we were in trouble. Now that our difficulties are out in the open, I hope we can all work together to solve them!"*

A comprehensive transition communication program uses various vehicles, written (memos, newsletters, and question-and-answer packets), electronic (videos, electronic-mail, and telephone hot lines), and in person (large or small group meetings, and one-on-one sessions). It also anticipates the many breakdowns in effective communication during transition, ranging from the distracting demands on people's time to the confusion as stress levels grow. A good rule of thumb is to "overcommunicate" by repeating the same message through multiple media. For example, announcements made on paper or by video should always be followed by in-person communications. The words in a written document may be interpreted in ways unintended by the sender; a lot of "wishful hearing" occurs during transitions. Effective communicators do not assume that their message was *received* just because it was *sent*. They check for accuracy and clarity of understanding. Yet this is especially troublesome for harried executives during a transition, who quickly grow impatient when they feel they have communicated adequately but come up against employees' insatiable thirst for information.

Transition communications should also be consistent across all levels. Senior management sets the tone through organizationwide communication that lays out the purpose and progress of transition activities. Local management reinforces these messages but also discusses their implications at the work group level. Always, and especially early in a transition, employees will have more questions than managers have answers. Managers should communicate what they know and be clear about what they do not know. A large part of their communication responsibility in a transition is to establish a climate of "when the information becomes available, you will get it." Employees understand that their immediate superiors do not know all the answers, but they want the peace of mind that comes from knowing they will hear the news in a timely manner.

Tell All You Can and Tell the Truth. In reality, there is a lot that can be told at all phases of a transition. Early in a merger, for example, the deal's rationale can be discussed, along with profiles of the merger partners—information about their products or services, customers, leadership, physical locations, and history. In a downsizing, a truthful account can be given up front of why the cuts are being made, whether they will occur in waves or in one layoff, how the organization will soften the blow for victims, and what to expect after the cuts. In any type of transition, an approximate timetable of when to expect key decisions can be communicated, along with the criteria being used to make the decisions.

As decisions are made, they can be publicized through formal communication vehicles (like newsletters, memos, and videos) and discussed through informal in-person sessions. Progress made in implementation should be promoted aggressively to provide tangible signs that the transition is indeed leading to a better organization. Even small wins can give a boost to people who have been cautious, or even cynical, about the transition's promised benefits. In the merger of two financial institutions, one in Europe and the other in the United States, culture clash cut deeply across national as well as corporate lines. We/they feelings were pervasive, and turf battles over who could call on what accounts prevailed at most locations. In the firm's small Asia division, representatives from the two banks joined together to call on a prominent prospect who had never done business with either side. Citing the combined resources of the two banks, the prospect became a customer. This relatively minor accomplishment was widely promoted through an article in the company newsletter and was recounted to various operating groups by the chairman during his travels. It became a symbolic focal point for what could be accomplished by cooperation between the two sides.

The value of transition communication transcends passing on information: it establishes a sense of trust between employees and employer that carries over into the posttransition organization. There will always be matters that managers are unable to discuss. Still, by acknowledging these areas and providing a reason why information cannot be forthcoming, employees will feel more fairly treated than if an obvious issue of concern is ignored by management. Also, circumstances may change during the months of transition planning and implementation, forcing a redirection in decisions already made. A steady flow of information will make such shifts more understandable.

The CEO of a distribution company wanted to establish norms of openness and timely communication during and after the acquisition of a slightly larger competitor. Through his own speeches and conversations, and in his column in a special merger newsletter, the CEO told employees that he could delay announcing merger-related actions until he was 100 percent certain of their likelihood, or he could communicate with people in a more timely manner. The trade-off of the latter approach, he cautioned, was that employees would have to accept that decisions conveyed in some early announcements might be changed if subsequent analysis warranted a better course of action. In feedback to the CEO, employees expressed an overwhelming preference for the early communication option and appreciation for the adult way in which they were being treated.

As merger planning proceeded, the transition task force charged with proposing a new operations design determined that the merger's cost savings target could be achieved by closing four of sixteen warehouses. The plan was accepted by the CEO and communicated to the work force. Employees at the twelve surviving warehouses breathed a sigh of relief. Just a few weeks later, however, the task force learned that a mistake had been made, and two more warehouses would have to be shuttered to hit the financial target.

In most organizations, an announced closing of two additional sites would generate anger at management for "putting people through the wringer," cynicism that "management does not know what it's doing," and distrust that "you can't believe anything management says." At the distribution company, a different reaction predominated. Employees at the two locations newly slated to be closed were shocked, but those at the ten surviving warehouses and at corporate headquarters heard management's explanation and accepted the midcourse correction as being a proper move. In this case, open and respectful communication up front helped management traverse a delicate passage in the transition process. It also established a precedent that reflected the CEO's desired communication norms for life after the merger.

Again, part of the communication challenge is to help employees understand that in exchange for receiving full and timely communication, they must be tolerant when changes in previously announced strategies are necessary. Throughout all transition communications, it is essential to be honest. Communicators should know that if they get caught in a single lie, their credibility is shot—and it takes a lot more time and energy to recover from distrust than to maintain a good communications climate.

Involve People in Managing the Transition. The Organizational Behavior 101 postulate that decision-making involvement breeds support for subsequent implementation holds true in a transition. There are both symbolic and substantive ways to involve people. In a merger, employees can take part in presentations to educate each side about the other, enter "name the new company" contests, or call up a toll-free hot line to offer their ideas. The friendly tone of Delta Airlines' acquisition of Western Airlines was underscored when Delta employees brought homemade baked goods to their Western counterparts at several airport locations. In a downsizing or culture transformation, large numbers of employees can participate in focus groups to voice their perspectives on opportunities and challenges associated with the change.

The most common form of involvement is to engage people in transition planning or implementation task forces. Employees who perform the work are abundant sources of ideas for how to integrate operations, reduce non-value-added work, or revise work procedures in line with new cultural norms. Where possible, it is important to "stack the deck" with employees who want to make the transition work and whose viewpoints influence those around them. Involvement in a task force may indicate to valued employees that the organization recognizes their contributions amid all the

craziness of a transition. There may be times, however, when someone cannot be taken away from work on core business requirements. In these cases, star performers must be reassured of their
value to the company so that they do not incorrectly interpret their
lack of involvement to mean that there is not a prominent role for
them in the posttransition organization.

Visit with People and Be Visible. "I do not understand why our
new president does not show his face around here more," wondered Michael, a staff attorney at a major television network,
where two major transitions—the arrival of a new president and a
major downsizing—were announced within a period of days. "It's
like a morgue here. Everyone's either frozen or depressed, and if
the president just walked around and took note of people, I think
we'd all feel a lot better. His office is just down the hall, but he
never comes out. But I sure see him talking to the outside world a
lot; he is always quoted in the trade papers and seen at industry
functions." Contrast this to Michael's feelings about his immediate
superior: "The head of our unit has been great, though. He is always pulling people out of their offices just to chat and see how
they are doing. We're all still nervous, but I'm glad that at least he
seems to understand that we are going through something that
makes us very nervous."

Management by walking around will never pay more dividends
than during a transition. People need more assurance and face-to-
face contact than in "normal" times. Their feelings of trust and security are enhanced by knowing that superiors have not forgotten
about their reports and are accessible if needed.

The norm in a transition, however, is for managers to avoid contact with their reports, especially in the early days. Some managers
feel inadequate in their capacity to allay employee concerns, so
they just stay away. Others are themselves worried about their fate
and sulk behind closed doors in their offices. One sales manager in
a downsizing firm purposely timed customer calls in the field to coincide with the layoff announcement at headquarters: "People are
going to be so worried that no work will get done anyway at headquarters, so at least I can visit some customers."

No matter how busy managers are with the details of the transition or how anxious they are about their own fate, they must make

the time to reassure employees face-to-face. Simple acts pay large dividends during difficult times: a pat on the back for a job well done, an acknowledgment of long hours put in, or an invitation to drop by the office if there is a need to talk. Some employees may take their superiors up on the offer to talk things through; many others, however, will be content knowing that their bosses are aware of the stress and uncertainty at hand and care enough to reach out.

Establish a Safety Net for Transition Victims. People whose jobs are eliminated in a merger or downsizing are the real victims in a transition. Some companies make concentrated efforts to find positions elsewhere in the organization for displaced employees. Firms that are laying off in one department but hiring in another may establish job banks and internal placement functions to match people with positions. Organizations in which technological advances have made jobs obsolete may offer retraining programs to prepare people for other positions in the firm.

Both approaches were combined by Household International, whose 16,000 employees operated a finance company, a bank, a mortgage company, an insurance company, and related businesses with $38 billion in assets when a 1990 decision to stop lending for commercial real estate and other high-risk commercial deals led to the elimination of 129 jobs. Hoping to save as many good employees as possible, the human resources directors of each Household subsidiary came together to form an employee placement committee. Displaced employees who had satisfactory performance ratings qualified for internal placement and received counseling on how to seek new positions; they were also given a list of openings in the company's growing businesses. To encourage managers to hire displaced employees, a temporary freeze was placed on outside hiring. Managers accustomed to selecting only people who were a perfect fit for their openings were urged to consider candidates who lacked skills that could be learned through on-the-job training. Because senior management support for the placement effort was evident, most managers jumped on the bandwagon and welcomed displaced people into their areas. Within a few weeks, most of the displaced employees had new jobs in the company.

There will not always be a place for all displaced employees, nor will companies always devote the time and resources required to set up and run an internal placement function. When the elimination of people and jobs occurs, it is common practice to offer some mix of adequate warning, severance pay, benefits extensions, and job search assistance (such as resumé preparation services, outplacement counseling, or job fairs.) These and other efforts to soften the landing of transition victims are important and benevolent acts for people in need. And they do have value in staving off potential lawsuits and influencing the perceptions of customers and other external stakeholders. The most critical reason for assisting victims, however, is to send a message to survivors that they, too, would be cared for if they were to become a victim.

The overriding objective of transition management is to clarify and, if necessary, revise employees' perceptions of the psychological relationship between themselves and their employer. How a transition is managed sends a message to employees—by design or by default—about what they can expect from the company in exchange for their contributions. This includes expectations ranging from standards of communication and involvement in the organization to norms for treating people who may no longer be needed.

In their unfrozen state during the transition, people are especially impressionable. Thus the work of managing the human side of a transition must be put on a par with such other responsibilities as integration planning in a merger or work flow analysis in a rightsizing. People look for "hard" evidence of the extent to which tangible improvements result from transition. In a merger, this could be economies of scale or new opportunities based on cross-fertilization between the two sides; in a downsizing, the elimination of unnecessary work or the outplacement of poor performers; in a change of leadership, revised strategy and renewed confidence; or, in a culture transformation, tighter links between words, behaviors, and rewards. But people also size up *how* the transition is managed and draw conclusions about how people are treated in the company. A critical responsibility in successful transition management, then, is to show survivors what their fate would be if a similar event affected them and, importantly, to help them assess the situation at hand and gauge reasonable attitudinal and behavioral responses over the long haul.

Realistic Expectations in Transition Management

No person or organization will ever bat one thousand in the transition management game. Stress will never be totally eliminated, and unconditional commitment will never be generated. There are too many decisions to be made, competing demands to be balanced, and irrational human responses to be handled for anything near perfection to be attained. Realistically, if people can be assisted to a fair degree in reducing the amount of stress they experience and helped to consider how the posttransition organization is worthy of their commitment, then transition management can be considered successful.

Managing the human side of the transition reduces employee stress and its debilitating effects on individual well-being, team productivity, and organizational performance. It also lessens the cynicism, distrust, and depression that can prevail during transitions. Moreover, effective transition management generates excitement about charging up the hill to capture awaiting business opportunities. Invariably there will be unintended fallout—memories of former colleagues who have fallen, pains of wounds garnered in the trenches, fatigue left from recent battles, and fears of what may lie ahead. These and the other unintended consequences of the transition must be acknowledged, worked through, and let go of before the work force is ready to make a successful run at new business opportunities.

Part 2

Recovery

5

Recovery after Transition

Organizational transitions do not have abrupt endings. In a merger, for example, some employees may encounter immediate and substantial change, but others may wait months or even years until an integration task force makes recommendations about their departments. Then, as changes are implemented, they invariably produce reverberations that ripple through other parts of the organization. No sooner do merged or acquired employees learn they still have a job than they find themselves thrust into an even more stressful and drawn-out period of struggling to meet business objectives in an environment of confusion and chaos.

In a downsizing, survivors mourn the loss of former coworkers and mentors and cope with getting work done with fewer resources. Over time they develop new mental models, revise work expectations and career aspirations, and adapt to new realities. In organizations engulfed by culture transformations, the change process creeps ahead slowly as employees cope with the mixed messages sent by simultaneous forces for the old and new ways of doing things.

Despite employees' ongoing need to assess and cope with transition-related changes, senior management comes to the point where it has had enough talk of merging, downsizing, or transforming and declares the transition "over." These executives have let go of the old organizational order and are well on their way to accepting the new order. They are excited by what they see ahead—a merged operation with increased efficiency and clout, a decreased head count and reduced cost structure, or a more pervasive service orientation. They do not want to hear any more about lingering postmerger culture clash, layoff survivor sickness, or resistance to change. They are also anxious to realize the improved business results expected to follow from the transition. But where are the middle managers, frontline supervisors, and rank-and-file employees? Odds are they are still holding on tightly to the old order.

This chapter examines the individual adaptation that must occur for an organizational transition to be completed. In particular, it looks at why people hold on to the old organizational order and what can be done to help them feel more confident in accepting the new order. Some people are so battered following a transition that they are insecure about their ability to move successfully from the old to the new. Others do not let go of the old because they lack a clear vision of what lies ahead. Still others hear the words that describe the new order but do not see how it will benefit them personally. For all people, however, there are factors that make the known more comfortable than the unknown, even when the old has proven obsolete and the new offers great promise.

Phases of Adaptation

Individual adaptation to transition occurs through three phases: holding on to the old, letting go of the old, and accepting the new. Throughout these phases, every person and organization encounters forces for maintenance of the status quo and forces for growth (see Exhibit 5.1). These forces tend to operate counter to each other, with a constantly shifting balance. Early on the maintenance forces predominate and are expressed in outright resistance to change or, at best, the absence of a will to act. Over time, the growth forces tend to dominate and provide the necessary impetus for letting go and adaptation.

Further, as Exhibit 5.2 shows, adaptation is experienced by the employee at the organizational level as movement from the old to new organizational order, and at the individual level as change in one's personal situation. In the *holding-on* phase, the predominant forces are those for maintaining the old order and resisting the

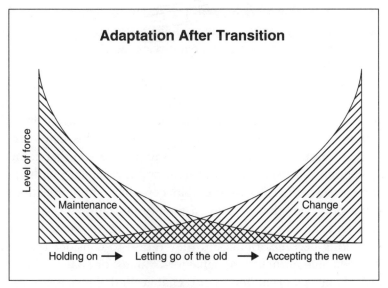

EXHIBIT 5.1

threat to the individual's current known state. The person perceives real danger in the form of a threat to self-preservation. The seeming unavoidability of this danger results in an emotional state of helplessness and, in some cases, panic. The person feels confused, cannot fully grasp what is happening, and consequently can-

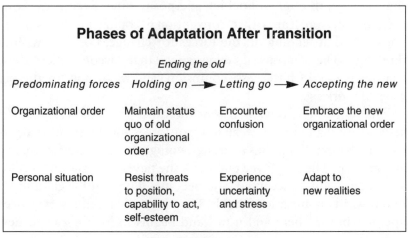

EXHIBIT 5.2

not adequately plan to cope with the situation. The threat of danger to accustomed ways of doing things, personal position, expected cause-effect relationships, capability to act, and self-esteem is overwhelming.

The individual attempts to fortify the old ways of doing things in order to shut out or control the threat. Trying to go on as if things have not really changed—that is, avoiding or denying reality—he or she is likely to indulge in wishful thinking. This helps reduce anxiety, at least in the short run. Any thing or person that counters this experience is perceived as a threat and is reacted to with anger. In some cases, efforts to assist employees—like communications or training programs that describe a new organizational order—may be met with put-downs and resistance. During this stage individuals' thinking becomes rigid, and they refuse to consider the possibility of change in their own behaviors, values, or goals.

Over time, external forces for change and internal forces for growth and development overcome the maintenance and resistance forces, leading to the second phase—*letting go*. The employee discovers that some of the valued ways of coping are no longer successful. A renewed encounter with reality occurs, followed by a renewed period of personal uncertainty and stress. This is an experience shared by many managers in firms engaged in reengineering efforts. Intellectually, they recognize the potential for improvements in work processes; emotionally, however, they are frightened by the specter of change. The individual hopes to exert some control through politicking and positioning. Eventually, however, the person learns that conventional coping mechanisms do not succeed at fending off the forces for change, nor does wishful thinking. The emotional experience that accompanies these changes is one of bitterness, confusion, and mourning for the old ways of working.

Finally the individual arrives at the third phase of *accepting the new*. More than just the weakening of forces for the status quo, arrival at this phase implies a strengthening of the forces for change and growth. The employee embraces the new organizational order: it is understood, is accepted, and becomes a beacon for guiding action toward organizational goals. On a personal level, the employee operates in the "here and now" and begins to look ahead to new realities.

After accepting the new organizational order, employees grow more comfortable with their position in it. They begin to modify their self-image and develop a renewed sense of worth. New mental models are developed, delineating both expectations and limitations in the organization. As sense is made of the new order, and as individuals see that they can cope with it, anxiety and depression lessen. Employees figure out what they can accomplish in the new organization and what their available resources are.

Ending the Old: Holding On and Letting Go

Moving through a transition is a lot like swinging on a set of rings (see Exhibit 5.3). The organization wants the individual employee to progress from the old to the new, a goal that may or may not be consistent with the individual's desire, ability, or motivation. With one hand securely fixed on the first ring, the employee is expected to grab onto the next. Below, however, the ground is hard, and no safety net is in sight to soften any fall. Few except the truly courageous or truly foolish will let go of the first ring until they have a reasonable degree of confidence that they can successfully grasp the one ahead. The individual employee can take some actions to increase the chances of success, but there will always be some hang time in midair without the security of holding on to either the first or the second ring. For some, this may be an invigorating feeling; for most, however, it is scary and uncomfortable. The expected consequences of hitting the ground keep the employee's grip tightly on the first ring.

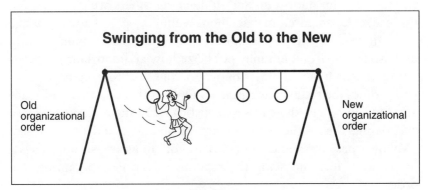

Swinging from the Old to the New

Old organizational order

New organizational order

EXHIBIT 5.3

Adapting to Loss

Before people can contribute to on the upside of a transition, they need to let go of what they have lost. Employees in an acquired company lose their premerger company identity; in a downsizing they lose coworkers and mentors; and in a culture transformation they lose accustomed ways of doing things. Accordingly, these people need to mourn the loss of their company, coworkers, and cultures. Such grieving follows the contours of reactions to death so aptly specified in the work of Elisabeth Kubler-Ross, whose studies of terminally ill patients and their families found repeatedly occurring stages of reactions.[1] These stages are often used by employees describing their experience of organizational transition.

First, there is denial of the loss. Executives may fantasize that a hostile raider withdraws its unfriendly takeover bid. Employees may deny their vulnerability to a downsizing by reminding themselves of how valuable they are to the company and how it could not function without them. At an acquired entertainment firm, a middle manager excitedly ran through the halls shouting, "I've got a copy of [the buying company's] organizational chart and there is no one who has my job. I'm going to survive this thing!" The buyer did not have anyone doing that job because they did not value that function, and the manager was included in the first wave of people to be terminated. Then comes a period of anger at company leaders ("How could they allow this to happen to us?"), at the acquirer ("What gives them the right to do this to people?"), and even at oneself ("Why didn't I see this coming?").

Next comes strategizing and bargaining. Unrealistic schemes for maintaining the status quo and influencing others are developed in this stage. An acquired management team may plot ways to change the acquirers before they themselves are changed; a manager in a downsizing environment may publicize how an important project is ahead of schedule and under budget in an effort to protect jobs. Finally comes the stage of acceptance. Only at this point are individuals ready to accept their losses realistically. In the context of death and dying, this is the achievement of an inner and outer peace: "My time has come, and I'm ready to go." In an transition, this is a preparation for embracing the realities of the new organizational order.

Demotivation After Transition

Employees will resist letting go when their mental models, developed under the old organizational order, predict a lack of success in moving from one ring to the next. Any combination of three conditions may reduce employee motivation to let go of the old organizational order and accept the new (see Exhibit 5.4). First, the employee may feel incapable of making the move from one ring to the next ("Even if I give it my best shot, there is a good chance I will fall"). This assessment would be based not only on general and historical perceptions of one's capabilities, but on recent episodes of reduced capacity to act during the transition. A person who felt unable to influence their situation or whose work suffered due to competing demands or unavailability of needed resources will see less connection between how hard they work and how well they do. This is what led David, the marketing manager from Mazda discussed at the beginning of Chapter 4, to go from thinking about his position with Mazda as a productive, mutually rewarding relationship to "just a job." Sixty-five-hour workweeks and success in upgrading Mazda's image in the marketplace did not influence the marketing team's vulnerability to being laid off. The result among

---

Links Between Transition Mismanagement and Reduced Employee Motivation

Transition Conditions	*Effect on Employee Motivation*
• Lack of control • Competing demands • Limited resources	*Inability* (employee feels unable to complete tasks even if giving best effort)
• Unclear vision • Little evidence of improved organization • Heightened cynicism • Lessened confidence	*Undesirability* (employee does not find new organizational order attractive)
• Broken promises • Changing psychological work contract • Increased distrust	*Unpredictability* (employee does not expect to benefit from or in the new organizational order)

EXHIBIT 5.4

survivors was a "why bother" attitude, since hard work did not seem to contribute to keeping their jobs.

Second, the employee may not find what awaits at the second ring to be worth the risk of letting go of the first one ("I physically can make it to the next ring, but how will I be any better off over there?"). The perceived attractiveness of life on the second ring will be reduced if during the transition no clear vision of the new organizational order was developed, if little evidence was produced to back up promises of a new and better organization, or if, as a result, levels of cynicism grew and confidence fell in how the employee viewed management.

The merger of two large organizations provides an excellent example of how not having a clear vision of the new organizational order inhibits letting go of the old. In this case, as in all mergers and acquisitions, a clash of cultures took hold as employees from both sides came to revalue key aspects of their business and ways of doing things.[2] Company values, policies, and systems that had always been taken for granted became much more important as executives reflected on what they might lose in the combination. Moreover, there was a tendency to differentiate one's own company from the other firm and to stereotype and denigrate the other side's style or culture.

True to culture clash form, managers from the merging companies put down aspects of each other's culture. Managers from one side reeled at the bureaucratic controls that ran untethered in the other. Managers from the side with the strong bureaucracy, in turn, worried about too little control over their freewheeling counterparts. Yet, people from both sides also saw the merger as an opportunity to enhance their own cultures by replacing outmoded, unproductive, and uninspiring ways of doing things. As one manager put it, "I don't necessarily support having our ways retained, but I can say for sure that I don't want to see their culture winning out. The real opportunity is to come up with something different than either side had in the past."

Unfortunately, the criteria defining a new order were not articulated by the combined organization's leaders. Senior executives were contending with their personal transitions and learning to work with one another and with new reports. The CEO was satisfied with masterminding the deal and did not see building a new postmerger culture as part of his transition management responsibilities. This task would be passed on to the president when he took over the reins in two years. In the meantime, transition task forces suffered from having no clear statement of the values, critical success factors, and operating principles to guide integration decision making. Had there been a shared vision of a new order, task force meetings could have been forums for assessing gaps between the current organizations and the desired end state. Instead, they were reduced to us-versus-them battles as participants held onto their old organizational orders. As word of this moved through informal communication channels, employees saw no clear advantage in accepting the new and therefore tightened their grip on the old.

A third form of demotivation after transition results when the employee does not believe that any personal rewards or benefits are likely to be realized by making the leap ("why should I bother moving forward when management won't deliver on its promises?") If a transition altered specific commitments previously made to the employee (regarding career advancement, compensation, or job assignments), generally changed the psychological work contract, or enhanced distrust toward management, then the employee is apt to be suspicious of new vows.

For example, Martin, a talented executive with a stable position in the computer peripheral industry, was wooed away by a competitor promising an opportunity to build a new product area from scratch. He was assured of the firm's commitment to this "product that will lead us into the next century." Before making the jump, Martin negotiated carefully to obtain sufficient levels of funding and autonomy in running operations. Martin came on board, hired staff, and made excellent progress in product development. Within a year, however, the company acquired another firm with a relatively mature business in Martin's product area. In a "reverse merger," the acquired management team was put in charge of Martin's new product. When Martin confronted his boss about the broken promises, he was told how the acquisition merely confirmed the company's commitment to this product area and that he should learn to be a team player. Martin's reaction was to withdraw psychologically:

I went through the motions, but I really was not producing much work. A couple of times I saw where I could make a difference in what these guys where producing, but I didn't feel any ownership over what they were doing, and I just didn't bother to contribute. Yeah, it hurts my ego, but I'm being paid pretty well for doing nothing! I'm biding my time until another offer comes along, but I don't know what I can do to prevent getting jerked around again.

The inability to find obvious benefit in the new organizational order also describes the plight of many IBM employees in the 1990s. These workers thought they had joined an organization committed to lifelong employment relationships. While intellectually some may accept changing business realities, emotionally many are stuck as they struggle with the altered psychological work contract at IBM and the uncertainty about what to expect down the road.

With little expectation that the next ring (the new organizational order) is attainable, is worth reaching for, or is the source of some payoff, employees will be slow to move forward. This underscores the potential for the residual effects of mismanagement to dwell in the organization long after the transition is considered over. It also reflects the difficulty of managing organizational transitions, as well as employees' tendencies to focus on the costs of a transition rather than the potential business and personal benefits. In IBM's case, the company is right to reduce its cost base and, concurrently, to bring its historical psychological work contract more in line with today's competitive realities. This is necessary to the company's long-term profitability and may eventually enhance employee job security and compensation levels. But the move is not without a cost to short-term employee morale and productivity.

Similarly, the computer peripheral company did not intend to hurt Martin, nor was it even concerned with the progress of his group; in fact, the senior leadership was more than pleased with the pace of new product development. The company received an unsolicited offer to acquire a competitor with current financial problems but tremendous product strengths. The CEO jumped at this opportunity and assumed that his subordinates, including Martin, would be as excited as he was about the integration opportunities. IBM, Martin's company, and others must make these organizational transitions to succeed, but they must also make a concerted effort to help employees embrace the changes.

Inattention to Letting Go

Along with individual forces for holding on are organizational forces that inhibit progress through the letting-go phase. Many reasons account for why the need to end the old is not sanctioned in organizations following a transition. To begin, the legitimacy of the need for ending the old ways may be denied by those with the capacity or authority to accelerate adaptation. While human resources professionals and first-line supervisors may witness the pain being experienced by employees, along with the resulting distraction from performance, executives—concerned about the future—overlook the need to let go of the past first. Many managers are blinded by their personal agenda for getting out of the blocks quickly following a transition. In a merger, acquired managers hope to impress new bosses. After a downsizing, managers hope to reduce their vulnerability to further cuts. In the case of culture transformation, senior managers hope to please higher-level executives by looking as if they are "walking the talk" of the new way of doing things. Each instance breeds the fallacy of getting people's behavior in line by putting their noses to the grindstone and producing results. The hoped-for acquiescence, however, is invariably blocked by personal forces for holding on to the old.

In some organizations where the process of letting go of the old first is understood but not wholeheartedly embraced, allowing people to deal with their feelings is dismissed as an inappropriate use of time. This reasoning ignores the fact that people will go through the phases of ending the old with or without the organization's sanction. Time and attention will be diverted from work activities whether the individual goes through the process alone or with the support of the organization. Rather than deplete resources, an organization-sponsored program can actually reduce the time required to end the old order by accelerating movement toward letting go.

Executives may also question the expenditure of money on a letting-go program when the organization has just endured a painful pruning of costs. Their doubts are sometimes echoed by employees, like the administrative assistant who (during a lunch break at a postdownsizing grieving program) asked her CEO, "How can you justify spending money on this hotel room, lunch for everybody, and an outside facilitator when we just laid people off and you told us we have to find even more ways of cutting costs?" The CEO gave an exemplary reply:

> While it has been a painful decision to terminate some employees, and the other financial sacrifices we have to make are substantial, we will never cut back on investing in our employees. The competition is only getting stronger out there, and if we want to be a survivor in this industry, our people have to get stronger too. We have come here today to help you cope with your feelings about where we have been and what we are going through, but also to help you identify how to be more successful as individual contributors in the future. This is only going to help us become a more competitive organization, and I always will pay for that.

There are also more deeply rooted reasons why most organizations do not attend to the letting-go process. These include culturally grounded fears of exploring aspects of the preconscious or unconscious self or of feelings like helplessness, vulnerability, rejection, or anger—especially in a work setting. This is hardly congruent with the "businesslike" behavior some executives extol following transition. Another very important reason why the letting-go process is often ignored is worth noting: senior executives have typically made progress in letting go before others in the organization have begun the adaptation process. Senior executives may have been involved in secret pre-merger negotiations, deliberated the need for a downsizing, or pondered the cultural transformation well before the transition was announced to the overall organization. In each case, they have had a head start in the process of psychologically rejecting the old organizational order.

As Exhibit 5.5 shows, those at the top levels in an organization begin their process of moving from holding on to the old to letting go and accepting the new well before employees at other levels. Senior executives, those with the most at stake, often have the most intense reactions to a transition and experience strong forces for maintaining the status quo. They adapt to change and mourn their losses through what typically is a private process, but one that consumes personal attention and time. Significantly, however, their adaptation process is accelerated by the high degree of control they enjoy relative to others in the organization. Senior executives are

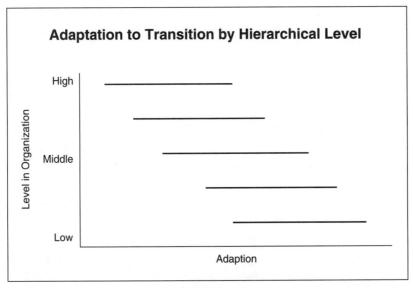

EXHIBIT 5.5

the architects of transition; they understand why change is needed and where it is headed. All other members of the organization have a lot less influence and a lot more uncertainty when it comes to adapting.

By the time executives at the top of the organization are looking ahead to new realities, people lower in the hierarchy are only beginning or, at best, in the middle of their adaptation process. In large organizations, transition implementation may not ripple down to the lowest levels for quite some time. Many employees do not experience their first wave of transition-related change—and thus do not *begin* their adaptation process—until senior executives have put the old behind them and are well on their way to accepting the new. When lower-level employees are just beginning to contend with holding on and letting go, senior executives have repressed memories of the pain and confusion of leaving the old behind and, as a result, are unsympathetic to others' needs for holding on. Having let go of the past, they are concerned with the future. Either because they are impatient to move on or because they refuse to accept consciously the pain of their own personal transition, executives sometimes forget that a new beginning requires ending the old order.

Readiness for Change

Traditionally organizational change agents (including consultants, internal training and development professionals, and executives acting on their own) have introduced change using a "future orientation." They diagnose the present situation, state the goals of the change effort, and develop and implement a plan for moving from here to there. They assume that the client organization and its people are at a starting point of acceptance—an assumption that is dead wrong on the heels of a transition.

The failure to recognize and address formally the need for holding on is a principal reason why so many change programs have difficulty maintaining their momentum. Little if any attention has been given to *working through* the potent need to hold on to the old organizational order and to avoid the powerful feelings that changed circumstances can trigger. The deeply felt experience of frustration, loss, grief, anger, helplessness, and depression has been almost completely ignored (except possibly at a relatively superficial level called "resistance to change").[3]

The need for individuals, groups, and organizations to hold on to what they are accustomed to is powerful. Not to be aware of this, to ignore it, or to try to override it guarantees failure to those charged with changing organizations or motivating individuals after a transition. An organization's employees will either be so saturated with change, filled with anger, or stuck in denial that they will not accept even the most carefully designed program for moving on to the new order. Furthermore, cynicism and distrust toward management will only grow when employees are confronted by yet another fad or program that is insensitive to their current psychological frame of reference. Rather than assuming that employees are psychologically prepared to accept a new order, successful change agents will facilitate movement through the three phases of the adaptation process.

The Venting Meeting

An essential part of a program to help people loosen their grip on the old and prepare for the new organizational order is the venting meeting. By raising awareness and accelerating learning, this meeting heightens people's understanding of how they are dealing with adaptation to a transition. The objective of the venting meeting is to facilitate the letting-go phase of the adaptation process. It accomplishes this by helping people along the three steps of letting-go.[4]

Consciousness Raising. The venting meeting alerts employees to common patterns of organizational and individual reaction to transition and, in particular, the personal adaptation process. This shows that reactions to loss and crisis are to be expected following a transition, and acquaints employees with the holding on–letting-go-accepting the new sequence. The goal is to help employees acknowledge intellectually what they are personally holding onto and to help them become aware of their reasons for doing so.

Reexperiencing. The reasons for and implications of holding on become truly understood only when they are expressed experientially. Talking through where they have been and what they are currently experiencing as a result of the transition helps employees bring their feelings to a conscious level. This is typically an emotional and highly charged process, in contrast to the more intellectual level at which initial consciousness raising occurs.

Mourning. The psychological process of letting-go is completed through an active mourning of what is being left behind—old ways of seeing and doing things, lost hopes and expectations, and the loss of what was once satisfying, meaningful, or simply familiar. This mourning is sometimes accompanied by remorse—a sense of guilt for the time wasted, the life that could have been but will never be. Yet it also instills a sense of renewal and rebirth, and an acceptance for what lies ahead. From the most primitive to the most modern cultures, there has always been a recognized need for rituals to carry individuals from one phase of the life to another. Mourning is a key facilitating ritual in the process of letting go of the old and accepting the new, at the organizational as well as at the individual level.

Benefits of a Venting Meeting

A venting meeting provides many benefits that are derived from mourning rituals. First, it validates the experiences of employees who are coping with loss in their personal situation and adapting to the death of their old organizational order. The mere acknowledgment from the organization that there is a *need* to mourn legitimizes the emotions and feelings experienced by employees as they cope with loss and change. Second, the venting meeting gives people guides for dealing with and moving through an uncomfortable experience. The venting meeting is a visible forum in which a group of people come to see that holding on to the old, although normal and natural, is a maladaptive response to new organizational realities. It is a turning point at which people let go of anger and blame and take personal responsibility for accepting their situation in the new organizational order.

Third, bringing people together to share in the venting meeting establishes a bond among members of the group. The tendencies to turn inward during times of crisis, to constrict communication, and to restrict decision-making involvement are replaced by a reaching out to each other as members of a community. Fourth, the venting meeting accelerates the pace at which people let go. Many (and sometimes all) members of the organization share the experience at the same time and the same place. The group members are at once providers and receivers of support and coping strategies. Finally, the venting meeting clarifies and confirms to those who may be stuck in denial that something is being lost. The dramatic scene of watching others acknowledge that the old order has ended weakens enduring forces for maintenance of the status quo.

Venting is distinct from bitching. Bitching is blaming, while venting raises up, legitimizes, and works through feelings. Employees who actively work through the stages of consciousness raising, reexperiencing, and mourning are better prepared to accept new realities and move forward. For a work force that is banged up and burned out after a transition, a venting meeting is a forum for healing and renewal. In organizations that have experienced wave after wave of transition, whose workers' threshold for dealing with stress, uncertainty, and disorientation has been saturated, a venting meeting also serves the critically important function of helping people wring away the built-up consequences of dealing with ongoing change.

The meeting also helps people come to terms with ambiguous organizational endings. If the organization ceased to exist, then the individual member could begin a process of mourning and letting-go. When an organization's structure dies but its identity lingers—

through bankruptcy proceedings, a merger, or bailout—this is a less obvious transition. The mourning component of the venting meeting transforms what might be perceived as a lingering hope for survival into a finite experience of death: an event that can be dealt with, adapted to, and eventually moved on from.

A venting meeting by itself does not complete the letting-go process, but it can be a powerful facilitator to accelerate adaptation to transition. Depending on many variables (including elements of the company culture, the extent to which the transition disrupted the old organizational order, and the skills of facilitators), a venting meeting may only address a portion of the letting-go process. For example, the reexperiencing of pent-up emotions may be too extreme for some corporate settings; as a result, a venting meeting may focus only on consciousness raising. (This does not eliminate the need for all steps of the letting-go process to occur.)

Alternatively, if an atmosphere of safety and openness can be established in the venting meeting, people will jump at the opportunity to express their feelings. The internal pressure built up over months of uncertainty and stress, combined with the acknowledgment that these reactions are legitimate, creates a tremendous need for people to talk about what they are going through.

Design Considerations

Several factors must be considered in designing a venting meeting, especially when prevailing conditions in a transition (like restricted communication and heightened tension and stress) result in reduced levels of trust and openness in the organization. These factors include issues pertaining to what should be covered in the program's content and who should be invited as participants.

Learning Methodology. In a venting meeting, consciousness raising initially occurs through presentations or presession readings. This is reinforced during the reexperiencing and mourning steps through discussions, role plays, and simulations. In designing a venting program, however, a decision needs to be made whether the target audience will respond best at the intellectual or emotional level (or some combination of the two).

While an emotional reckoning is important to the reexperiencing process, the members of a work team may initially be strongly uncomfortable with expressing their feelings a group of peers. In this case, the most that should be expected from a meeting is some consciousness raising and, perhaps, a written (as opposed to spoken) and individually focused exercise such as having people write down their behaviors, emotions, and perceptions in response to the transition and note their current feelings about the transition. At the very least, this gives people insight into the extent to which they have moved through the adaptation process. Often, however, the need to vent will take over and a spontaneous and energetic expression of feelings will ensue in even the most "closed" of organizational settings. This occurred in a consumer products firm several months after the integration of a major competitor. It seemed that everybody had something to be upset about in this transition: lead company managers (who for three years running were told that merit pay increases would be minimal due to the poor economy) were angry about the high price paid for the target and the generous employment contacts given to its executives; acquired managers resented the arrogant attitude of their counterparts from the lead company; and everyone was turned off by the highly political staffing process and the top-heavy organization that resulted (all senior executives were retained following the merger, while stiff cuts had to be made at middle and lower levels to meet postmerger cost savings targets).

Senior line executives recognized that divisions between people from the two sides were lingering and that cynicism and distrust in the organization were not dissipating. They scoffed, however, at the notion of what they assumed would be a "touchy-feely" venting session. Instead they consented to sponsor a series of "Rebuilding After the Merger" training workshops for middle managers. The workshops were promoted to managers with no mention of venting or letting-go in the course description or objectives. Knowing of managers' strongly negative feelings about the merger, the workshop leader attempted to create an environment of trust and openness during the session. In each of twenty sessions the floodgates opened and emotions poured forth. Considerable anger at the leadership and with the integration process was expressed. Even people who did not speak up during the sessions benefitted from their attendance; one manager who was quiet said to the facilitator afterward, "I thought it was only me feeling this way. It really surprised me that all these people feel the same way. I was worried something was wrong with me, because no one ever talks about this stuff."

After about ninety minutes, a collective sense came over the group that venting by itself would not change their situation. Rather than sit back and wait for senior executives to manage the recovery process, these managers themselves would have to step up to the plate and take responsibility for leading recovery in their work areas. This phenomenon was replicated in each of the twenty sessions. Admittedly, after the first couple of sessions the company grapevine talked up the venting aspect of the program, and attendees at later sessions came with some expectations for venting; to senior management's credit, they did not attempt to terminate or alter the sessions. As the chief financial officer later said, "Hey, if that's what people need to do, then that's what they need to do."

Degree of Confrontation. Substantial resistance to open discussion may hinder the purpose of a venting meeting, even when the meeting is wholly endorsed by organizational leadership. Therefore the proper degree of confrontation to elicit the optimum amount of venting is another consideration in designing the session. (Confrontation here refers to an encounter, as in confronting facts—*not* a clash or showdown between two parties.) Exhibit 5.6 shows various levels of confrontation that can be used to facilitate venting, differing by the degree to which they are overtly relevant to the situation at hand. The most purely relevant—and thus most confrontational—level is that of data collected from the client organization itself. These data may take the form of findings from interviews conducted with employees to determine their feelings about the transition, results from an employee attitude survey, or archival data such as financial reports or personnel records. Data drawn from the organization are the most powerful way to confront the presence of transition fallout within an organization and its people, countering such classic sources of denial as the resistance underlying statements like "Let me tell you why things are different with us . . ." Data collection has some up-front costs in terms of both time and money, but data collected from the organization may be the most potent way to grab people's attention and accelerate their involvement in a valuable meeting.

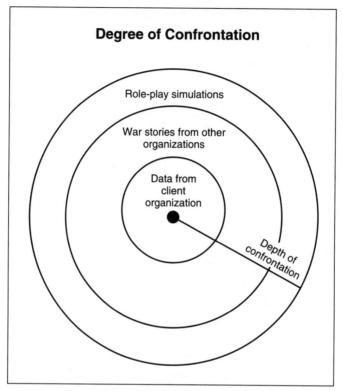

Degree of Confrontation

Role-play simulations

War stories from other organizations

Data from client organization

Depth of confrontation

EXHIBIT 5.6

Despite a history of outstanding financial results, a financial services firm headquartered in New York City never capitalized on chances to cross-sell across product areas. The CEO and other members of the firm's executive committee hoped to use a restructuring of business units as an opportunity to promote behavior change in the organization. They targeted the firm's trading group as ripe for producing even greater profitability through aggressive cross-selling. In this group, conflict historically raged between product managers and relationship managers—the product managers cared only to get the deal done and move onto the next customer, while the relationship managers protected long-term associations with their customers. Despite structural and attempted cultural changes, managers continued to play by the old rules. The executive committee sought assistance in getting the managers to let go of their old behaviors and attitudes and to accept a new organizational order characterized by cooperation across groups. One component of the plan to facilitate letting-go was a venting meeting. "These are New York City traders we're talking about," warned one member of the executive committee in response to the proposed meeting. "They will run right back to the trading floor if they feel their time is being wasted."

To get at the issues quickly, the venting meeting was designed to be highly confrontational. Interviews were conducted with a sample of traders from each business unit, with a summary of key findings presented at the beginning of the meeting. Direct quotes from the interviewees clearly showed agreement with the concept of cross-selling, but also the stubbornness of old behaviors. "Look," commented one trader in his interview, "I know the firm will make more money if we sell multiple products to the same customers, but I don't see what's in it for me." "I don't know those guys [in the other product area], and I'm not about to bring them to see one of my customers," reported another. Moreover, unreserved comments by product and relationship managers about each other were reported to the group. Product managers regarded relationship managers as "out of touch with reality" and "lazy." Relationship managers, in turn, described product managers as "willing to sell their grandmothers to make a deal." Captured by the intensity and relevance of the data, not one of the meeting attendees left the ensuing venting session to return to the trading floor!

A lower level of confrontation begins with the dissemination of war stories from other organizations. These stories can be colorful and relate well to the situation in the client organization; managers are especially attentive to how others before them have grappled with adaptation issues. The facilitator must guide the group carefully from an examination of adaptation dynamics elsewhere to a discussion of what is going on within their organization and among themselves. When anecdotes from other organizations are being served up, it is critically important that they pertain to the specific kinds of transitions experienced by managers in the audience. People trying to cope with the aftermath of, say, a downsizing demand relevance to their situation, or they will throw up an added barrier of resistance to what will otherwise be perceived as a generic or irrelevant program.

Another less confrontational technique is the role-play simulation. If skillfully led, simulations can be excellent learning opportunities and vehicles for generating discussion of issues in the client organization. For example, the combination of two computer companies, dubbed in the press as a "marriage made in heaven," became a living hell. The deal got off to a bad start when the "merger of equals" agreed to by the two CEOs was interpreted differently by their respective management teams. The acquiring CEO intended the term to mean that his side would determine integration plans but let managers from the other company participate in implementation planning meetings. The CEO from the target company, however, assumed the language implied mutuality in all merger-related decision making.

Each CEO prepared his management group according to his view of the agreement. When managers from the two companies met at the first integration planning session, which occurred before the deal's legal closure, those from the lead company were stunned when their counterparts from the acquired company spoke up and offered their views. The acquired managers, in turn, were angered by the arrogance and power plays of those from the lead company, and they stormed out of the meeting. When word got back to the senior executives about the conflict, the lead company's CEO could not understand the "insubordination" displayed by the other side, and the target CEO called his board of directors to see if the deal could be stopped.

Financial problems in the target company left the board with no choice but to accept the merger. The lead company's CEO took over the reins of the combined firm, and integration planning went forward in what all involved now called an acquisition and not a merger of equals. Despite the rocky start, many managers from the acquired side accepted positions in the postmerger organization. During integration planning and implementation, animosity between the two sides remained thick. The CEO earnestly wanted cooperation within his management team, but months of patience and one-on-one conversations with key subordinates did not pay off. Managers from both sides continued to avoid each other and failed to identify the synergistic opportunities that were supposed to arise from the merger. Finally the CEO announced that he was going to take the top three layers of his executive team to an offsite meeting to break down the cultural barriers.

The two-day meeting was built around a role-play business simulation. Executives were grouped according to their premerger affiliations, with those from the lead company assigned to "LittleCo" and those from the target company put into "BigCo." Immediately prior to conclusion of an intense day of business simulation—these were aggressive managers who wanted to win any game as much as they did in the real business world—the facilitator announced that BigCo had agreed to acquire LittleCo. The facilitator did not have any more information, but he promised that he would get some by the next morning. Then he called a halt to that day's simulation and invited the participants to the cocktail hour.

At the bar, managers could not leave their simulation roles behind. Players from LittleCo (in real life, the managers from the lead company) huddled together to speculate about what their new owners had in mind for them. Players from BigCo (the acquired managers) gathered in their own cluster, making big plans to integrate their new possession.

The role play continued the next morning with a series of simulated merger negotiation sessions. The facilitator instructed executives from BigCo to handle this acquisition in what was described as the firm's norm of assimilating target operations into their own way of doing things. He also directed the LittleCo group to do their best to hold out for as much autonomy as possible. Each side designated two members to serve as merger negotiators. It became clear after a few rounds that merger negotiations were headed nowhere. BigCo players grew angry at the lack of cooperation from their acquired counterparts; LittleCo players disdained their new owners and regretted having to report to, in the words of one manager, "such close-minded, unyielding people." Before long, BigCo negotiators could take no more: in the midst of one negotiation session they fired LittleCo's CEO and turned to the rest of the LittleCo management group, asking, "Who wants to be next?" On that note, the facilitator ended the simulation.

A spirited discussion followed the role play. Real-life acquiring managers expressed newfound appreciation for the plight of acquired executives; their counterparts coldly replied, "See how it feels?" The ensuing dialogue was infused with anger and resentment as managers from both sides recalled upsetting episodes from the early days of their real-life merger planning. Eventually, however, the emotion of the exchange retreated into a more passive sense of understanding and acceptance. One acquired manager expressed empathy toward counterparts from the buying side: "I can see how you would get all caught up in dominating the action if you thought that was your charge." The problems of the past could not be erased, but a new respect for the other side's perspective was generated along with a regard for the necessity of coming together as one team. As a group, the managers committed themselves to burying the hatchet. While the offsite meeting did not change the behavior of the managers overnight, it weakened the forces for the status quo and significantly strengthened the forces for change. Most importantly, it was the psychological turning point needed by the lead company's CEO to get people to accept his vision of a merged company benefiting from the strengths of both sides.

Ceremonies. Ceremonies are powerful tools for bonding people who are adapting to a transition and for accelerating their acceptance of the inevitable change confronting them. A variety of ceremonies have been used in conjunction with venting meetings. Many build on the theme of death and involve burials or wakes. Others celebrate the "good old days" left behind through such techniques as placing items in a time capsule.

A ceremony is not a surrogate for venting. Rather, it is a dramatic method for marking the transition from old to new. In organizations where the target audience is deeply uncomfortable with confronting issues in a public forum, a ceremony can emphasize the need to let go of the old at a lower level of emotional risk. Ceremonies, though, sometimes are rejected out of hand by executives who regard them as too exotic. The choice of whether to integrate a ceremony into a venting meeting agenda depends heavily on the organizational culture and climate.

Attendees. A few important rules guide the decision of who should attend a venting meeting. One is to never have people and their direct superiors in the same session. (The exception to this rule is the case of the top team in an organization—the senior executive and his or her direct subordinates. In groups with sufficient trust and maturity, the venting meeting can be successfully managed.) Employees will rarely express their deepest feelings if their boss is looking at them from across the room. This is not meant to deride the work of leaders who have built trust across hierarchical levels in their teams, but it is prudent to err on the side of creating as safe of an environment as possible for people to speak up in venting meetings.

When a superior persists in wanting to attend a venting meeting with his or her work group, a simple warning that this might hinder open discussion usually suffices at getting him or her not to attend. Sometimes superiors have a genuine interest in understanding what is going on with their people; this need can be satisfied through the offer of an anonymous summary of key points made during the meeting. The report can also include any ideas that may have been discussed in the session for facilitating the adaptation process within the work group, including what kind of resources or support are needed from the leadership. Another option, if the participants at a venting meeting consent, is to invite the superior to attend the last half hour of the meeting to hear a summary of the issues raised by the group. Again, this should be an anonymous report in which only summaries of the group's work are presented, rather than anyone's individual responses.

Some superiors may be adamant in their insistence on attending the session, usually with the wishful assurance that "my people are not afraid to speak their minds in front of me." If the executive persists despite advice to the contrary, his or her presence can be managed so that the impact on openness is minimized. The easiest way to do this is by creating breakout groups and placing the superior in one that includes either other senior attendees (if a venting meeting involves people from various work areas, then the superiors can all be put into one group) or the personalities from the group who would speak out no matter who was in the room with them (this provides the added advantage of keeping aggressive talkers from dominating the other groups).

Another rule is to make the session voluntary. No one should be forced to attend a venting meeting; nor, once the meeting has begun, should anyone be put on the spot and compelled to participate. Remember that even those who remain silent in a venting meeting report vicarious benefits from hearing how others are dealing with adaptation.

The question often arises whether to keep work groups intact during venting meetings or to bring people together from various parts of the organization. There is no definite rule here; sometimes scheduling realities dictate who will attend which venting session. Whenever possible, however, it is helpful to make the group as heterogeneous as possible. Meetings held after merger implementation are enhanced by bringing people together from the two premerger sides. This symbolizes the need to join together as one team and creates a bonding opportunity to assist in breaking down stubborn we/they dynamics. Following internal restructurings and transformations, a venting meeting with attendees from various departments or business units increases lateral communication and lets people see how employees in other organizational units are dealing with similar adaptation experiences.

Bringing people together from different units also acts to reinforce the new organizational order when it calls for stronger ties across groups. This was the case at the entertainment conglomerate MCA, where its diverse business groups (including movie production, television program distribution, and theme park units) traditionally enjoyed substantial autonomy in management systems and human resources practices. Mirroring corporate leadership's call to increase uniformity in the management of operating units, managers from various business groups were scheduled together in the venting sessions. In addition to the other benefits, attendees reported how the meeting helped them realize that counterparts from other areas of the organization shared some of their transition concerns, discover new ways of approaching shared problems, and develop a sense of camaraderie with people from other areas.

Guidelines for Conducting Venting Meetings

A venting meeting can be a powerful tactic to help people weaken their psychological attachment to the old order, release pent-up anxiety and frustration, and come together to counter the look-out-for-number-one tendencies that predominate during transition planning and implementation. For these benefits to be realized, however, the organizational community must regard the venting meeting as a safe milieu for expressing their deepest and truest feelings. In organizations that sponsor a series of meetings for various groups of employees, the impressions brought back and discussed through informal channels by attendees of the first few sessions will strongly influence whether others regard the meetings as something to look forward to or something of which to be wary.

Openness of communication, trust, and risk taking—qualities essential to the success of a venting meeting—are not bountiful in organizations during and after a transition. Therefore suspicion of and outright resistance to the notion of venting should be anticipated. In situations where people have become burned out, angry, or frustrated about their ability to achieve success in the new organization, there may be employees who will jump at the opportunity to release these feelings. More often, however, people will arrive at an organization's initial venting sessions with a healthy cautiousness, especially if restricted communication and distrust have been the norm during the transition. With some careful planning, the venting meeting concept can gain the respect, appreciation, and eager participation of the work force.

Be Conservative. Initial venting meetings are so consequential in establishing the frame of reference through which employees view subsequent sessions that it is important to "stack the deck" to ensure a successful meeting. Usually this means using outside professionals to facilitate the meetings. Outsiders help establish the credibility of the process by documenting that many organizations recognize the negative consequences of transitions and use venting meetings. Outsiders also reinforce the sense of anonymity and confidentiality in the process, thus encouraging suspicious or cynical employees to speak up. If an organization has a cadre of people who can be trained to facilitate the sessions, then these internal resources can be used once outsiders have established the credibility of the process.

Maintain Flexibility. When designing a venting meeting, it is always important to consider where people are coming from as well as where they are going in a transition. That is, the methods used in the venting should have a reasonably good fit with the old organizational order. If a pretransition corporate culture disdained confrontation and openness in communication, then it is doubtful that a group of people will embrace the notion of a venting meeting with open arms (or open mouths). Too large a discrepancy between what people are accustomed to and what is planned for a venting meeting can hinder participation. A skillful facilitator will test the degree of confrontation, assess attendees' comfort level and responsiveness, and proceed in a manner likely to produce the greatest amount of participation. He or she will also be ready to abandon initial plans when a group proves more or less open to the venting than originally anticipated.

Insure Confidentiality. An atmosphere of confidentiality must be maintained to make the large majority of participants comfortable with venting. At the opening of the meeting, address the issue head-on and establish norms that whatever is said in the meeting will remain in the room unless otherwise agreed to by the full group. Usually a direct statement from the facilitator about the necessity for respecting one another's confidentiality suffices. Should the group choose to have some kind of report of issues sent to senior management after the session, only use a format presenting group summary statements. At no time should the facilitation identify any individual's personal comments or provide enough detail to trace the source of the comment.

Give Examples. Get the ball rolling by sharing stories of transition-related issues from other organizations. Most people are uncomfortable with their feelings toward the transition and blame themselves for being in this negative situation. They will not readily volunteer how they feel if they suspect that it is somehow wrong to have or speak out about feelings of anger, vulnerability, and incapacity. The best way to confirm that these are normal reactions is to share experiences from other settings. This is accomplished as part of consciousness raising prior to the venting portion of the meeting.

Treat People—and Their Pasts—with Respect. Participants in a venting meeting may be at different places in their journey toward ending the old order and accepting the new one. Those holding on to the old order may be resentful at "traitors" or "sellouts" who have moved on with their adaptation; those ready for the new may be frustrated with the "laggards" or "troublemakers" who have yet to let go. The venting meeting is a forum for tolerating diversity in adapting to a transition—people are allowed the space to verbalize what they now are experiencing. Additionally, the venting meeting is not a place to overly criticize the past. Part of the letting-go process may entail coming to understand why past practices are unsuited for current or future business challenges, but this can be done without ridiculing or slighting what was once appropriate.

Venting Meeting Agendas

A venting meeting can range in length from one hour to a few days, and it can be scheduled on an ongoing basis or held as a one-time-only affair. After the acquisition of Western Airlines by Delta Airlines, lunch time brown bag venting meetings were sponsored for Western employees on a weekly basis. These were held at Western's former headquarters in Los Angeles until employees no longer needed a group setting to facilitate their personal letting-go processes. Following an internal reorganization at AT&T that combined its information systems and communications divisions, a single three-day offsite meeting was designed to help people let go of the old order and accept the new one. The objective of a single meeting is to alert employees to the adaptation process, accelerate their movement through it, and get them to deal with it consciously on their own or seek other assistance for support, rather than to work through the entire process in a group setting.

Exhibit 5.7 provides a menu for preparing the venting meeting agenda. Not all components are intended to be used in all meetings, either because of their poor fit with the organization's culture or due to time constraints. The full agenda typically requires roughly two days of work, but it can be expanded to three days if strong holding-on forces are anticipated. Alternately, the meeting can be condensed to one full day or less if components like the mourning ceremony or the feedback session with senior management are dropped.

Set the tone and atmosphere of the venting meeting early on by clarifying the meeting's purpose and objectives, establishing the facilitator's credibility, and loosening people up through an icebreaking exercise. Icebreakers like asking people to draw their current feelings about organizational life on a piece of paper or to describe them as a food or television program succeed at getting people to open up and participate. Then raise awareness of the adaptation

---

Venting Meeting Agenda

I. Introduction
  • Meeting objectives
  • Facilitator's background
  • Icebreaking exercise

II. Presentation on organizational and individual responses to transition

III. Breakout group assignment
  • Identify key issues affecting this transition
  • Prioritize issues for discussion

IV. Full group meets
  • Breakout groups report lists of high-priority issues
  • Consensus developed regarded key issues for discussion

V. Discussion of key issues

VI. Mourning ceremony

VII. Presentation on guidelines for managing self and/or others during recovery period after transition

VIII. Individual assignment
  • What I can do to facilitate recovery
  • What the company needs to do to facilitate recovery

IX. Breakout group assignment
  • Consolidate "what I can do" and "what company can do" lists

X. Full group meets
  • Breakout groups report lists
  • Consolidated lists prepared

XI. Feedback session with senior management

EXHIBIT 5.7

---

process through a presentation that educates attendees on organizational transitions and their impact on employees: the underlying environmental forces, unintended consequences, of models of individual adaptation, and other topics that either reveal or confirm what employees have been experiencing.

The presentation usually is met with considerable head nodding and verbal confirmations of how the discussion applies to the attendees' situation. In some settings the attendees may be bursting at the seams, ready to let out their feelings in an emotional and energetic catharsis. In others, however, a more conservative approach is taken by conducting a breakout group exercise that acts as a segue between the consciousness raising and reexperiencing components of the meeting. The intention is to build up employees' comfort level with the venting process. Attendees are assigned to small groups—people typically feel more at ease in a small group and feel more responsible for contributing to the group discussion—to identify and prioritize the issues from the presentation that are most pertinent to their personal situation. A lively exchange usually ensues and continues until the facilitator persuades the members to return to the full group.

Venting at MCA

At a venting meeting conducted with middle managers at MCA, breakout group members were asked to respond to two questions: (1) What are the critical changes affecting MCA today? and (2) What are the short- and long-term impacts of change on people and on business at MCA? Managers cited such major changes as the acquisition of their firm by Matsushita, the weak economy, and changing technologies and business markets. They discussed a mixed bag of positive and negative consequences associated with these changes. The weak economy, for example, resulted in a salary freeze but also an opportunity to determine ways to work smarter.

The change talked about most passionately, however, was not any actual event but the shift at MCA from the known to the unknown. Comments in the breakout groups characterized how managers feared the unknown, were uncertain how changes would affect them, and felt powerless. Through the discussion, most attendees reexperienced anger, stress, and feelings of betrayal by their historically paternalistic leadership. What concerned these middle managers most was that their bosses were not doing more to help them cope with the transition. Many shared the dispiriting perception that MCA cared less about its people than ever before in its history. In responding to the second question, breakout group members discussed the expected impact of these changes on people and business in MCA. Summarized in Exhibit 5.8, the responses reflected the emotional tenor of the small group discussions: managers perceived a mostly negative impact on people and on the business in the short run, but they expressed mostly positive expectations for the long term.

Sample Issues Discussed in Breakout Groups

Impact of Change on People

Short term	Long term
Lower salaries	Greater career opportunities
Limited career opportunities	Increased personal flexibility and adaptability to subsequent changes
Decreased morale and productivity	
Loss of key talent	Cross-cultural exposure
	Reduced career opportunities for women
Unclear management direction and goals	Restricted salaries
Increased stress	

Impact of Change on Business

Short term	Long term
Weakened image	Global competitive advantage
Loss of decision-making power	New technology
Loss of key creative talent	More efficiency
Loss of direction	New direction

EXHIBIT 5.8

When the venting meeting participants return from their break-out meetings and the full group is again convened, each break-out group reports its list of high-priority issues. The full group achieves consensus regarding the key issues in this particular transition and organizes them into a set of discussion items to guide the reexperiencing portion of the meeting. Now comes the emotional highlight of the venting meeting, as the facilitator leads a discussion that addresses salient issues weighing on the employees. Following the consensus list of items is less important than letting the group go where it wants with the discussion—invariably, one issue will bleed into the discussion of another. The depth of the discussion will vary according to the skill of the facilitator and the openness of the group. The full reexperiencing step rarely occurs at one meeting. Still, the moderator may take advantage of the presence of the group and conduct a mourning ceremony to facilitate bonding, supportiveness, and acceptance of the end of the old order among the attendees.

In addition to covering the three steps of letting-go, the venting meeting may include a module that readies people for their responsibilities in the new organizational order. This is typically the case when the organizational leadership is concerned about finishing the meeting on a positive note. Although the mourning process itself may end in a celebratory fashion, much like a traditional Irish wake, the notion of grieving retains a negative stigma in most organizational cultures. To help people look forward and feel optimistic about their chances for success, then, the venting meeting can close with a segment on preparing for the new organizational order.

After a symbolic pause in the meeting, a break or lunch, the focus turns toward the future with guidelines for managing the recovery period following the transition. In meetings involving nonsupervisory employees, this could be in the form of suggestions for managing oneself during recovery. Typically these include some mix of tactics for continuing the work of letting-go process and adapting to the new organizational order. When the meeting involves participants who manage other people, guidelines for managing subordinates during recovery are presented along with those for managing oneself. An individually focused exercise to get people to distinguish between areas they can and cannot control helps attendees not to fixate on matters beyond their influence.

At MCA, the distinction between what one could and could not control was underscored by asking each attendee to prepare two lists by themselves: (1) what they as individual managers could do to better manage recovery, and (2) what the company could do to better manage recovery. In breakout groups, people consolidated their lists and, in a final assembly of the full group, integrated them into lists of "what I can do" and "what the company can do" (sample results of these lists are presented in Exhibit 6.5).

At MCA, these lists—along with the summaries of responses to questions about change and its impact on the company's people and business—were presented to senior management in a written report. In other firms, the venting meeting sometimes concludes with members of the senior management team making a scheduled appearance to hear the findings firsthand from participants. This symbolizes leadership's genuine interest in what people have to say

---

Suggestions from MCA Managers on How to Manage Recovery

What I Can Do to Manage Recovery:

Maintain a positive attitude and communicate that to my staff.

Communicate my anxieties to my boss.

Disseminate accurate information on a timely basis.

Be open to ideas/suggestions from my staff.

Introduce staff to job duties not normally assigned to them, so that the group gains an appreciation for all responsibilities handled in their area and can handle work of absent employees.

Set realistic goals for myself and my staff.

Reassure valued employees.

Be flexible.

Share the highlights of this program with my staff.

Take a day off and recharge.

What the Company Needs to Do to Manage Recovery:

Issue quarterly reports (similar to press releases) from senior management on results of meetings with Matsushita.

Tell employees *why* things are happening.

Set consistent policies for each business group in areas of benefits, evaluations, etc.

Combine similar or like functions.

Consider job sharing as an alternative to layoffs.

Use focus groups to invite employees' ideas.

Recognize achievements.

Develop incentive programs to boost morale.

Look more at the long term.

EXHIBIT 5.9

---

about recovering from transition, but also lets executives hear the issues in employees' own words and with their emotions attached. Prepare executives for this portion of the meeting by reminding them that this is the attendees' meeting, not theirs. Their role is to be active listeners during the reporting-back session—that is, first to show empathy for where the attendees have been and what they are experiencing, and second to convey that they heard the employees' ideas about how the company could help them manage the recovery process. This contrasts with the knee-jerk executive response of feeling compelled to reply to every issue presented. Executives may wish to respond to a handful of timely issues, but their task is to listen to employees and take away from the meeting a clear sense of what people have been through and what resources and support they need to move forward with their adaptation to the new organizational order.

Venting at AT&T

Rhea Serpan was excited to learn of his appointment as head of the western region of AT&T's network operating group, the newly formed unit created by the internal merger of the company's communications and information systems (IS) divisions. He also understood the necessity for change. Strategically, the combination would give AT&T customers "one-stop shopping" for their computer and communication needs; financially, savings could be realized from resulting economies of scale. Serpan was less confident, though, about making one team out of people who "grew up" in two very different business climates.

The communications group, composed of veterans of telephone companies in the predivestiture Bell System days, enjoyed years of market leadership, customer loyalty, and a track record of high-quality products and service. Its management, however, was somewhat complacent and, at least in the eyes of some executives, was not responding quickly or appropriately to competitors. By contrast, the information systems group was a new venture that had yet to achieve profitability. IS managers were seen as risk takers but had a reputation for being insensitive to both people and bottom-line concerns.

Through the months of merger implementation, Serpan's concerns about people from the two sides coming together were justified. Three factors in particular frustrated him and his efforts at realizing a new organizational order. First, strong we/they dynamics persisted between the two sides. Each group continued to feel that the other's management style was inadequate to the needs of combined operations. Second, executives were not reinforcing Serpan's direction within their work areas. They had little experience in managing change of this sort and even less self-confidence that they could mold a new way of doing things. Finally, there was a strong orientation toward holding onto past identities and practices rather than building something new. With the considerable changes following the divestiture of the Bell operating companies, managers were inclined to retain familiar people and practices rather than look to make further change.

Serpan knew that his only hope of building a new organizational order was contingent on speeding his top team's adaptation process. Consequently he commissioned a three-day meeting to facilitate letting go of the old order and accepting the new one.

As a first step, each of the eighty managers in the combined division was interviewed, individually or in a focus group, and completed a questionnaire assessing his or her feelings about the ensuing change. It did not take much prodding in interviews to get managers to talk about differences between the two sides. Communications people regarded themselves as the winners in the internal merger and their counterparts as losers, based on the two sides' financial performance. Communications people also believed that they were led by "professionals," while information systems executives were "mavericks." By comparison, managers from the IS side felt that they were performing as well as could be expected given their relatively recent entry into the market. Moreover, they attributed the success of the communications group to traditional customer loyalty and not to the ability of its management.

Both sides acknowledged an upside to the combination, including increased benefits to customers and more opportunities to advance in the company. Yet they also saw the downside. Nearly two-thirds of the surveyed managers expected that the combination would lead to a substantial downsizing; one-half reported less job security; and only one-third felt that people from the two sides would have equal opportunities to advance in the newly merged unit.

Still, most managers expressed a wait-and-see attitude in response to questions about whether the integration would capitalize on the strengths of both organizations. The survey also revealed a major deterrent to joining together: only 23 percent of the communications managers said they trusted IS people, and just 17 percent of IS managers trusted their counterparts.

A three-day retreat was scheduled, with the first day devoted to consciousness raising about the adaptation process and beginning the reexperiencing step, the second day dedicated to continuing with the reexperiencing step and conducting a mourning ceremony, and the third day focused on the future with a series of presentations on the structure, policies, procedures, and expectations of the new organizational order.

The first day began with a presentation on common patterns found in organizations and people engaged in transition. Then key findings from the survey and interviews were presented. This put the issues on the table, using the words and responses of the people in the room. No one at the meeting could deny that the issues raised in the presentation were applicable to their own situation. Five factors emerged as central to the success of this internal merger:

- The degree to which the merged divisions managed the integration process well (in terms of communicating, providing chances for people to participate in decisions, and building ownership of the change)
- The level of energy and enthusiasm the managers had and developed in their people (for example, minimizing burnout, addressing concerns about limited growth opportunities and worries about whether another shoe would drop)
- The quality of direction provided (such as developing a sound business strategy and a workable implementation plan)
- The degree to which the managers educated one another about their businesses (including developing knowledge regarding each side's products, the new boss's expectations, and criteria for success)
- The degree to which the managers addressed the clash of cultures and created trust with their counterparts

The eighty managers were then broken into ten groups, two covering each issue, to clarify their expectations and concerns about how their division would approach the assigned issue. The groups were asked to recommend (1) what, as individual managers, they could do to address that issue to recover from the integration, and (2) what they needed from senior management in the way of leadership, structure, and support. The full group reassembled, and each small group reported its recommendations. The session concluded with each manager preparing a personal action plan and selecting from the roster of recommendations how they were going to lead the transition back in their own functions. The regional director made a commitment to take the groups' feedback to senior management in the form of his personal action plan.

The highlight of the second day was a "graduation" ceremony. After the managers discussed their ideas for successful integration in small groups, they were brought back together as a large group, and each manager was asked to write down "the three *worst* ways in which the integration could affect me personally." Each also received a sheet of stationery with his or her pre-integration letterhead and an old business card. Managers were then asked to stand and were led outside where a wooden coffin awaited. Off to the side, a marching band sounded a somber funeral march.

One by one, each of the 80 managers stepped up to the coffin, crumpled his or her worst case lists, letterhead, and business card and tossed them in. As the last manager stepped back from the coffin, the group was startled to hear a low, grumbling noise. Slowly, a one hundred-ton paver rolled around the corner and headed straight for the group. At first the managers stood paralyzed, unsure of what was to transpire. The band broke into a rousing rendition of "On, Wisconsin," and the paver veered toward the wooden casket, flattening it and its contents. Spontaneous cheering broke out among the executives as the paver rolled back and forth on top of the coffin.

Abuzz with excitement, the managers were asked to return inside. As they entered the building, they were handed academic caps and gowns and instructed to put them on. Ushers assembled the managers into two orderly lines and marched them into an auditorium where banners proclaiming "Congratulations, Graduates!" awaited them. Once all were seated, their regional director welcomed them and embarked on the classic graduation speech: "The day has come for which we have all worked so hard to prepare you. It is now your turn: our destiny lies in your generation's hands!" The managers sat quietly, absorbed in the speech, understanding the meaning of these words for them. Then the ushers brought one row of "graduates" at a time to their feet and marched them up to the stage. There, Rhea Serpan presented each one with a diploma, a "Master's of Merger Management," and a graduation gift—a share of company stock. After all proceeded across the stage and back to their seats, the group turned the tassels on their caps from left to right and proclaimed that they had graduated into their positions as leaders of the organizational recovery process.

Moving On

Before people can look ahead to new challenges and opportunities, they have to end what used to be. Before they can become a different type of employee, accepting their new personal situation as well as the new organizational order around them, they have to loosen their grip on their old identity, including all of its trappings and perceptions.

But employees who have ended their attachment to the old still have a way to go in completing their adaptation after a transition. As the next chapter tells, they must contend with an awkward period of feeling out new methods and roles. This reignites feelings of stress and uncertainty, but it is a critical—and creative—step in molding the new organizational order.

Approaching the New

After loosening their grip on the old organizational order, employees are closer to the last phase of adaptation after a transition—accepting new possibilities and ways of seeing and doing things. A rare opportunity is at hand to revise the negative or limiting ways of working and to construct a new organizational order.

Hang Time

Progress from ending the old to accepting the new is not instantaneous; the employee still contends with competing forces for the status quo and for growth. Although resistance to change gives way to adaptation, the forces for maintenance are sustained by the confusion and uncertainty of life beyond the old organizational order and personal situation, and by the inability to comprehend quickly the changes that take place as the new order is implemented. This is a period of slow internal psychological transition, the inevitable hang time that occurs when one has let go of the old ring but has not yet grabbed onto the new ring. Management consultant William Bridges refers to it as the "neutral zone":

> This is the no-man's-land between the old reality and the new. It's the limbo between the old sense of identity and the new. It is a time when the old way is gone and the new doesn't feel comfortable

yet. When you moved to your new house, or got the promotion, or had the baby, the change probably happened pretty fast. But that is just the external situational change. Inside the psychological transition happened much more slowly, because instead of becoming a new person as fast as you changed outwardly, you actually struggled for a time in a state that was neither the old nor the new. It was a kind of emotional wilderness, a time when it wasn't clear who you were or what was real.[1]

This is a difficult period for many people adapting to organizational transition, several managers have dubbed it the "twilight zone" in reference to the frightening qualities from which they would like to escape. Unless the phenomenon of hang time is understood, people in the process of adapting to a transition will mistakenly conclude that the lack of stability they feel means something is wrong with them. Some will panic, tighten up, and brace themselves for a fall. Others will lurch back toward the old ring, or grasp for the new one before it is within reach. Some, however, will recognize the fluidity of hang time and see it as a chance for creativity, renewal, and development. They will patiently try to accept the awkwardness and uncertainty as an opportunity to learn the perceptions and patterns of behavior that characterize the new organizational order.

Forces for maintaining the status quo, including long-held ways of thinking and acting, will never fully be erased. Individuals will attempt to respond to new situations as they always have. But during hang time, as people become increasingly aware of their patterns, they recognize when they are on the edge of responding in what now will be a maladaptive manner. The only way to learn this is through trial and error, either by oneself or by vicariously watching others being rewarded or punished for certain behaviors. Eventually, emerging mental models of life after transition come to be confirmed or discarded.

From the ashes of the old organization comes a new base and fresh momentum to begin anew the march toward revised organizational objectives. For individuals this could be new roles, relationships, and behaviors; for teams it might mean new missions and new operating procedures or standards; throughout the organization this implies a new architecture, new culture, new vision, and new ground rules aligning people's behaviors. The new organizational order takes actual form, and innovative ideas, institutions, and integrations are created.

Managing the Hang Time

There will be a lag between the articulation of the new organizational order and its realization as people experiment with methods for bringing it to life and learn what it truly implies. While this hang time between the old and new is uncomfortable and disorienting, it is also the best moment for innovation and renewal. As will be discussed in the next chapter, developing an organizational context that allows for experimentation and learning enhances the creative and effective use of hang time. One requirement to make the most of hang time is to review established policies and procedures carefully to ensure they will not hinder adaptation. The "rules" that prevail during hang time most likely were set up under the old organizational order, when things were not as fluid as they are in the transition to the new. Policies about temporary job assignments, job classifications, time off for training, who can make what kind of decisions, and so on may require revision.

Having some short-term goals for people to aim at provides checkpoints along the way toward desired longer-term outcomes. Hang time can be discouraging for those looking for quick improvements. It is important to give people a sense of achievement and progress; this helps counter the feelings of self-doubt that prevail during hang time. Do not promise, or expect, high levels of productivity during hang time, this will only set people up for failure. Everyone loses when ambitious targets are not met after transition: managers look bad, employees' self-confidence erodes even further, and executives get upset. Team leaders may have to educate superiors on limitations to productivity during hang time, as well as sell them on seeing how success at meeting a more attainable target (which builds people up) is worth far more in the long run than failing to meet a "stretch" target (which brings them down).

Finally, it is important during hang time to restrain the impulse (common during times of ambiguity and disorientation) to push prematurely for closure. It is tempting to rally everyone around immediate "wins" to offset uncomfortable feelings, but a greater price eventually gets paid when quickly implemented solutions fail to provide true breakthroughs in performance, quality, or effectiveness. The best way an individual, team, or organization can "use" hang time is to prepare for a successful, perhaps even graceful, arrival at the next ring. This recovery from the unintended consequences of organizational transition is an ongoing process of learning and renewal. It requires experimentation and risk taking, but it results in greater capacity.

Accepting the New

As people move through hang time, usually several months after a merger, downsizing, or other transition event has begun to be implemented, forces for accepting the new strengthen. By now employees have learned more about their personal fate and have grown more familiar with the situation within which they are working. In an acquisition, this may be more insight into how the lead company operates; in a downsizing, it could be a knowledge of how to get things done given limited resources; and in a reengineering, it is likely to mean thinking in terms of work processes rather than functional tasks.

This openness to change and to considering the new organizational order was markedly evident in the views of executives involved in a major bank merger after sufficient time elapsed to allow for moving through the stages of holding onto and letting go of the old order. An initial round of interviews with upper-middle-level managers, conducted one month after the merger announcement, had exposed two major themes: first, considerable anger at senior management for their actions in what the outside world saw as a perfect merger; and second, substantial uncertainty about what might have to be given up personally (including positions on executive committees, power, influence, independence, and perks).

A second round of interviews conducted six months later found that with very few exceptions, managers were less focused on the past and on what they had lost (or thought they would lose). Instead, they were more oriented toward new opportunities. Questions about "What is going to happen to me?" were supplanted by "What are we building here?" Concerns about surviving the merger were displaced by worries about missing an opportunity to build a truly great institution. As one manager noted. "We have a chance to become *the* great bank in this country, but we are not being pressed to do this." "We need to turn merger planning up a notch," claimed another. Others reflected on the adaptation process. As one senior vice presented commented, "Most of us have lost something in this merger, but we are getting over that. We now need something *new* to belong to—what is the new company to be?" A business manager was more specific in her need for clarity of the new organizational order: "What are the rules for appropriate behavior in this organization? How do I know that what I am doing is what is expected of me and what will make me successful in the future?"

Redefining Personal Success

Beyond matters of structure, product or service mix, and procedures, the direction of where the organization is headed includes a new definition of how personal success is achieved in the organization. Part of the work of building a new organizational order is to help people understand and adapt to personal changes. That is, even as the newly emerging organizational context remains poorly defined, people can learn about how they need to change to align their behaviors and expectations with the new organizational order. This is indispensable in helping individuals guide their personal efforts toward organizational goals.

A starting point for doing this is likely to be a redefinition of what personal success means in the new organizational order. In the past, success may have meant steady ascendancy up the corporate ladder; in the future, it may be defined as simply retaining one's job. Success in the old organizational order may have been measured in terms of the percentage increase in base pay, whereas in the new order it may be counted according to the size of a bonus paycheck. In essence, this means altering the mental models people use in assessing and reacting to their work environment. In the new organizational order, people may have to accept that they must persevere in their tasks even without a sense of feeling fully equipped with information or other resources to get the job done or that the menu of rewards available to them will not be as generous as it once was. As always, however, people will still be influenced by the extent to which they perceive efforts on the job to be rewarded.

The upside here is that the emergence of a new organizational order provides an opportunity for leaders to strengthen what may have been a weak link in the motivational chain under the old order.

While individual employees must recalibrate what they can expect from their organizations for being a member and for performing at reasonable levels, so must organizations recalibrate expectations of what it means to be a member. One obvious lesson from the years of organizational MADness is that people need to look out for themselves. Employees can no longer expect the paternalism and womb-to-tomb employment that organizations once offered. Instead, they have to accept primary responsibility for managing their careers.

The organization, in turn, cannot have it both ways by changing the terms of the psychological work contract to a more transactional and temporary relationship, yet expecting employees to dedicate themselves unequivocally to organizational needs. If the organization is going to change the rules, then it must expect people to change how they play the game. The organization owes its employees an explanation of how and why the rules are changing. More than this, it must help employees adapt to those changes through the process of experimentation and learning. Yet the burden does not rest entirely on the organization. Individuals must take the initiative to understand where they can exert control and to experiment with new ways of doing things.

Personal Change and Development

In particular, people need to restore their levels of self-esteem and self-confidence, which are eroded during transitions, to the point where they believe in their own ability and are optimistic about their chances to succeed—whether that success is realized within or without their current position or employer. This puts people in a proactive mode, making something of and for themselves rather than placing themselves at the mercy of the organization. The resulting motivation ideally gets applied to both individual and organizational needs: employees *feel a sense of control* and *look upon the work situation in new ways* to produce their best effort to succeed personally and to help the organization move toward its goals.

A Sense of Control

Perceived loss of control over one's work situation lies at the core of unintended and maladaptive responses to organizational transition. Thus the foundation for accepting new realities following transition is identifying where one has and does not have control, accepting this, and moving ahead accordingly. By focusing where one has control, one can rebuild a sense of personal efficacy. More importantly, one can avoid being distracted and demoralized by what lies beyond one's sphere of control.

When assessing themselves and their situation following a transition, most people look at their glass as half empty rather than half full. They bemoan control that has been lost or was never had. Yet when asked to articulate where they *do* have control, people discover their ability to influence some of the most important components of their work situation:

• **Career.** People can make an effort to identify career options, both inside and outside their current employer. This requires realistically assessing career alternatives and possibly revising personal expectations and dreams for one's future. It certainly requires letting go of traditional definitions of what constitutes a successful career. In the event there are no immediately clear paths to promotion—a strong possibility in the 1990s—a lateral move may be a boon to longer-term career mobility and job security. A transfer to another department provides new skills and experiences; the more hats a person can wear, the more valuable he or she is to an employer. Organizations need employees who are broadly skilled and whose assignments are wide rather than narrow. Thinking through "where the action is" in one's current organization and attempting to transfer to a growing business area (or at least one that is likely to be buffered from severe downsizing in the foreseeable future) may preempt personal vulnerability.

If no immediate alternatives to the current job are available, a person can enroll in courses or training programs to learn new skills and enhance future employability. Or one can network with people who may have leads for job openings. Even just updating one's resumé in anticipation of future need is a way of exerting control.

• **Performance.** Increasing numbers of people view their work as just a means to a paycheck while they look elsewhere—to recreational activities or voluntary work—for the personal satisfaction they no longer receive at the workplace. Their compensation is just that: an extrinsic reward that compensates them for the time they give up to be on the job. One way people can take control is to recast their experience at work as a source of meaning, personal challenge, and other intrinsic rewards. Doing well on the job in spite of all that is going on beyond one's control can be a source of personal pride, as well as a decent coping mechanism.

• **Work team.** Managers at middle and lower levels may not be able to control the decisions coming out of the executive suites, but they can influence how their work groups recover from the unintended consequences of a transition. During recovery, managers and supervisors have a chance to show true leadership. Whether or not they are receiving it from their superiors, managers and supervisors can control the extent to which they share information, listen, project excitement, direct energy, show empathy, model vulnerability, and are patient toward their subordinates.

• **Relationships.** Managers also can control the extent to which they reach out to peers in other parts of the organization. Developing new relationships with colleagues facilitates communication, enhances problem-solving capacity across work groups, and creates an important support network. It also reduces dependence on senior managers to coordinate across areas, freeing them up for their leadership responsibilities.

• **Attitude.** Every person in decent mental health can influence how he or she looks upon the circumstances and situations in his or her life. Employees can control the extent to which they adopt a perspective that views the posttransition period as an opportunity for growth and development. They make a personal transition from viewing what they are (or might be) losing to taking account of what they are gaining. For managers and supervisors, this may be new leadership and team management skills; for other employees, it may be new analytical and problem-solving capabilities. For all, it is the acquisition of a sophisticated and realistic knowledge of the new realities of the workplace.

• **Stress Management.** People are responsible for and should take control over their own stress management during recovery. The cumulative nature of stress—its effects being most debilitating when a series of small disruptions to the status quo add up—means that even when they are adapting to positive personal and organizational change, people are susceptible to stress reactions. The individual can manage levels of experienced stress in one of three ways. First, he or she can eliminate the source of stress, (for example, by changing jobs). If eliminating the stressor is not a practical alternative, a second option is to change attitudes about it: the job may not provide desired career advancement opportunities, but it may be the source of excellent benefits like health insurance and child care reimbursements. Finally, one can experience the stress but ameliorate its impact through exercise, meditation, participation in a hobby, or some other form of stress management.

One of the most effective stress management tactics during recovery is to keep a personal journal of one's experiences, emotions, and learnings. Regular entries written in a diary or spoken into a tape recorder raise awareness of emotional experiences, bring the mental process into the behavioral realm, and add a dose of discipline to the process of learning from one's situation. Reflection helps individuals to pause and think through their experiences. The benefits span both negative situations (writing about anger and jealousy helps people control those and other negative emotions, rather than have the emotions control them) and positive events (thinking through the cause-effect relationships underlying desired outcomes promotes personal learning).

By looking out for themselves and controlling opportunities to learn, employees gain an additional benefit during recovery: they make themselves more marketable for job opportunities inside and outside their current employer. Managers and supervisors who compete for scarce job openings with others possessing solid technical skills can distinguish themselves from the crowd by documenting leadership and managerial skills honed during recovery. Employees who can discuss in job interviews the contributions they made to team accomplishments during recovery demonstrate a positive attitude and a track record for success in the team environment that characterizes the new organizational order for many employers. This is an important point: team orientation, creative problem solving, and transition management skills are among the core competencies that organizations increasingly are looking for in new hires. People who can control the extent to which they learn and change with the organization today are going to be all the more attractive to the employers offering tomorrow's jobs. Learning during recovery, then, is a way to control (at least to some extent) one's employability in the future.

Based on studies of managers recovering from mergers and acquisitions, professors Anthony Buono and Aaron Nurick report that one of the most effective ways to help people come to terms with their spheres of control is to guide them through a set of questions in a process consultation mode.[2] The goal is to prompt employees to identify (1) the exact nature of their problems and concerns, (2) what it will take to resolve the situation, and (3) whether they currently have or might be able to generate appropriate resources to deal with the situation. This enables people to distinguish those aspects of their work environment that they can and cannot control, and to identify the areas that can most effectively be managed through action or through a change in attitude. When people concentrate on those areas where they can exert some influence, they can be encouraged to work constructively on potential solutions. While some of these may be relatively minor in nature, by building on a series of small successes people can begin to appreciate more fully their sphere of control and, in turn, increase their self-confidence and self-esteem following a transition. Hang time thus seems less frightening and becomes more fluid.

José, a marketing manager, survived two waves of head-count reductions following a telecommunications merger. His work, for the most part, was the same after the combination as before, but he now had a new boss from the other side in the merger. José was happy to have a position in a company that, as a result of the merger, was poised to be a leader in the development of new technologies, yet he was not sure if or how he would see any personal benefit stemming from the combination. He accepted a consultant's offer to guide him through the issue identification and resolution process. José identified his primary problems and concerns as (1) the absence of a career path in the new organization, (2) dismay over a new boss who did not know José's track record of past innovations and con-

tributions nor seemed to be making much effort to become ac-
quainted with new players on his team, and (3) a fear of losing his
job if poor financial results mandated a subsequent wave of layoffs.

When asked how he could resolve the concern regarding the lack
of a career path, José acknowledged that this issue was beyond his
control and would require attention from human resources experts
or members of the firm's senior executive team. To resolve the next
issue—a new boss unfamiliar with his capabilities—José listed some
steps he could take to remedy the situation. First, he decided he
would do with his subordinates what he had wanted his boss to do
with him: spend time getting to know people, ask them what they
had accomplished in the past, and find out what they were looking
forward to in the near future. José hoped that this practice would
somehow get reported to his own boss, perhaps by one of the
boss's former underlings who now was part of José's team, but he
recognized that this was only slightly probable. Still, José felt he
was doing something that would help him establish his own leadership position, which was enough reason for José to commit to it.
Second, José intended to prepare a portfolio of past work and present it to his new boss. Although worried that this might be regarded as too pushy, José felt that doing something to promote himself
was better than taking no action and remaining anxious. José got
added mileage out of preparing the portfolio by using it as the basis
for a speech he volunteered to deliver to a marketing professionals
group in his city. This was a way to gain some visibility with potential employers in the event that his third concern, being hit by another wave of layoffs, came true. None of these actions were dramatic or earth-shattering, but they helped José develop a sense of
control over his situation and increased his self-confidence that he
could work toward some personal success.

Kim was a manager in a financial services firm for thirteen years,
and she figured she always would be a manager. Her department
grew to seventy-five people; then, following a merger, her company
decided to relocate her operation to another city. Kim figured she
and her family would be miserable in the new city, so she stayed put
and took a gamble. She looked through the company's career opportunities listing and was drawn to a notice for an employee assistance specialist. The position required five years' experience in
human resources; although she had no such experience, Kim ap-

plied anyway and got the job by persuading her future boss that her years as a manager had taught her the techniques necessary to communicate one-on-one with employees. The lesson here for other managers is to be creative and do not limit oneself to a narrow sense of what one can do. Skills are more transferable than most people suspect. Kim *reinvented herself* with success. She did this because she let go of the expectation (developed under the old company organization) that people were rewarded for loyalty; instead, in her own words, she was "prepared every day for my job to disappear."

A Fresh Perspective

Succeeding within the framework of the new organizational order requires that people change along with their work context. Most of the ways in which people can take control of aspects of their work situation require looking at them with a fresh perspective. Managers building bridges to other departments have to abandon old organizational practices of running everything up the flagpole before taking action. Individuals who include options outside the company in their career planning activities are ignoring old taboos about what it means to be a loyal employee.

People must not be restricted by the confines of the old organizational order when defining and living by the new order. Rather, they have to seek challenges, take risks, and look for new ways of doing things. Recovery is an excellent time for individuals in historically weak staff functions in organizations to "show their stuff." Members of human resources departments with reputations in the old organizational order as "paper pushers" adding little or no value can break out of that mold by searching for new ways to serve the organization. The director of training at a transportation conglomerate had been frustrated by years of budget cutbacks that limited his group to offering only the most basic technical skills courses. After a major restructuring, he took the initiative to sell business unit heads on training programs to develop more general managerial and leadership skills. Eager for some intervention to recover from unintended consequences of the restructuring, the executives readily commissioned the design and delivery of a sequence of new training programs.

Sometimes looking for fresh perspectives means accepting limitations. Individuals who joined an organization for promotional opportunities or job security may have to redefine their expectations. "What does it mean to me to be unable to fulfill career aspirations?" and "What do I really want from my working life?" are questions that only the individual can answer for himself or herself. By answering them, however, he or she gains a new perspective and can move forward. For example, Beth, an engineer who joined an aerospace firm with dreams of one day managing a project team, survived wave after wave of downsizing following spending cuts in the defense industry. She came to grips with the inevitability that she would not become a manager anywhere in the foreseeable future. She then asked herself why she wanted to manage and identified two factors: helping others learn and making more money. From the loss of her career ideal, Beth came up with a new plan. She transferred to the company's training department to satisfy her desire to help people learn and set a goal of gaining employment, in about three years, with a training consulting firm to address her desire for greater income.

Executive Support for Letting Go and Moving On

Employees need adequate time to work through their adaptation to transition. This is becoming increasingly clear to executives who recognize the necessity of letting go of the old before moving on to the new. They endorse the adaptation process in their organizations in both implicit and explicit ways. First, these executives subtly factor insight into the adaptation process into their business planning and leadership actions. They develop realistic business expectations that allow time for people to identify psychologically with the new organizational order. They remind upper- and middle-level managers that their employees may still be moving through the stages of adaptation and that a dose of patience with people who are holding onto the old may be warranted. Second, these executives sponsor formal programs to accelerate the rate at which people work through their reactions to loss and crisis. Instead of paying lip service to human reactions to transition, these executives dedicate resources and provide expertise to assist employees in working through the holding-on and letting-go stages so that they can arrive at the point of accepting the new order.

Executive Orientations

Some leaders who sanction adaptation processes are guided by humanistic values that show respect for the individual and the integrity of the organization. Other leaders come to acknowledge the adaptation process through a more practical route: they have seen the debilitating effects of previous transitions on employee well-being and organizational performance and seek to minimize the fallout from subsequent transitions. The CEO of a manufacturing firm anticipated distractions from performance and other unintended consequences of an impending downsizing after he saw how a merger and two reorganizations in a three-year period devastated employee morale, customer service, and profit margins. He directed his human resources staff to ready a formal plan to help survivors deal with their losses *prior to* the general announcement of the reduction in force.

Whether motivated by their personal values or their organization's financial results, executives who recognize the need to end the old before accepting the new share some basic orientations. They recognize that signs of mourning and coping with loss and crisis may not be apparent, especially soon after transition. Many managers and employees who do not want to be labeled as weak under pressure will attempt to put on a facade of being all right. Others are stuck in denial. Still others are numbed by the overwhelming effects of multiple waves of transition. Executives who successfully lead their troops through and out of transitions do not assume they know what their people are feeling. Instead, they create an environment in which people can risk expressing what they are experiencing. In turn, these leaders are able to distinguish between the natural need to vent pent-up emotions and antagonistic bad-mouthing. They do not take what they hear as a personal attack. Instead, these executives recognize that sanctioning the letting-go process will result in employees who appreciate their leadership's sensitivity and willingness to take the heat.

Executives who address the adaptation process also demonstrate respect for people's pasts—the old organizational order from which they have come—and direct their subordinates to do the same. This is most obvious in an acquisition, where the lead company's culture dominates over that of the target, but it applies to all transitions in which people have to let go of the past. Successful acquirers know that one of the best ways to help people let go of their old ways of doing things is to show respect for that culture rather than denigrate it. Allowing acquired employees to pay homage to what they are leaving behind helps them release their psychological attachments to it. In contrast, lead company managers who put down the acquired company and its culture inadvertently strengthen resistance to change among acquired employees who are proud of their past and see their self-worth at stake. Even in other types of transitions, expressions of respect for the old organizational order allow people to accept the new order without a loss of self-esteem. In contrast, put-downs of the old order prompt employees to dig in and defend where they have come from.

Leaders who sanction the need to let go acknowledge that "you pay now, or you pay later" in recovering from the unintended consequences of organizational transitions. Intervening early in the adaptation process, when resistance is relatively weak and minor issues have not yet festered into major problems, requires fewer resources than does addressing stronger counterforces later. These executives have patience and a realistic sense of the time scale that guides the adaptation process. They put aside the typical value placed on short-term results and quick fixes, acknowledging that Band-Aids will not heal the deep-seated wounds experienced by people during transition.

Importantly, executives who support programs to facilitate letting-go recognize that their behaviors during and immediately following a transition are potent signals to employees about the new organizational order. Actions speak louder than words as employees create mental models about life after the transition. One company conducted an extensive set of employee focus group interviews, inviting complaints about inefficiencies in the old order. In addition to identifying short-term issues, this signaled how, from that point forward in the new organizational order, employees at all levels shared responsibility for locating cost savings opportunities.

Modeling openness and trust does more to create that climate as part of the new order than does talking in those terms. Embracing the concept of letting-go of the old before accepting the new is one of the most compelling ways in which leaders send a message to employees that they recognize what people have been through during a transition, what they now are dealing with during adaptation, and what they will be contending with during recovery.

Recovery and Revitalization

Moving on after transition is never a return to the way things used to be. Rather, it is setting sights on the next ring and determining where and how one can increase the odds of grasping it successfully. Moving from one ring to another requires ability, agility, and timing; so does moving from the old to the new in organizations today. Adapting to life after a transition is never easy for people, but the process can be facilitated by helping people to stop holding onto the old ring, to see that the new ring is within reach, and to believe that they can make the leap.

Just as the individual passes through phases in adapting to a transition, so does the organization. *Organizational recovery* is the period of bouncing back from the unintended consequences of the transition. It coincides with the individual passage through the phases of holding on, letting-go of the old, and moving ahead. At the organizational level of activity, it involves changes in mindset and behavior that create a context for realizing the new order. As such, recovery clearly is the middle step in the unfreezing-changing-refreezing process.

Organizational revitalization is the set of activities that sustain the new order by resuscitating individual employee spirit, team performance, and organizational effectiveness. Revitalization may involve modifications in perceptions, practices, policies, and processes. It is the "refreezing" step that reinforces desired changes in the organization and its people.

The next set of chapters describes efforts organizations can take toward recovery and revitalization after a transition. Chapter 7 offers a framework for creating a context for recovery, while Chapters 8, 9, and 10 discuss ways to revitalize individuals, teams, and systems. This framework assumes, of course, that people have let go of the old and are ready to reach for the next ring.

Creating a Context for Recovery

As individuals pass through the phases of adaptation after a transition, they require a sense of what the new organizational order is about. That is, to let go of the old ring, they need to have a new ring in sight to latch onto. This places a great importance on clear statements of the direction of and guidelines for the new organizational order; these bring substance to looking upon work and its requirements in fresh ways. Direction and guidelines also delineate the boundaries within which people should exercise control in testing new methods and developing new mental models. All of this is part of the experimentation and learning that must occur during hang time. Individuals will not take the risk to experiment, and organizations will not benefit from what can be learned, unless leaders develop a supportive environment for doing so. Clarifying direction and guidelines and supporting experimentation and learning are the key tasks that create a context for organizational recovery after a transition.

Unless a context for recovery is set, the organization will not move from the old to the new order. The organization may contain bright spots; there may be excellent departments or excellent groups. There may also be bright and capable people who realize the need to do something positive, yet they are rarely able by themselves to make a real difference. Individuals may be able to do their piece a little better by paying more attention to customer needs or eliminating an unnecessary report. But none of these isolated actions will transform the basic routines of the organization, allow it to learn, and help it to recover from the unintended consequences of transitions.

To avoid a slow organizational decline caused by emotional and intellectual paralysis after transition, individuals who want change have to translate their desire for action into a collective will and a collective purpose. Individual aspirations and activities have to be mirrored by groups, aligned with departments, and supported by organizations. This requires the genuine support of senior leadership as evidenced through active and committed management of the recovery period after transition.

Recovery at Majestic

You may recall the case of Majestic Manufacturing in Chapter 1. Historically regarded as an excellent employer, Majestic attracted well-skilled and highly motivated employees who were committed to achieving company goals. In exchange for their loyalty and hard work, the company provided employees with job security, liberal benefits, and regular pay increases and advancement opportunities. Then, beginning in 1985, Majestic experienced four major transition events in a five-year period, including the acquisition of a competitor, two significant restructurings, and a voluntary reduction in force. Shortly thereafter CEO Justin Jordan conceived his vision of making Majestic the premier company in its industry. He engaged a strategy consulting firm to conduct a companywide value-added work analysis and commissioned a training company to deliver a program on the "continuous improvement process" to all Majestic managers. Thousands of hours and millions of dollars were spent on training programs and consultant fees.

Jordan's intentions were honorable: enhance the firm's competitive position by transforming the way people thought and acted on the job. As he charged ahead to pursue his vision, however, he left his work force behind. No one in the company, his direct reports on the senior executive team included, knew what he meant by "premier company." Middle managers, unsold on its benefits, resisted application of the continuous improvement process back on the job. Burned out by round after round of transition, Majestic employees rejected the value-added work analysis as nothing more than a euphemism for "more layoffs ahead." Inadvertently, the CEO had torn the fabric of the psychological relationship that bonded employer with employee. Employees viewed the attempts at transformation as follies yielding pain with no gain. They became confused by the sequential introduction of jargon like *premier company*, *value-added*, and *continuous improvement* and grew cynical of management's capacity to lead in any way other than "flavor of the month." And after promises of no layoffs following the merger were broken, employees distrusted their leadership and always kept one eye anxiously looking for the next swoop of the layoff ax.

Recovery Strategy Design

With the external economy continuing along its sluggish pace and internal efforts to transform the company proving ineffective, Jordan made the difficult decision in January 1991 to implement Majestic's first-ever involuntary reduction in force later that year. To spearhead the planning and implementation of the downsizing, Jordan turned to the most trusted member of his senior team, executive vice president André Lloyd, a veteran Majestic employee with close ties to both line and staff groups. When Lloyd received the job of coordinating the 1991 involuntary reduction in force— tagged a *realignment* by the CEO—vivid memories of how the voluntary reduction in 1990 debilitated the morale and spirit of the Majestic work force leapt into his mind. If a voluntary reduction produced a severe case of layoff survivor sickness, Lloyd reckoned, what would be the impact of an involuntary program just one year later?

Lloyd set out to design the components of the reduction in force—severance packages, outplacement services, communications packets, and the like. He knew he had to do much more, however, than soften the landing of the layoff victims: he had to help the survivors recover from the downsizing as well as the cumulative effects of ongoing transition and turmoil. Lloyd invited a consultant with experience in working with layoff survivors to spend a day with him and brainstorm what a recovery strategy at Majestic might involve. Their work together would eventually extend over the next several months.

On the day the consultant arrived at Majestic's headquarters, Lloyd intercepted him in the hallway and warned him—only half-jokingly—not to let on to anybody in the building that he was a consultant. "People have had it up to here with consultants," cautioned Lloyd, "They'll lynch the next consultant they see, if they don't lynch me first for bringing another one in!" He relayed Majestic's recent history, describing the acquisition, subsequent restructurings and voluntary downsizing, and the CEO's call for Majestic to become the premier company in its industry. His tales of the value-added work analysis and continuous improvement programs were all too familiar: lots of time and dollars spent on studies and training, little on follow-up or real change.

Lloyd knew that the challenge facing Majestic was not just to help people get over their reactions to this round of layoffs, but to change employees' expectations about working at the company. He spoke of the real need to transform the Majestic culture. The realities of doing business in the 1990s no longer would support the paternalism of the old organizational order; competitive pressures mandated newer, smarter ways of working. Lloyd concurred with the "premier company" premise—to keep pace with the competition, Majestic would have to embark on a process of continual renewal to enhance product quality and customer service while keeping costs in line—but he reeled at both the poor manner in which it had been introduced by Jordan and received by the work force.

The consultant shared his observations of unintended transition consequences and described the many ways organizations can prepare for and implement downsizings, help survivors adapt to life after the cuts, and use the transition as an opportunity to build a new organizational order. Although Lloyd acknowledged the fallout from the 1990 voluntary downsizing at Majestic and expressed his fear that the 1991 involuntary program would have similar results, he was discouraged by the consultant's laundry list. "These interventions seem appropriate enough," he said, "but our people have been through so much change lately. I don't think they can handle any more programs or processes." The consultant concurred, even if employees were able to absorb more jargon and tactics, the residual effects from misfires of previous programs would interfere with recovery efforts.

Lloyd and the consultant reached a temporary stalemate. The involuntary downsizing would set off emotional shudders in employee ranks, but employees' tolerance for change and uncertainty was at a new low and impeded the delivery of responsive interventions to help them adapt to the transition and build a new organizational order. Two specific roadblocks to a recovery strategy surfaced: employees were saturated with the turmoil of recent events and they were in no frame of mind to deal with yet another program, no matter how much it might help them and their company.

As Lloyd and the consultant continued to exchange ideas, they found a way to break through the first roadblock. The model of people having to let go of the old order before accepting the new one caught the executive's attention. To counter their saturation with ongoing organizational change, Majestic employees had to release their pent-up anger, resentment, depression, and other sentiments. The company could help its managers loosen their grip on the old order by providing a forum in which they could vent their concerns and loosen their attachment to old expectations and identities. Thus the first component of the strategy for recovery at Majestic was a series of venting meetings to help downsizing survivors let go of the emotions and issues built up over years of change at work.

Lloyd had gone out of his way to let the consultant know that the recovery approach would have to be hidden. Announcing that it was "downsizing recovery time" would only strengthen the second roadblock—resistance to what would be seen as the latest management fad. The goals of recovery had to be accomplished without raising the process to the level of a new program or introducing new models, concepts, or buzzwords. Lloyd's persistence on this point led to an idea for removing the second roadblock. Although Majestic managers had never really implemented it, they had already been through continuous improvement (CI) training and knew the process. Why not tap into the CI language and tactics already familiar to managers?

As introduced in Majestic, continuous improvement called for identifying a customer, measuring that customer's needs, intervening to meet those needs, and subsequently measuring the extent to which they were met. The second component of the recovery plan, then, was to get managers to use the CI process as a guide for their efforts to rebound from the psychological trauma of downsizing, clarify work roles and responsibilities, and set in place the organizational capability and individual motivation to achieve premier-company status. To accomplish this, managers had to regard employees as customers with a need to recover after downsizing. Managers would be asked to measure employees' recovery needs, design an intervention to meet those needs, and subsequently evaluate whether employee recovery needs were met.

If managers were going to regard their employees as customers, traditional respect for hierarchical authority—a cornerstone of the Majestic culture—would have to be put aside. The challenge was to speed up this process without overburdening a group of very busy people who had been subjected to one new program after another and were now about to go through a major downsizing that would disturb both work flow and employee well-being.

Recovery Program Design

First, however, Lloyd had to sell CEO Justin Jordan on the need to recover after the impending involuntary downsizing. As in most large bureaucracies, bad news had not risen to the top in Majestic, and Jordan had little idea that his employees were burned out on change and had not lined up behind with his premier-company initiatives. Lloyd commissioned a small project for the consultant to interview a sample of Majestic managers. The unintended consequences of multiple transitions and the lack of alignment with his vision became clear to Jordan as he read the summary report, and he endorsed the recovery plan.

A month before the layoff was to be announced, Lloyd convened a steering committee of human resources (HR) professionals to guide the recovery program. Eight senior HR representatives—two each from Majestic's headquarters group and three strategic business units—joined Lloyd and the consultant on the steering committee. Key criteria in choosing the eight included intellectual capacity and willingness to look to the future with open minds. The involvement of HR professionals broadened the talent engaged in designing the program and increased informal communication back to the business units.

The steering committee made some basic decisions, like opting to limit the recovery program initially to a pilot business unit. Then, as the group got down to discussing design options for the program, one member suggested that the human resources department itself model desired behavior by using the CI process to design the recovery approach. HR representatives agreed to regard their constituent line managers as customers with a need to design recovery programs in work teams. To measure managers' needs, these HR representatives would conduct focus group interviews to identify areas in which managers felt they could use assistance. This was a sharp break from Majestic tradition, in which HR had unilaterally designed programs and interventions. Getting line managers to participate in the program design—"going to the customer"—demonstrated that this effort was different from those before it. One week after the downsizing announcement, focus groups with a sample of surviving managers were conducted to assess their views of recent changes in the company, current levels of employee morale and organizational effectiveness, anticipated consequences of the downsizing, and what would be needed to rebuild individual spirit and team cooperation. Internal organization development experts from the HR staff conducted the focus group interviews.

In the focus groups, managers discussed what had to be considered if the recovery efforts were to reap true benefits. They expressed three needs most frequently: letting go of pent-up frustration, divorcing themselves from old ways of doing things, and being given the time, help, and opportunity to design ways to work smarter. Managers acknowledged an understanding that their old ways would not meet new competitive challenges, and that the downsizing presented an opportunity to identify better ways of working. They were frustrated, however, by the lack of time available to design and implement any of these new techniques. Many managers expressed high levels of burnout and apathy during the interviews, an indication of how deep their feelings of helplessness were. Others talked of their disillusionment with faddish programs that led to no real change, and their skepticism that the 1991 realignment would be different.

Capabilities Development Workshop

After discussing the focus group findings with the steering committee members, the consultant proposed a two-day capabilities development workshop. The workshop would be designed expressly to address managers' needs to release their pent-up emotions and thereby free them to design recovery strategies for their work groups.

The first day of the workshop was a venting meeting to facilitate the letting go of emotions and attachments to the old organizational order at Majestic. After a celebratory dinner—a symbolic respite between the first day's emotional work of letting go of the past and the intellectual challenge of designing the future—the second day of the workshop aimed to begin giving managers the time and resources they said they needed to design recovery strategies in their work areas. The day began with a videotaped message from CEO Justin Jordan. In it he recognized the unintentional consequences of years of ongoing transition but also acknowledged that the road ahead would be dotted with pain, confusion, and occasional disappointment. Jordan noted that all members of the Majestic community would have to see these as inevitable results on the path to a new organization and urged managers to view them as opportunities for learning and improving rather than signs of failure. To underscore this point, he used his own rollout of the premier-company concept as a case of how good intentions sometimes fall short but still provide an opportunity for learning. He confessed some personal lessons: the importance of communicating more clearly what "premier company" meant, selling people on its benefits, and enlisting people in creating ways to realize it on the job.

Jordan proceeded to describe the values underlying his concept of premier-company status and showed how these values related to business goals. He did not hide the limitations of the new organizational order, bluntly saying that the old days of paternalism could not be retained in today's business environment and, while efforts would be made to cross-train employees and place them with opportunities in emerging businesses, the company would continually have to assess staffing levels to achieve its vision as the industry price leader. But, Jordan quickly added, the long-term benefits of this industry leadership would mean an important competitive advantage for the firm and enhanced opportunities for creativity, personal development, and rewards for surviving employees.

Following a short discussion of managers' reactions to the video, a senior trainer from Majestic reviewed the continuous improvement training managers had received several weeks earlier. As shown in Exhibit 7.1, the model was adapted for use with employees as internal customers. Managers were asked to follow this model but told they could have complete creative control over how it would be applied to their particular work area. To aid the managers, the trainer worked through each step of the process and outlined prototypes for building recovery strategies.

Linking Continuous Improvement Process with Recovery

Continuous Improvement Process	Recovery Action
Identify customer and needs	Define "customer" as employees in your work group who need to regroup following downsizing
Measure customer's needs	Measure employee regrouping needs following downsizing • Employee attitude survey • Focus groups • Unobtrusive measure (e.g., records)
Clearly define work process that provides products and/or services to customer	Design an intervention to address employees' needs to regroup
Close the gap between work process output and customer's expectations	Implement regrouping program
Develop capability to measure and compare work process output to customer's expectations	Conduct ongoing assessment of the extent to which employee's regrouping needs are being met
Change and improve work process, inputs, resources, and work environment to improve the outputs	Provide ongoing feedback and continuous improvement in the work process following downsizing

EXHIBIT 7.1

- *Identify customer and needs.* Managers defined their "customer" as the members of the work team reporting directly to them. Customer needs might include, but not be limited to, rebounding from the psychological effects of downsizing, clarifying new work roles and responsibilities, and establishing organizational capability and individual motivation necessary for business success.
- *Measure customer needs.* Managers received detailed information on various measurement approaches, including employee attitude surveys and focus group interviews. They were offered an array of available standardized questionnaire items and focus group interview protocols, but they could choose other measures if desired. Considerable time was spent on identifying sources of archival data, including production and personnel records.
- *Design intervention.* While the actual design of interventions to address employees' recovery needs would be contingent on measurement results, managers received examples of possible activities. These were primarily in the form of vignettes of how managers in other downsized organizations helped their work teams recover. The trainer encouraged managers to go beyond these examples and be creative in designing their own interventions.
- *Implement interventions.* Managers heard a brief presentation on the do's and don'ts of fostering change in work groups. This included such issues as communicating the rationale underlying decisions, showing people how they can benefit personally from organizational changes, and reinforcing changes through rewards.
- *Conduct assessment and provide feedback.* Managers reviewed their measurement tactics to ensure that they allowed for ongoing assessment of the extent to which employees' recovery needs were being met. Without overwhelming managers by forcing them to look too far down the road, program trainers stressed that the purpose of the CI process was to provide continuous feedback and improvement in the work process after downsizing. Managers began to recognize the process as a vehicle for ongoing change, not as a one-time-only reaction to the downsizing.

Managers then designed a draft of recovery approaches for their work areas. One HR professional from the steering committee was assigned to work with each manager, to coach them on how to adapt the prototypes to their situation, review the initial draft, and schedule appointments to revise the plan for implementation.

The draft recovery approach designed by the manager of the business unit's order entry department exemplifies the work produced. The manager identified telephone order entry personnel as his customers, who had a need to maintain timely and accurate customer service in spite of a 12 percent reduction in head count. The work group's specific needs covered both issues directly related to the work process and group dynamics that appeared as unintended consequences of recent tough times in Majestic:

- Identify work essential to maintain performance standards
- Identify work conducted by now-terminated employees
- Determine creative approaches to conducting essential work
- Overcome fear of another wave of downsizing
- Minimize group tension and conflict developed during the downsizing
- Rebuild spirit and excitement previously characteristic of the work group.

To secure a baseline measure of his customers' needs, the manager planned to use three methods. First, focus groups would be conducted with a sample of order entry staff. These groups would probe the impact of downsizing on the team's work process by assessing changes in work flow and the extent to which tasks were not being performed as well or as often as they were before the downsizing. Second, a questionnaire would be designed and administered to all team members. This would measure such individual issues and group dynamics as motivation, personal distress, intragroup tension and conflict, communication, and opportunities to influence the work process. Third, objective measures would be collected to assess individual well-being and team performance. These would include organizational records indicating rates of absenteeism, tardiness, accidents, voluntary turnover, order accuracy, customer complaints, and employee grievances.

This manager looked upon the recovery as an opportunity to foster positive change while overcoming the lingering problems of downsizing. Though he recognized the need to examine measurement findings before committing to a plan of action, the manager pondered the intervention stage of the recovery process. He began to consider activities like weekly meetings with his work team to address specific issues identified during measurement and an external customer advisory board. An initial meeting would be held with his work team to feed back and understand measurement findings before moving on to the next task of prioritizing needs to be addressed.

Recovery Program Results

In meeting the general objective of helping Majestic and its people rebound from the debilitating effects of a downsizing, these beginning steps of the recovery program yielded some specific benefits. First, the recovery effort legitimized the human pain experienced at Majestic over the last several years. Concepts like layoff survivor sickness were openly discussed and confronted. Employees learned that their psychological reactions to a traumatic organizational transition were normal, and they also learned how to deal better with those reactions in themselves and their work groups.

Second, the recovery program gave managers and employees a shared sense of responsibility for recovery after downsizing. It broke down traditional expectations that addressing employee needs was the exclusive responsibility of HR and not of line managers. The program also helped shift the Majestic culture from a reactive to a proactive stance in dealing with employee issues as various levels of management became involved in anticipating and addressing strong employee reactions to the transition. The recovery also reinforced Majestic's shift from a paternalistic culture to one in which the organization and all its people shared responsibility for steering through change. It demonstrated that Majestic and its employees shared a common interest in rebounding from a downsizing in a creative and productive way.

Finally, the capabilities development program nurtured the self-confidence managers needed to lead recovery in their work teams. It helped managers distinguish between areas in which they did and did not have control, and it involved them in taking action where they did have control—in designing recovery strategies for their own work areas and handling their personal reactions to life after downsizing. It also stressed the need to abandon their old ways of approaching work. The world had changed and would continue to change; commitments and identities that led to success in the past were no longer likely to produce it in the new organizational order. The self-confidence instilled in managers carried over to aid many in leading their troops through subsequent waves of transition.

Creating the Context for Recovery

While not suggested as a textbook approach to managing transition and recovery, the Majestic case does highlight an effective ability to help a group of people who had grown angry, cynical, and pessimistic to loosen their attachments to old emotions and ways of doing things and contribute to the definition and building of the new organizational order. To be sure, Majestic employees still had a great deal of anxiety and uncertainty as they attempted to contend with the disorienting and confusing hang time between the old order and the new one. Yet a collective sense of progress took hold within the Majestic work force in the weeks and months following the capabilities development workshops. Managers returned to their work teams with renewed optimism and excitement about the future, but also with a realistic sense of the hard work ahead of building a new way of doing things. This sense of renewal and readiness for recovery was in part attributable to the letting go among managers of old, pent-up emotions. Additionally, however, it was due to the conditions present in Majestic that coordinated efforts at the top, middle, and bottom levels of the organization to create a context for recovery. A context that supports recovery helps people move through hang time toward accepting the new organizational order and, ultimately, positive organizational change. Eight characteristics are necessary for a context for recovery.

1. Organize Work Around the New Organizational Order—Direction and Guidelines. Managers and employees contributing to organizational recovery must have something with which to align their actions on the job. Two components of the new organizational order—direction and guidelines—give people a sense of what really matters in the new organization and a larger picture to keep in mind while concentrating on their daily activities. Direction is a clear statement of where the organization is headed, a destination to be reached via transformation or changes. Guidelines are more specific indications of the values and behaviors necessary for how the organization will reach its direction. Together, direction and guidelines help managers and employees understand those activities that contribute to the objectives of the new organizational order and those that do not. They also clarify which aspects of work are open to local assessment and revision and which are fixed and off limits to local variation. Posttransition organizations that lack direction and guidelines for the new order disable employees from acting because there is no contextual basis for people to know if their actions help or hinder the achievement of organizational goals.

Compare the two rollouts of Justin Jordan's vision of premier-company status in Majestic. In the first he dropped the phrase on the organization and then proceeded to bring in consultants to conduct a value-added work analysis and trainers to teach continuous improvement. No wonder employees were unreceptive to either intervention: the direction was ambiguous, with no specifics on where the organization was headed, how it would get there, or how attaining the vision would benefit individual employees. At the second rollout, Jordan more carefully and clearly communicated what *premier-company* meant, took time to sell people on its benefits, and enlisted them in creating ways to realize it on the job. He also gave people some guidelines to understand what would matter most in achieving this new vision: responsiveness to customer needs, innovation in new product development, smart usage of information technologies, and constant retraining and renewal of employees. The direction and guidelines gave people an understanding of where the company was headed and the contributions expected of them.

2. Aim High. The context for recovery is supported by a norm that encourages all organizational members to search for high-quality answers and not settle for the easy way out. Clear expectations must be set for fundamental changes in the way work is approached, organized, and managed rather than incremental modifications to the status quo. Too often compromises and trade-offs characterize how decisions are made in organizations after a transition. Employees who avoid the vulnerability of risk taking or are too burned out to give their best shot will settle for easy resolutions rather than press toward innovative problem solving. In addition to the obvious problem of producing low-quality decisions, this rekindles cynicism, pessimism, and other forces against the new organizational order as it signals that valid improvements are not being made during recovery.

In Majestic, a training program on group creativity and decision making was offered to any work team interested in enhancing its issue identification and problem-solving ability. The course covered impediments to the group decision-making process, exercises for enhancing creativity, and methods for realizing the appropriate conditions for optimal decision making.

3. Accept Responsibility. Executives in organizations are often keen to fasten blame anywhere but on themselves. When things do not go as hoped, they sometimes blame the business environment, sometimes the decisions of previous top management, and sometimes the failure of current middle management to implement decisions made by the top team. While there may be an element of blame rightly attached to these groups, it distracts from the true issues at hand. A new organizational order can occur only when executives, managers, and employees accept that fundamental change is needed and that they—and only they—are ultimately responsible not only for the organization's failures in the past but for its success in the future.

This is a matter of getting people to stop placing blame for the past and to start accepting responsibility for the future and how they are going to get there. This attitude is critical to creating a context for recovery, as it encourages employees to take responsibility for their own behavior and performance. To foster this mindset for managing change, organizations must promote inquiry and exploration and remove stigmas attached to making mistakes. Failure must be recognized as being an integral part of learning about the new organizational order; it is a painful but powerful way to learn. Successful organizations tolerate individuals not having an answer, but expect that people work together to find the answer rather than pass the responsibility. These organizations also eliminate the barriers and traditional obstacles to sharing power. Executives, managers, and supervisors are rewarded for enabling others.

At the same time, employees are rewarded for assuming additional responsibilities.

4. Reject Programmatic Change. CEO Justin Jordan's initial efforts to achieve premier-company status were stymied by managers' rejection of programs like continuous improvement. As is the case in many organizations, there was no action taken in work teams to reinforce the process learned in the CI training program. Much more than this, however, CI failed at Majestic because of the anger manifested in perceptions of it as management's "flavor of the month." Continuous improvement was never seriously considered by Majestic managers as a helpful tool for enhancing customer service or organizational effectiveness; rather, it was derided as yet another senior management folly. Similarly, the structural changes proposed by Jordan in the late 1980s to streamline decision making and reduce bureaucracy failed to produce any behavioral change, as managers and employees continued to abide by the guidelines established under the old organizational order.

Jordan knew that change was required to adapt to new competitive realities, but he misunderstood how to bring it about. His assumptions underlying his initial effort to develop a new organizational order resembled those of most senior executives attempting organizational renewal. They think that promulgating company-wide programs—mission statements, corporate culture programs, total quality programs, and new pay-for-performance systems—will transform organizations, and that employee behavior is changed by altering a company's formal structure and systems. One study of organizational change, finding the exact opposite to be true, concluded that "the greatest obstacle to revitalization is the idea that it comes about through company-wide change programs."[1]

5. Focus on the Work Itself. The saturation effect following transitions, in which employees' threshold for dealing with stress, uncertainty, and disorientation is taxed up to and beyond its limits, interferes with people's ability to learn and apply new programs or processes. No matter how conceptually sound or pragmatically applicable a total quality management or empowerment intervention may be, people will perceive it as an irrelevant distraction rather than as a method to help get the job done. Similarly, efforts that start with changes in structures or systems will be second-guessed, put down, and sometimes even ignored by employees. Moreover, precious time (and usually lots of dollars) will be wasted as mandated changes stagger down from the top.

An essential condition in developing a context for recovery is to get people to focus on the work itself. Their attention is centered on aligning tasks, roles, responsibilities, and relationships with the critical business needs of the new organizational order. Employees concentrate their energy on their work, not on some abstraction like "empowerment" or "culture." At Majestic the capabilities development workshop was not an indoctrination session to force-feed managers the continuous improvement process. Rather, it was a forum to help managers diagnose where change might be needed in their work areas and plan how to go about the transformation process with their employees. The continuous improvement process, already familiar to managers, was offered as a prototype and not insisted upon as the only course to follow.

As the work itself is examined and aligned with the new organizational order, changes in structure or systems may follow. At Majestic, after the order entry department manager implemented his design for assessing and responding to employees' needs for recovery, employees themselves took on the responsibility to identify work essential to maintain performance standards. One proposed recommendation required changes in the computerized order entry system. After review by management from both the sales and MIS departments, appropriate changes were made in the information system. Note the sequence here: the system change followed changes in work, not the other way around. As initial architects of the change, order entry employees saw its benefits and took ownership over its successful implementation.

6. Emphasize Local Design. Successful organizational change is often initiated in local teams and then spreads through the organization. At Majestic the focal point for designing change was at the work group level within the pilot business unit—managers of work groups attended the capabilities development workshop and managed the change process back in their teams.

Abandoning conventional assumptions of organizationwide programmatic change and of structural change producing behavioral change means that the more successful strategy of endorsing and nurturing change at the local level can be supported. This is effective for a few key reasons. First, local managers are intimately familiar with their work technology and group dynamics. A senior executive or general manager cannot understand the intricacies of a particular business unit, function, or work team. They may have a sense of what the new organizational order should feel like, but any efforts to direct the change effort will limit the latitude available to local managers to achieve a design for recovery that truly builds toward the new order.

Second, local design means that managers and employees at the work group level take more ownership over the recovery process. At a time when perceived lack of control is a major concern for organizational members, local design allows people to feel more like architects of change rather than victims of it. They actively contribute to diagnosis and planning the change strategies associated with recovery, rather than passively sitting back and taking what senior leadership mandates. Finally, the very fact that individual managers are willing to accept responsibility for getting things done right through involved group effort signals, in most work organizations, a move away from the old way of doing things. Aside from the content of what is being changed, the process involving personal responsibility and group involvement managed locally is itself likely to be a quality of the new order.

7. Encourage Coordination and Communication. Throughout the implementation of recovery plans in work areas in Majestic, work groups learned from the successes and failures of others. Frequently, the way one work group dealt with an issue provided some insight for another. This exchange of information occurred both through informal sharing sessions among the human resources coaches and in such formal ways as a monthly recovery newsletter and occasional large group meetings. The newsletter kept people informed about ideas generated in various business areas and updated them on progress of implementations. Retreats and meetings set up to facilitate the exchange of information across groups provided time for managers to consider how creative solutions designed in one area might be applicable in their own or generate variations more suited to local application. Other corporations use steering committees to encourage interdepartmental cooperation.

In addition to spreading useful ideas, communication and coordination across work areas in organizations recovering after a transition may nip emerging conflicts in the bud. When two work groups are approaching the same issue, they can join forces to find a mutually agreeable solution rather than each going off in their own direction.

As the implementation phase is entered, coordination across work areas is typically necessary to realize true change. The modifications made in Majestic's order entry system required close working relations between the sales and MIS groups. To enhance coordination, an ad hoc organizational arrangement was made to transfer an MIS staffer to the sales area on a full-time basis.

8. Provide Resources. Even when commitment to recovery after transition is solid, forces remain that run counter to building the new order. Among these are pressures to produce short-term business results and frustrations that derive from inadequate resources to assist in developing and carrying out recovery plans. Busy managers and employees need assistance in aligning work with the new order. At Majestic, this assistance came in the form of three sets of resources—time, coaching, and prototypes. The business unit selected for the pilot recovery program was chosen in large part for the general manager's commitment to provide time for managers to attend the capabilities development workshop and for work teams to go "off line" on a regular basis to assess and plan changes to work. The business unit head could not see how to produce significant improvements in productivity or quality without an initial investment of time. The organization's commitment of time was matched by employees in several work areas. Majestic people became so involved that many regularly used their lunch hours and stayed into the evening to contribute to recovery activities.

To enhance the likelihood of success in local recovery efforts, professionals from Majestic's human resources staff coached managers in the design and implementation of their plans. Coaches met with managers on an ongoing basis after the capabilities development workshops, and they could also be called upon to facilitate employee work group meetings or to identify other resources to assist client groups in their work. One coach, for example, researched what other local firms were doing in the area of work innovation and arranged for a small group of Majestic employees to tour their facilities and learn from their experiences.

While the local aspect of recovery planning always was stressed at Majestic, managers could avail themselves of prototypes to guide their efforts. At the capabilities development workshops, a variety of approaches to assessing and planning changes were reviewed by trainers and other human resources professionals. Some managers followed these prototypes verbatim, and a few rejected what they heard completely; the majority, however, built upon and refined the models presented.

Building the Capacity to Learn

The enduring benefit of organizational recovery is not the capacity to charge up a hill and capture the opportunity at hand immediately after a transition, but to create an organization capable of adapting to a changing competitive environment and charging up hill after hill—each with its own terrain, hazards, and rewards. To do this, the organization has to monitor its behavior continually, gain insight from its own experience and that of others, and adjust the way it operates. In short, it has to have the capacity to learn.

Experimentation and Learning

Recovery after a transition requires experimentation and learning at the organizational, team, and individual levels. Experimentation is critical if the organization, team, or individual is to meet the challenges posed by an increasingly complex external environment. There are no clear-cut paths to success. Only by trying different approaches and learning from these efforts will the organization, team, or individual find its way.

Learning is important for other reasons. The continual search confirms that a different and better way of doing things is indeed emerging. It reinforces the concept that change is pervasive in the current and future business environments and that to retain the best chances for personal success, individuals had better be prepared to change also. Mirroring the process at the organizational level, individual contributors have to monitor their behavior, gain insight from their experiences and the experiences of others, and adjust the ways they operate. This is an ongoing process that builds capacity at all levels in the organization and revives spirit and confidence. Finally, experimentation establishes standards that "good" may not be good enough. Experimentation implies a permanent need to search for the best modes of operating. Simply being good at something may not be sufficient for longer-term success; competitive pressures are likely to require excellence of execution.

Individuals cannot do this on their own; they must be supported by their top and middle management. At AT&T's Network Systems Group, a unit employing one-fourth of the company's work force, a new strategic intent of going global and growing the business began in 1991. To communicate this new order, help people link their job activities with the new strategic intent, and enhance the leadership capacity of middle and upper managers, the group's president commissioned a program that embraced and reinforced the process of learning by experimentation. Managers came to the program having conducted presession assessments of what was and was not working well in their areas and in which aspects of what was not working they could make a difference. This became their "personal challenge." After a training program involving cognitive and experiential techniques, each manager met with four to six peers in a mentoring group to assess their personal challenge and experiment with implementation alternatives before committing to follow-up action. The managers also received 360- degree feedback from their superiors, peers, and subordinates regarding their own leadership behavior and, in particular, their capacity to encourage a learning orientation in their work teams. The basic message of the program was that the company that succeeds is not the one that avoids mistakes; it is the one that makes mistakes and learns from them quickly. Ellen Walton, who helped design the program, said, "The philosophy in my organization is 'try it.' If it does not work, we learn from it and move on. It takes a supportive boss to do that."

Learning Versus Copying

An important distinction exists between true learning and mere copying. Popular best-practices studies help educate an organization on the variety of procedures and activities that prove successful elsewhere. Reflection on what is working elsewhere, however, does not replace the need for organizational experimentation and learning. What works well in one organization may not be the best way forward in another context. At most, copying can lead an organization to yesterday's best practice. Moreover, it will not build an internal learning capacity to help the organization and its people contend with ongoing change.

This also holds true for the dissemination and copying of the best practices within organizations. It is ideal when experimentation and learning in one part of the organization can reap additional dividends through applications in others. Realistically, however, consideration has to be given to how a practice developed elsewhere applies to a group with different dynamics and potentially different business conditions. Once again, the adage that "you pay now or you pay later" holds true. Time spent up front on analyzing the fit of practices developed elsewhere (including how to modify those practices before implementation) versus locally generated options can save the eventual usually more substantial costs of coming to terms later on with an approach that simply was not appropriate for the situation at hand.

When organizations focus their energy on easy-to-copy tactics or faddish techniques rather than on more fully understanding their situation, the concepts underlying the techniques, or their fit, change does not last long. Organizations in recovery faces a paradox: the greater the need to recover, the greater the desire to see some significant change in short order. The faster one wants to see results, the more one is attracted to implementing tactics and techniques rather than carefully building a context for recovery. The more amenable a tactic is for instant use, however, the more likely it is not to be very different from what prevailed under the old organizational order.

Leading Recovery from the Top

How does a context for recovery get established in an organization? Begin by taking the lead of those who have likened the merger, acquisition, or downsizing process to a kidney transplant: it must be planned and carried through very carefully, and the convalescence must be closely supervised if the organism is to avoid rejection.[2] When the convalescence stage is reached, the patient goes through a slow and careful process of accepting the new organ, adjusting to life-style changes, and recuperating from the debilitating side effects of major surgery. On one level, posttransplant recovery entails the body's physical acceptance or rejection of the kidney and its ability to fight off infection. On another level, posttransplant recovery occurs as the patient psychologically adjusts to life after the surgery and accepts new realities that include both limitations and benefits. For example, the patient may have to come to terms with the loss of participating in sports or eating particular foods. Alternatively, the better-functioning organ may allow the patient to engage in behaviors and activities not possible before the surgery.

Both the physical and the psychological aspects of post-transplant recovery involve considerable learning by trial and error. The physician collects data through extensive presurgery testing and planning and draws from personal experience and insight to devise a program of what drugs to administer and in what dosages to facilitate recovery. Ultimately, however, it is how the patient's body metabolizes and responds to the drugs that determines the protocol that works, and this can be determined only by ongoing experimentation and monitoring. And while the physician, therapists, and family and friends can offer support, it is the patient's own character—his or her patience, tolerance for frustration, and persistence through the trial-and-error process—that will influence the rebuilding of self-confidence and the psychological acceptance of the behaviors in which he or she can safely engage.

The postoperative recovery process mirrors the posttransition recovery process in organizations. A CEO, president, or business unit leader can steward the process, but it is ultimately the employees themselves who will accept or reject the new order through their own process of trial and error. A leader—even when equipped with the best intentions and best prescriptions—cannot force organizational change, just as a physician cannot compel the body to accept a transplanted organ. Nor can a leader mandate the adoption of new behaviors congruent with the new order; that only comes from learning the cause-effect relationships and establishing new mental models derived from the trial and error experimentation of adapting to that new order.

Much has been written in recent years about the senior executive role in the organizational change process, with various characterizations of the "visionary leader," the "transformational leader," the "charismatic leader," and even the "magic leader."[3] Effective leadership at the most senior organizational level is essential when people are reluctant to tamper with the tried and tested cause-effect relationships and to bring to life the vision of the new order. Yet traditional manifestations of "tough turnaround" leadership—that is, "taking the helm" by introducing programmatic change or making structural or systematic alterations and hoping that behavior change follows—have proved ineffective.

In contrast, executives who successfully lead the recovery process after a transition recognize that they do not change organizations. What they do is create a context within which managers and employees change their own work areas and behaviors. Still, the leaders understand that the stewardship of recovery requires a delicate balance between flexibility and direction: the flexibility required to allow local change efforts to flourish, and the direction required to guide change within acceptable parameters. Leaders can contribute to the development of a context for recovery in the following ways:

Be Involved Without Being Obtrusive. Senior leadership must accept responsibility for the realization of a new order without imposing it on people. This gets to the heart of what is meant by creating a context for change rather than mandating it. The leadership role is to provide the resources for local change planning and implementation efforts and the guidelines to align work with the new order. In addition, senior leadership actively promotes teamwork and a sense of shared fate, and it facilitates the acceleration of learning from one unit of the organization to another. Here, however, the temptation to force learning from one part of the organization to the other must be kept in check. Leadership visibility is important to demonstrate interest in the recovery process and the importance of it to achieving a new order, but the real stars of the show are the local change efforts.

Project Excitement. One characteristic of organizational life dissipated during the MADness of the 1980s and early 1990s is the sense of employees that they are contributing to something special. Most people want to identify psychologically with their workplace, not merely trade hours on the job for a paycheck. Senior leadership has to put some of the excitement back into the workplace by rallying people, motivating them to act, expressing confidence in the organization's and its people's ability to succeed, and celebrating accomplishments along the way to the new order.

Following a merger of two medical centers that involved the elimination of many jobs, a physical move between two campuses, and the exacerbation of long-standing conflicts between groups—for instance, between nurses and doctors, management and hourly employees, and ancillary services and direct patient contact staff—the chief administrator acknowledged she had a bitter work force on her hands. She recognized the prevailing negative mindset as a hindrance to her efforts to build a high performance system, and she set out to help people recover from the transition. Along with clarifying expected standards of performance on the job, sanctioning a process for designing change within and across teams, and other actions to create a context for recovery, a large part of the administrator's efforts went into rallying people about the excitement of creating a new and special organization. She took care to remind people constantly, in group meetings and in one-on-one conversations, of the rare opportunity to design and build a new organization. She also repeated her confidence in their ability to design and implement standards of service that exceeded benchmark standards in the health care industry. The administrator also injected fun into the process—for example, dropping into work group meetings with pizzas. She offered symbolic rewards for time spent on designing positive changes, such as giving out passes to a local movie theater or gift certificates to restaurants so that busy employees could celebrate with their family and friends.

Food and fun, however, are no substitutes for the satisfaction of making a positive contribution to one's work situation. In an auto parts manufacturing firm, burdened in the 1980s by the plunging fortune of the American car industry, the plant general manager generated excitement after three downsizings in four years by calling on employees to take control of their future by contributing to improvements in productivity and quality. This was their chance to emerge from the pack as a preferred provider to automakers.

Direct Energy. It is not good enough to get people excited; their energy has to be directed toward what matters most. Leaders creating a context for recovery ensure that employees understand the priorities as well as the fundamental ways in which work is to be organized, approached, and managed. At Majestic, the CEO's articulation of guidelines—including innovation in new product development and smart usage of information technologies—focused managers' efforts on creating change in their work areas in a way that contributed to organizational priorities. At the medical center, enhanced teamwork was underscored as a critical success factor and as a key criterion in evaluating proposals for changing working arrangements. Yet employees also heard in no uncertain terms that cost containment was of paramount performance in an environment of perpetual change. At a profession services firm, managers and employees, beaten down by a succession of leadership changes and cost-cutting efforts, rallied around not a general call for enhanced business results but a specific mission to place profitability above growth in determining new business directions.

During recovery an atmosphere of give-and-take between leadership and local managers provides ongoing feedback in both directions. Leaders may learn something from a local change effort that modifies their vision and guidelines or should be factored into change efforts in other areas. While the administrator's original architecture of the merged medical center called for separate facilities for inpatient and outpatient care, she listened to the radiation departments recommendation to combine all services in one location to achieve substantial cost savings. She then asked all other groups to consider if physical consolidation would contribute to enhanced cost savings and patient services within their departments. This illustrates also how the new order is not typically a static vision, but a moving target that keeps pulling behavior and decisions closer and closer to its center.

Motivate from the Inside. Successful leaders know that real influence is a matter of winning over peoples hearts and minds, not controlling the overt behavior of their muscles and bones. Genuine motivation, the kind that is truly needed to charge up a hill, is not derived by dangling a carrot in front of good performers or holding a stick over poor ones. It comes only from people committing themselves to a special cause. The credos of the most successful companies are positive affirmations of the employees, customers, products, and services of the company. They emphasize values that go beyond profitability. Adhered to on a daily basis, they build pride of belonging and meaningful purpose among employees. As a first step in responding to reduced employee morale and operating results following its series of transitions, the professional services firm drafted a statement of the companys direction and values. The statement, in addition to clarifying the company's commitment to not straying beyond its core business and leadership's direction of profitable growth, spelled out the values that would guide attainment of the strategic goal including honesty, integrity, hard work, and courage. As Steven Brown notes, leadership's job is to embody the purpose of the new order, not by preaching it but by making it the basis of all decisions and testing proposed solutions by answering these questions: Will this strategy or change build pride in my people? Will it build belief in our products and services? Will it build belief in the company?[4]

Say It Again and Again. Nothing has been more overcommunicated in management literature than the need to overcommunicate to employees. But the message still has not been heard. A 1990 *Wall Street Journal* survey of 164 chief executive officers found that, although they acknowledged that personal communication helps create more employee commitment to change, 86 percent said other demands prevented them from devoting more time to communicating.

Communicating during recovery extends beyond formal channels of newsletters, memos, videos, and group presentations produced by staff specialists to a personal commitment by senior leadership to ensure that people do the following:

- Comprehend the new order and guidelines for achieving it
- Accept that the old organizational order, although not wrong, is no longer the best way to achieve organizational and personal success
- Learn about recovery successes in other parts of the organization and how they apply to their own situation
- Understand why decisions are being made and see how these decisions contribute to the new order
- Sense the leader's personal excitement about new possibilities and achievements and are themselves "catching the fever"
- Are themselves communicating with each other in a multidirectional, comprehensive, open, relevant, and timely way

Another facet of leadership communication during recovery is the sharing of information that, in the old organizational order, had been available only to top management. In most companies this includes information like frank assessments of the organizations or business unit's financial results and competitive position. Information sharing of this kind is a symbolic way of rebuilding the trust that was likely to have eroded during the transition. No matter what the content, in order for communication to be a tool in creating a context for recovery, it must encase consistent messages across multiple media and provide some upward feedback to ensure that the messages were heard and understood. Many organizations have used individual interviews, focus groups, and questionnaires to track employee reactions to posttransition communications just as they would track customer sentiments following a marketing change.

Show Empathy. Even when they have let go of the old, employees suspended in hang time remain grappling with change and with making sense of the new order. It is naive to think that employees will embrace the new order without some experience of threat, hesitation, and other fear-based reactions. Beyond merely acknowledging this reality of human adaptation, leaders benefit from displaying empathy toward the situation of others in the organization—being aware of sensitive to the thoughts and feelings of their experiences during recovery.

To be credible in the recovery process, leaders must demonstrate a gut-level understanding of what it is like to be an employee during and following a transition. To know this, a leader must be in touch with the concerns of employees. Understanding their day-to-day experience means knowing what they worry about, what excites them, what frustrates them, and what they are thinking, feeling, and needing as they do their work. This empathy can only come from spending time with employees across levels and departments.

Be patient. Executives who successfully lead the recovery process after a transition understand that change will not happen overnight. To create a new order is to change fundamentally the organization's culture, and cultures change slowly. Each step of the way takes time—creating a context for change, clarifying and communicating the guidelines to align work with the new order, determining and availing resources to support local change planning and implementation efforts, facilitating learning from one part of the organization to others, and actively promoting teamwork and a sense of shared fate along the way. Of course, none of this can occur until people first let go of the old order, itself a time-consuming process.

Executive disdain for this slowness contributes to the customary preference for programmatic or structural change. Mandating a change gives leadership the illusion that its wishes have been implemented and supported, when in reality forces for maintenance are providing substantial resistance. Nonprogrammatic change may take substantially more time up front, but it eliminates the back-end resistance that so often defeats organizational renewal.

Anticipate Mistakes. Ask people to discuss the most potent sources of learning in their professional development, and they are likely to talk about how they learned from their mistakes. This is a stressful but tremendously effective way to learn whether for a kidney transplant patient discovering new capacities, a child learning how to ride a bicycle. a consultant determining how to deal with clients, or an employee attempting to understand and contribute to a new order. Leaders set expectations: "We will fall down a lot, and it's going to hurt sometimes. But we are in this with you, and we will do what we can to pick ourselves up, learn from our mistakes, and move forward." Importantly, senior executives must ensure that their direct subordinates also display this tolerance and patience in their words and actions.

Model Vulnerability. Leaders will make mistakes along the way, too. "Walk the talk" here means that senior executives should own up to their personal missteps and miscalculations. They model vulnerability and the effective process of learning from those mistakes. Anything less reinforces cynicism and suspicion of leadership's true intentions. An organization cannot adopt a learning mode unless its most senior executives do the same.

Certainly Majestic CEO Justin Jordan's acknowledgment of his mistakes in the initial rollout of his premier-company vision and what he learned from the experience was a dramatic move in a company that historically deflected self-scrutiny. Equally powerful at the professional services firm was the receptiveness of the CEO and the entire management committee to feedback that they had failed to follow through on past efforts to implement espoused values and that their current team dynamics, if left unchecked, would in all likelihood interfere with any future rollouts. This vulnerability was projected front and center at an offsite meeting where the next layers of management convened to review the initial draft of the statement of direction and values. The facilitator kicked off the meeting by reporting key findings from interviews he conducted with a sample of the attending managers. Included among the factors presented as inhibiting the company's new direction were explicit statements taking the top management team to task for their past behaviors and current dynamics. The other managers in attendance were impressed by their leaders' acceptance of this feedback. During the course of the three-day meeting, they shifted their focus to their own role and away from what the management committee needed to do to promote successful change.

Implement Change at the Top. Senior leadership must assess how change elsewhere in the organization affects its own team, as well as the implications of the variety of local changes on overall company structure and systems. Once local changes reach a critical mass, the CEO has to be ready to transform his or her own work unit as well. The company's structure and systems must be put into alignment with the new management practices that have developed. Otherwise, the incongruence between local changes and static top management will cause the recovery process to break down.[5]

It is the exceptional leader who embraces change from elsewhere in the organization and implements it in his or her own team. New skills, capabilities, styles, and value orientations may be required at the top to nurture the recovery process as well as to manage in the new order. A change in the top team is a dramatic move, but one that may be essential for recovery and reinforcement of new ways of doing things. A major force for the status quo is that the members of the top team typically are products of the very systems, structures, and values that the new order seeks to change.[6] And past loyalty and performance are difficult for senior executives to overlook when it comes to assessing the staffing of their top team. Yet there comes a time of reckoning when the leader must either embrace the new order in his or her actions or somehow rationalize ignoring it. Either action sends a clear, strong, and obvious message to the overall work force.

Managing Recovery in the Middle

Actions taken to create a context for recovery may be especially threatening to middle managers who see their traditional authority at risk. They, like others in the organization, must align their work with the new order and adapt to change. To a greater degree than most, however, middle managers are likely to experience a sense of loss as they see the responsibility for planning and implementing change shared across traditional boundaries, both lateral and hierarchical. These managers may have worked hard at advancing in the organization, may be frustrated by a sense of being stalled in their ascent to still higher levels, and may resist giving up the traditional trappings of their position. Opportunities to participate in its design aside, middle managers might perceive the new order as something resulting in their giving up more than they gain.

Increased employee decision making and team self-management were among the guidelines for a new order given to middle managers at Engelhard Corporation. To offset middle managers' resistance and answer their questions of "What's my role in empowerment," the company sponsored a six-month training program to teach managers in its Huntsville, Alabama, metal catalysts plant how to delegate authority, facilitate meetings, encourage consensus building, and handle unusable employee ideas without discouraging future suggestions. The point of the program was to underscore corporate commitment to the new order and help speed middle managers' adaptation to the new way of doing things. Recognizing that training was not a panacea and wanting to avoid sending the message that this was a "flavor of the month" management strategy, the company kept close attention to managers' behavior on the job. After giving them ample time to align with the new order, Engelhard fired several department managers who refused to change their management style.

Firings may be necessary to deal with middle managers—or, for that matter, senior managers—who do not adapt to new organizational realities. To avert this fate, however, middle managers can assess their readiness for change and prepare themselves for recovery in a few key ways.

Seize the Opportunity. Organizational recovery based on nonprogrammatic change implies that the responsibility for its success extends beyond senior executives. Managers in the middle must seize the opportunity being handed to them by top management to orchestrate change on a local level. They grasp the responsibility they are offered, have the courage to take risks and experiment, ask for information and resources when needed, constantly test and expand the edges of their influence, and have the common sense and loyalty to use their newfound power to contribute to the organizational good and not just advance their own selfish interests.

Trust in Oneself. Even though they themselves are among the key dissidents who thwart programmatic change efforts, middle managers feel insecure without a format to follow when given the responsibility for contributing to change. Certainly middle managers need the skills, information, and prototypes for participating in the recovery process that can be provided by senior executives, staff specialists, and external consultants. Yet these managers must also pull from their own knowledge, experiences, values, and creative processes to free themselves from both organizationally dictated and self-imposed barriers to self-expression. Middle managers who play their roles well in organizational recovery see themselves and their people as powerful and creative individuals who, through years of hierarchical and paternalistic management, fell out of the habit of displaying or experiencing their full ability or potential. This may be a stretch for a cadre of people whose self-confidence has been wounded during transition, but it is the only way in which they and their organization can truly recover.

Learn New Ways of Managing. One way to build self-confidence in one's ability to manage during recovery is to acquire new skills and insights, especially in the area of team management. Managers often are well versed in technical skills but in no more than the most rudimentary of managerial skills. and these latter proficiencies tend to be limited to how to manage individuals. Recent research shows that successful middle management during recovery comes down to learning a new kind of management: managing groups, removing barriers to group performance, and helping groups resolve conflict.[7] There are a variety of ways to pick up new management insights, including attending courses, reading literature, talking with managers from other groups or organizations, and learning from the mistakes and successes of others. Still, these insights should not be applied verbatim. What has worked well in one context may not necessarily transfer to another; they are merely models and ideas to prompt a manager's own thinking about what will work best in his or her work area.

Be Proactive. A middle manager who sees the need for recovery after a transition but who works in an organization in which senior executives deny or ignore the need will have to risk being proactive in building the context for positive change. There are a growing number of cases in which recovery is initiated by middle management without a sanction from the top. Although senior management may not have formally articulated a new order, savvy middle managers recognize changes in the external environment or company direction and align their work teams with this evolving organizational order. In some of these instances middle managers act in somewhat covert ways, keeping recovery activities low-key until improvements can be documented. In others, middle managers are overt, lining up resources and support before launching their local efforts. In both cases, middle managers take proactive action because they accept that old ways of approaching and organizing work in their areas would not meet new challenges. These are courageous middle managers willing to get the right things done through involved group effort.

Keep Perspective. Managers who do not just merely survive a transition but who truly triumph amid the turmoil develop a singular ability to keep things in perspective. They distinguish between what they can and cannot control and between what does and does not matter to them, and they focus their attention and actions appropriately. They have listened closely to the explicit and implicit messages from senior leadership and understand which activities are consistent with the new order and which are not. This perspective helps managers concentrate their own efforts and those of their work team. It also buffers them from too much self-criticism when confronted with a situation beyond their control, as well as from too much distraction from what really matters when faced with competing demands and overwhelming time pressures.

From Recovery to Revitalization

With a work force that has relinquished its grip on the past and is ready to grab onto the new, executive leadership and managerial action can combine to develop a context for recovery. When the direction, values, and other components of the new order are articulated, employees can participate in designing and implementing ways to align their individual and group activities in the new direction. Over time people learn about the new order, how they fit into it, how they can succeed in it, and what they can expect from it. Learning and changes that occur during the swing from the old ring to the new one, however, must be reinforced if they are going to remain and flourish as part of the new order. As the next chapters relate, characteristics of the desired new order can be refrozen in a manner that builds on recovery by revitalizing employee spirit, team performance, and organizational systems in the pursuit of business success.

Part 3

Revitalization

8

Revitalizing Individual Spirit

Organizational communications expert Roger D'Aprix believes that excellent companies are excellent for one of three reasons. One is simple luck—having the right product and being in the right place at the right time; examples from the past include Polaroid and IBM. Their inevitable problem is that time catches up with them, and they have few resilient resources and relevant experiences that enable them to compete against lean and hungry competitors. Another reason for successful performance is commitment to the customer: the sort of obsessive service ethic that permits some companies to "think out of the box" and do what it takes to keep the customer happy. They refuse to get sidetracked by policies and practices. L.L. Bean, H.L. Gore, Hewlett Packard, and Levi Strauss are examples of such firms.

But for D'Aprix, the best examples of excellence come from those companies that have a vision of where they are going and focus every resource and every worker in that direction. General Electric and UNUM, an insurance company based in Portland, Maine, are organizations that have come through adversity by being highly focused and highly strategic. These types of companies are instructive for thinking about revitalization after a transition because they offer insight into rebuilding individual motivation following difficult times.

Faith, Hope, and the Motivation to Act

From work with organizations that have rebounded from adversity, D'Aprix concludes that committed, productive employees share three qualities. First, they have *faith* in their leadership and in their organizations, as well as in themselves. That faith, in turn, makes them *hopeful* and generally optimistic about the future. From that base of faith and hope, they produce their best effort to succeed personally and to help the organization move toward its goals; that is, they have the *motivation to act*.

Executives can revitalize their organizations and people after a transition by restoring faith and creating more hope. How do they do that? The process of ending the old and accepting the new provides clues to the answer. Leaders must get employees to see that the old organizational order is inadequate or ineffective in dealing with current and future business realities while they inspire confidence in the new organizational order. This is an ongoing need during recovery and revitalization, even when formal interventions like venting meetings have been used to aid in the letting-go process. Forces for the status quo and for growth are constantly operating, and effective leadership of organizational recovery requires weakening the former and strengthening the later.

Restoring Faith and Creating Hope

Beginnings start with endings. To truly let go of the past, people have to believe that it no longer serves them or their organization well, that there are personal advantages in accepting change, and that a sound vision exists for where the organization is headed.

See That the Old Way No Longer Works. The organizational environment has changed so much that new ways must be invented to cope with new market forces. This is the problem that has never been successfully attacked in the U.S. auto business. To this day in Detroit you can find hundreds of auto workers and executives who deny that there is a quality problem, or ever has been, with American-made cars. Today's organizational leaders must share a clear sense of the market place and the forces that are acting so powerfully on their companies. To put this another way, they must make the case for change.

Articulate a Vision. The leader must articulate a vision of where the organization is headed, what will matter in getting there, and how people can play a role in making it happen. He or she must inspire and excite people with this vision. Many American companies have done this poorly, trivializing the power of an exciting vision. There have been so many inadequate or unfruitful "visioning" exercises in recent years that a backlash is forming against their use. A front-page *Wall Street Journal* article in 1993 dubbed vision as "overrated" and cited "no nonsense" Chrysler Corporation CEO Robert J. Eaton as an example of an executive who disdained the process of articulating where his organization is headed.[1] Yet the article went on to describe how Eaton had clarified his desire for the company to "stay healthy" along with his personal ambition to be "the first chairman never to lead a Chrysler comeback." This *is* Eaton's vision, for the firm and not just for himself. And he gave clear orders on how Chrysler would achieve this vision, by concentrating on "nuts-and-bolts" management.

It matters not that something is called a vision and introduced amid hoopla and through charismatic style, but that employees hear clearly where the organization is headed and what its methods will be in getting there. Eaton did this well, and so must other leaders seeking to restore employees' faith in their workplace.

Or, Accept That There Is No Better Alternative. An alternative way to get people to embrace the new organizational order is to have them accept the fact that there is no alternative, or that other alternatives are far less satisfactory. Here again the leader must communicate a sense that the chosen organizational order is conscious, well considered, and the most likely to succeed. David Kearns at Xerox persuaded a whole company to embrace total quality and customer service by convincing them that the alternative could be the demise of the company. Thus the case for the new organizational order can be both positive and negative. The point is that during adversity Kearns held up a vision of a customer-oriented company making quality products as good as the Japanese. Why did he succeed where Roger Smith failed at General Motors? The difference was that Kearns understood the need to unite people behind his vision and to communicate it in word and deed. Smith was a prisoner of the GM culture, by his own admission: "I sure wish I'd done a better job of communicating with GM people . . . then they would have known why I was tearing the whole place up. I never got this across."[2]

See an Opportunity for Reward. After years of organizational MADness, transitions have come to mean less security or less opportunity for employees at middle and lower levels, but employment contracts with potentially huge payouts for senior leaders who stay or golden parachutes (also with princely sums) for those who leave. This disparity creates a sense of distrust of executives who escape the ravages of change. A better course is to hold out some tangible advantage for the employee in embracing change.

People will accept the new organizational order if they see the promise of an eventual reward for accepting change. This reward can be in any variety or combination of forms—extrinsic rewards of pay and benefits, opportunity rewards of learning new skills or moving into new positions, status rewards such as perks and promotions, and other intrinsic rewards like increased self-esteem or feeling part of an achieving team. If people come to associate receiving desired rewards with accepting change, this will confirm their faith in the new organizational order as a source of advantage for both the organization and themselves.

Motivating People to Act

Once people have faith in the organization's direction and ability to realize it. then they begin to feel excitement and to share a conviction that change is necessary. They are optimistic about the new organizational order and latch onto it, hopeful about their own future and that of their organization. People are psychologically ready to produce their best effort to succeed personally and to help the organization move toward its goals. Employee confidence, shredded by transition mismanagement during the days of organizational MADness, can be restored with both objective improvement in results and with the belief that the individual is a valued member of a worthwhile organization. Employee motivation to act in ways that achieve desired organizational goals is enhanced through three basic needs on the job.[3]

The Need for Job Mastery. People need to feel fully comfortable that they can perform the job that they are asked to do. Especially following structural and staffing changes in a reorganization— and when they are asked to realign their work tasks with a new organizational order—people need to feel they have the right tools and information to complete their tasks. They also must perceive a direct relationship between how hard they work and how well they do.

The Need for Job Predictability. Even in an environment of increasingly rapid change and turmoil, employees need to know that there are predictable consequences for job actions and job behavior. Note that predictability can mean ongoing change, provided this expectation has been set as part of the new organizational order. More often, however, employees will look for consistent treatment of people across situations and consistent consequences of their own actions. This counters the shock and distrust produced by downsizings in which good performers lose their jobs, take demotions, or receive reduced pay raises. Importantly, predictability reestablishes employees' expectations that effort will indeed be rewarded.

The Need to Be Part of Something Special. People want to do more than earn a pay check at the workplace. They want to belong to something great, something worth their allegiance. And people want to produce excellent results, not just for their own benefit but for their special team or group. The cynicism and distrust bred by organizational MADness have distorted this earnestness with selfishness and resentment at the workplace. As long as organizations continue to mismanage transitions, they can expect reciprocal reactions from employees that reduce individual commitment and organizational achievement. Alternatively, if executives recognize and respond to people's needs to feel recognized and valued as part of a recovery, then employees are more likely to give the organization their very best. This is the beginning of productivity and commitment. It is also the highest form of collaboration between employee and employer.

Individual Revitalization

In a skeptical age affected by countless downsizings and the eroding psychological bond between employer and employee, it may be difficult to believe that faith, hope, and the motivation to be part of something special are the watchwords for business success. Yet they come through when employees themselves discuss what is needed to recover from the disappointment and discouragement that linger after a transition. To be sure, survivors of organizational transitions use language that is much more tangible than that of "faith" or "hope," but nonetheless they speak of the need to reestablish trust and confidence in their employer, of desires to recoup from the past and move ahead in realizing personal and organizational goals, and of renewing loyalty and reenergizing performance at the workplace.

Interviews conducted with employees in ten organizations following transitions reveal a broad range of actions needed to recover from unintended consequences and contribute to new organizational objectives.[4] These interviews were conducted after transition turbulence had subsided and the subjects had already vented their anger in earlier rounds of individual interviews; for the most part the interviewees had let go of their need to deal with the past and were ready to look ahead to the future. Exhibit 8.1 lists the most frequently cited responses from these interviews, classified according to what employees need from their jobs, their work teams, and their leadership. (While the exhibit implies that certain needs are greater earlier or later in the recovery process, in reality many of these needs pervade both the short and long term. For example, communication is an essential need both early in the recovery period and over the long haul. Similarly, there is a constant need to "walk the talk," but doing so requires that a vision of the new organizational order be clarified early on.)

What Employees Need to Recover from Transition

From their job

Understand benefits
- Align work with new organizational order
- Learn what it takes to succeed

Realize benefits
- Fair rewards
- New skills and experience
- Career development

From their work team

Realize quick wins
- Participate in experimentation and learning
- Meet short-term goals

Feel part of an achieving group
- See new and better ways emerging
- Meet long-term goals

From their leadership

Realize trust and confidence
- Communication
- Empathy

Reinforce trust and confidence
- Walk the talk
- Fair and consistent treatment

Short term

Long term

EXHIBIT 8.1

What People Need from Their Jobs

Simply stated, transition survivors want to know what is in it for them to reinvest their trust in the workplace and psychologically recommit to the organization and its goals. Talented contributors are not satisfied with the basic exchange of doing a job for a paycheck; they want to see some higher reward in return for their contributions to their employer. In many respects, it is like a bride who, left at the altar once, wants some assurance that life will be better after the marriage and that the groom intends to do his best to make the marriage work.

The years of organizational MADness have made employees not only more cynical and suspicious but wiser to the realities of the new psychological work contract. They concede that there is no lifetime job security, no steady career ladder, and no escape from the possibility of ongoing downsizing and rightsizing becoming part of "business as usual." As a result, some want a clear idea of what they have to do to succeed on the job. For the most cynical, success in the 1990s is defined as minimizing the likelihood of being blindsided by a subsequent transition. But for others, the best and brightest among them, giving their heart and soul (as well as their brain and brawn) to their employers requires that they be convinced that some personal advantage is likely to result from organizational recovery.

Interviews with employees following organizational transition indicate that they want to understand how life in the new organizational order will be better and, in particular, how they can approach their work in a way that will allow them to realize benefits. In the short run, employees need to discern how they can align their work with the new organizational order. A supervisor in the nursing department of a health care organization that grew rapidly through acquisition wondered what direction she was expected to take her unit: "How does administration want us to prioritize cost cutting, service quality, and retention of nurses in a competitive job market? I have ideas, but I need some sense of which way we are going, because I want to make sure what I am building is coordinated with and contributing to the goals of the organization." In a manufacturing concern decimated by continual waves of downsizing and restructuring, a machine operator looked forward to finding new and better ways of approaching work: "I get a sense that the worst is behind us now, but we have got to make some improvements in how we get the job done. There's been a lot of talk about quality improvement and increasing productivity; that's good, but now we have to take the time and do it instead of just talk about it."

Employees also want to know what it takes to achieve personal success from performing their jobs in line with expectations. As a middle-level manager in a consumer products firm reported, "Look, I've given up on the idea that pay raises and promotions will come automatically around here. Those days are gone. But what do I have to do to protect my job and maybe get a shot at what new openings are available?" Another manager from the same company wondered, "What is going to distinguish the successful from the mediocre managers around here? I don't mind giving my all and working hard, but I want to know I'm doing the right thing. Give me a clue as to what [my business unit head] wants from me." And from a firm in the computer industry, the head of a project team sought "a final determination that the culture here is something I am comfortable with. How will people who do their jobs well be treated? I want a sense of certainty that I am in the right place."

Then, over time, employees want to gain the benefits of doing their jobs in line with expectations. They cite three specific personal benefits in particular. First, employees want fairness to prevail as the fruits of organizational success are shared. Fairness here refers to a hybrid of two dimensions: a reasonable chance for growth in pay, and equitable distribution across groups and levels. "No more of these fat bonuses for the guys upstairs while we get paltry 3 percent pay raises," demanded one manager. "I understand there is a shift in our industry from base pay to greater at-risk pay," observed another. "I'll play by those rules, but I want a fair shot at getting the prize if I hit the target."

The second benefit people look for from their jobs during recovery is the opportunity to gain new skills and experiences. People who have made it past transition and into recovery accept that from this point forward staffing needs are rapidly changing in organizations and that the individual employee must increasingly be responsible for training and development. A middle manager in a computer manufacturer observed, "It's been a rough road [living through the transition], but I've learned a lot about myself and about working in organizations today. I want assignments that will broaden my skills and increase my chances to be of value here or, if necessary, at another employer." A colleague at the computer manufacturer noted. "With fewer people around after the cuts, I'm expecting to get a wider variety of assignments and experiences as time goes by." This relates to a third benefit transition survivors look for from their jobs: enhanced career development opportunities. Interestingly, most managers distinguish between career *development* and career *advancement*. They recognize that the mergers, delayerings, and other restructurings that have flattened organizations have blocked upward mobility. Instead, they look to lateral moves as recognition of their contribution to their employers and to participation on special committees or task forces as opportunities to learn new skills or get exposed to new information. A trading manager in a U.S. financial services institution acquired by a European-based bank commented on his hopes to "be transferred to newly emerging product areas or foreign locations. With the globalization of business today, this could be a real boon to my career." The manager of a mature business line at the consumer products company put it succinctly: "Our product has seen its day, and I have demonstrated that I can produce for this company. Let's see what they do—if they just let me waste away here or transfer me where the action is."

What People Need from Their Work Teams

The work team is the focal point for achieving quick wins in recovering after a transition and the concrete evidence people seek to prove that life afterward will not just be different but perhaps better. Interviews reveal that both the process of participating with coworkers in experimentation and the outcome of meeting short-term work group goals are important. When asked what it would take to make him feel optimistic about being part of the posttransition organization, a manufacturing supervisor in a computer company replied, "Truly coming up with better ways of getting the job done. We all know that the old ways of doing things are what got us in trouble. Me and my team are the ones who know this work best; put us to work on thinking about improvements and that will get us excited." "I don't expect to change overnight, but starting to work on production improvements as a team will help," echoed a coworker.

Interviewees also note the power of a quick win in the form of meeting short-term goals. After working for nearly two years in an environment of depressing and discouraging results, the sales manager of a software publishing company stressed the need for some optimistic results to renew his group's spirits: "Don't give us a target that we can't meet. That will only give people the impression that nothing has changed despite all the talk about things being different. It's been a long time since we've had something to celebrate; making our numbers for the first quarter [after the transition] is a surefire way to get our group revved up."

As time moves ahead, transition survivors need to feel that they are part of a team that achieves its goals. Interviewees indicate they will assess their teams' long-term performance in two primary ways. First, they will look for new and better ways of doing things emerging from their process of experimenting and learning. "It's all right to talk about improving how we do things around here," noted a manager from a financial services firm, "but sooner or later we are going to have to make some changes. That will be encouraging." Second, they will watch for results, as a manager from an entertainment conglomerate reported: "The bottom line is just that— the bottom line. If we can turn our performance around and produce consistent financial results, then that should help everybody feel good—our team, our unit management, and our senior leadership." Importantly, transition survivors place particular emphasis on the performance of their work area. "I cannot influence our overall corporate results," offered another manager from the entertainment firm, "but I can make a difference in [our department]. Being part of a team that makes its contribution to the bigger scheme is all I can ask for."

What People Need from Their Leadership

Beyond personal growth and reward and work team enhancements and results, employees in posttransition organizations report a need to see their leadership make an effort at rebuilding trust and confidence. By far, the comment heard most often in interviews is about the need for communication. True organizational revitalization, from the employee perspective, rests to a large degree on the forthrightness of leadership to share information regarding business plans and goals, performance results, competitive insights, technological developments, and news of what is happening in other parts of the organization; knowledge not typically shared under the organizational order experienced by most interviewees. An operations vice-president from a computer firm noted, "If I've always felt segregated from the process, imagine how frustrated people below me must feel. We need visibility and connection with the top of the organization, and we could stand to have some across groups here, too." In addition to demonstrating trust of and respect for employees on the part of leadership, employees report that the newly shared information helps them understand how best to align their work with emerging business realities and to orchestrate team activities.

To complement the hard facts, employees also need some "soft" caring from their leadership in the form of empathy for people who are adapting to new realities. The MIS director at a financial services firm noted, "If our senior executives demonstrate respect for us and our situation by giving some indication they know what we have been and are going through, they would earn a tremendous amount respect from employees in return." Employees also want their leaders to express a recognition that trust and confidence need to be rebuilt after a transition, rather than act in a way that seems to take these qualities for granted.

To fortify trust and confidence over time, employees need to see their leaders' words reinforced by actions. Employees will keep a keen eye on the extent to which senior people in the company walk the talk of the new organizational order. An operations manager from a financial services institution warned, "You can have all the vision statements and communications in the world, but they don't amount to a hill of beans if leadership says one thing and does another." If they understand and accept new business realities such as limited resources and increased competition, employees will expect sacrifice and hardship as well as success and rewards to be shared in the future.

Enduring trust and confidence will depend to a large extent on leaders who operate in a fair and consistent manner. Again, the operations manager advised, "During the past couple of years this place was run by the principle of 'management by exception'— leaders make exceptions for themselves and for their favorite people. What they need to do now is act in a way that says `we are in this together.' If they do as they say, and if they treat people fairly rather than play favorites, then they will earn back my respect." Many interviewees shared a general perspective that leaders need to convey a sense of partnership along with fairness in moving forward after a difficult transition. A finance executive in the entertainment conglomerate represented this view: "Our people want appreciation that there is a reward mechanism for what they are being asked to do. When we win, we should celebrate the victories. When we lose, we should stand back and assess—ask the difficult questions—so we can get back on track."

The Limits of Vision

A well articulated vision of where the organization is headed plays an important role in revitalizing employee spirit after a transition and, when coupled with guidelines for desired values and behaviors, can direct employee actions in line with the new organizational order desired by the leadership. Most efforts to communicate corporate vision and subsequently direct employee behavior, however, miss the mark. In the typical scenario, a CEO goes offsite with a few senior executives to hash out a vision statement. Upon returning home, an article appears in the company newsletter heralding the arrival of the vision, a nice video is made to explain the vision in detail, and plaques are ordered so that each employees can have a constant reminder of the vision hovering above their desk or work area. Then the CEO and top team get back to the "real work" of running their business.

Employees want to learn more about the vision, how it will be attained, and precisely how they can contribute to achieving it. To convey an adequate degree of precision, middle managers and direct supervisors must reiterate the CEO's statement of vision. Employees prefer face-to-face communication about business information to other styles, and while senior executives must set the tone in communicating business information, employees want to hear directly from their immediate superiors.[5] Middle managers, however, are them-selves unclear of the vision and, following a transition, do not make a priority of learning more about it and communicating it to their peo-ple. Supervisors, the representatives of management most employees see on a day-to-day basis, are even further in the dark about the vi-sion. While newsletters, videos, and plaques are important supple-ments to face-to-face communication, they are not substitutes for the personal touch that employees seek and that is required to revitalize them. Moreover, without ownership over the vision, managers and supervisors are either cynical about the promise of a vaguely worded statement or threatened by the changes it suggests (or both), and they resist it rather than support it.

Eventually the CEO gets some kind of feedback—findings from an employee attitude survey, persistent nudging from the human resources director, or disappointing financial results—that indicates how people in the company are not clear where it is headed and have further lost faith in their leadership's ability to move the orga-nization forward. This only serves to frustrate the CEO. "Haven't I already told the people the vision?" asks the baffled leader. Yes, perhaps, but the CEO's message and intentions have not been real-ized on the job.

Articulating Vision

Vision statements need not be elegant. In fact, the simpler they are, the easier they are to communicate and the more accessible they tend to be for translation into on-the-job behaviors. This relates to another characteristic of effectively clarified visions: they specify lucid goals for improvement. At the professional services firm de-scribed in Chapter 7, for example, the specific wording that the firm "will reclaim a top 10 position in [its] industry" through "profitable growth" clarified that leadership was all for growth after years of flat performance, but not at the risk of affecting prof-itability. These phrases directly addressed questions about the com-pany's direction that had been on the minds of employees.

Frequently vision statements include the core values that should accompany efforts to attain the vision. Values represent what the organization believes in and how people should work with and treat one another. They are the attitudes that subtly sanction or prohibit behaviors on the job. Majestic CEO Justin Jordan's articulation of core values—quality and integrity in all endeavors, fairness in treating people, and leading the pack in innovation—was invaluable in helping people understand what he meant by his vision of premier-company status.

The process by which the vision statement is developed is as important to revitalizing people after a transition as the content of what it says. The extent to which an organization's vision and values are shared among top executives is an early test of how the vision will be received through the ranks and of how facilitative it will be in aligning people and their work around the new organizational order. If understanding of and support for the vision cannot be generated at the top, these outcomes will not be realized through the ranks. Take the case of a retail sales conglomerate that experienced multiple waves of restructuring as part of an effort to centralize decision making and rein in autonomy from business units. Before any effort was made to broadcast a vision to the overall work force, the chief executive used the process of articulating the vision statement as a method for facilitating team building at the top and for pronouncing his seriousness about his direct subordinates reinforcing the vision in their business units. A consultant conducted one-on-one interviews with the CEO and business unit presidents to identify issues, concerns, and priorities related to business direction and vision. At an offsite meeting with the executives, the consultant reported the interview findings and facilitated a discussion to align their perspectives about the desired end state for the firm. Key concerns of autonomy versus centralization were addressed head-on and examined through rounds of give-and-take discussion. As the CEO put it, "we now have a vision that is not just a bunch of words, but something that we all really believe in and will dedicate ourselves and our employees to achieving." Anything short of a consensus among the top team would have foiled implementation of the vision in the business units.

Living the Vision

Statements of vision and guidelines for action in and of themselves will do little to restore faith, create hope, or generate the motivation to act in a work force recovering from a transition. To facilitate revitalization, the vision must jump off the paper on which it is printed. It must become animated and integrated into people's actions on the job, not merely be spoken about or pointed to. This is called *living the vision*.

Exhibit 8.2 represents a model for living the vision through activity up and down the organization. It is built from the vision of senior leadership at the top of the organization but requires the support of each level from the bottom up. This activity at all levels engages people in living the vision. The top of the organization articulates a clear direction for the organization; managers and supervisors in the middle link business unit mission statements with the corporate vision and develop guidelines for employee behavior. Then, in work groups, employees translate the vision, mission, and operating guidelines into day-to-day operating procedures. This clarifies how employees can align their work with the new organizational order and provides an answer to the prominent question of how they can contribute to overall organizational success. Finally, working back up the pyramid, supervisors and managers review proposed new ways of approaching work to ensure they support the mission and vision and to provide coordination across work areas.

Living the vision aligns employee behavior after a transition not by mandate or directive, but by contributing to a context for recovery that encourages change at the local level. Living the vision enables employees to transcend their day-to-day work activities and see their contribution to the new organizational order. The process is what is most important—being on the way to the vision matters more than arriving. There are no targets or final objectives, as these would put limits on the organization's ability to learn and enhance itself.

Living the vision succeeds at rebuilding employee spirit following transition for a number of reasons:

- *High credibility*. Living the vision directly addresses employees' questions ("Where is this organization headed?" "How do I align my work accordingly?").
- *High validity*. Changes in work procedures are based on employees' own recommendations for aligning work with the vision, not some consultant's suggestion or some program's prescription for how to approach work.
- *High involvement*. Care is taken each step of the way to ensure

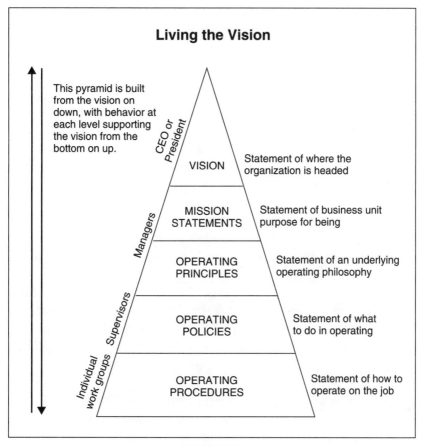

Living the Vision

This pyramid is built from the vision on down, with behavior at each level supporting the vision from the bottom on up.

CEO or President

VISION — Statement of where the organization is headed

Managers

MISSION STATEMENTS — Statement of business unit purpose for being

OPERATING PRINCIPLES — Statement of an underlying operating philosophy

Supervisors

OPERATING POLICIES — Statement of what to do in operating

Individual work groups

OPERATING PROCEDURES — Statement of how to operate on the job

EXHIBIT 8.2

genuine support for suggested revisions before the process is pushed to the next level.

- *High relevance.* The vision is linked with people's daily work situation.

These qualities contrast with common approaches to abiding by vision statements: visions can wither if people feel they must read tablets of stone passed down from above. Allowing people some say in developing initial vision statements, subsequent mission statements, and operating guidelines and procedures can help rev up energy and enthusiasm in the posttransition organization. This involvement provides the emotional glue that holds together the various parts of the organization and complements the strategic and financial plans in rebuilding after a transition.

Translating Vision into Mission

Once a vision is articulated at the very top of the organization, but before it is publicly announced, it should be tested with the next level of management. Again, if people at this level cannot understand and support the vision, rolling out the vision throughout the company will only spell failure. At the retailer, a "management forum" was conducted in which the corporate CEO presented the vision to the top teams from each business unit. In small groups, the executives generated questions about the vision and its implementation. Some discussion of semantics and other relatively minor matters ensued, but the group soon endorsed the vision as something they could and would support in their units.

Next, each team met and adapted the vision into mission statements for their business units. A mission statement is the business unit's direction and purpose for being, including what distinguishes it from the competition. One specialty retailer in the conglomerate's portfolio came up with a mission of "contributing to [the conglomerate company's] overall financial success by being recognized as the premier source of moderately priced ladies' sportswear." The teams also prepared work plans to create a context for recovery in their business units, to pave the way for moving the vision and mission statements through their organizations and soliciting employee feedback and involvement.

Only after plans were set for bringing it to life in the business units was the vision communicated throughout the retail conglomerate. This countered the tendency for vision statements to be rolled out amid fanfare, only to fade away as people's behaviors remain consistent with the old way of doing things. The vision communications strategy addressed how to involve people in translating the vision into on-the-job behaviors as much as it did the promotion of the vision statement itself. Additionally, communications were geared not merely to tell people but to sell them on the vision and the plan for living it, why the vision was important to the organization and its people, what the plan was for achieving it, and how people would be involved in living it.

Translating Vision and Mission into Operating Principles

The next step in living the vision is to translate the statements of corporate vision and business unit mission into operating principles to guide individuals' work on the job. Middle managers in each business unit meet to determine two important aspects of this process. First, they ensure that the business unit's mission statement clarifies principles for how work is to be approached. Operating principles, statements of an underlying operating philosophy, are derived from the vision and mission statements. These are general guidelines on how to approach work and align it with the company's direction, not unyielding instructions. In one of the business units in the large retail conglomerate, managers developed an operating principle that "we will be recognized by our customers for being responsive to their needs." Second, the managers determine how to continue the process into the next levels of the organization. They develop work plans within their areas to solicit employee input in clarifying operating policies and procedures that reinforce the unit's mission statement and the corporation's vision. After reviewing these plans with their bosses, any necessary revisions are made.

In the retailer, part of the implementation plan was to develop an internal resource group to help middle managers, supervisors, and employees align their work with the vision. In each business unit, a small group of line managers—chosen for their mix of generalist business skills, process orientation, and excellent communication skills—were taken off line and given one-year temporary assignments as resource specialists. After going through their own training, these resources provided information and tools to assist managers in areas such as gathering work-related data and writing clear operating principles.

Being a large organization, the retail conglomerate replicated the involvement of middle managers (in linking operating principles with vision and mission) at the next lower level of managers. Their charge was to translate operating principles into operating policies. Again, their work was submitted for review at the level above before being passed down. In the retailing unit, an operating policy of "regularly survey customers to assess their satisfaction with current products and service, and to determine their changing needs for the future" was aligned with the operating principle of being recognized by customers as being responsive to their needs. In smaller or flatter organizations, it may not be necessary to separate the tasks of developing operating principles and policies; rather, they can be combined in the work of middle managers.

Translating Operating Principles and Policies into Operating Procedures

Next comes the work of taking operating principles and policies and translating them into operating procedures—statements of how to operate on the job. Employee groups, usually integrated work teams, meet to discuss the corporate vision, business unit mission, and operating principles and policies to ensure their understanding. A manager from the business unit attends an initial meeting to explain the rationale underlying operating principles and policies and to solicit feedback regarding their relevance and applicability to work activities. Then, on an ongoing basis, employee teams meet to identify new operating procedures to align work behaviors with the operating principles and, ultimately, the mission and vision. Recommendations, which may include new ways of approaching work or ideas for eliminating unnecessary work, are prepared for presentation to and review by supervisors and managers. Periodic upward communication meetings are held to review employee recommendations and ensure that proposed new work activities support the mission and vision and are economically and technically feasible.

In the retail unit, employee groups recommended many ways in which the operating principle of "we will be recognized by our customers for being responsive to their needs" and operating policy of "regularly survey customers to assess their satisfaction with current products and service, and to determine their changing needs for the future" could be brought to life. These ranged from cashiers taking the time to solicit feedback from customers after transactions to the development of a customer satisfaction questionnaire.

Operating procedures are not rigid rules to be followed in an uncompromising manner. Rather, they are suggested guidelines for behavior on the job. In the retail stores, for example, if cashiers saw that customers were in a hurry, they would not bother them with questions about service standards. And while there is great license for creativity in developing operating procedures, employee groups need clear statements of vision, mission, and operating principles to the define the boundaries within which that license operates. This direction also contributes to the information work teams need to design work procedures that are likely to receive approval from the organization's regular decision-making authority.

Work groups need support in aligning work activities with the vision of where the organization is headed. Training programs are effective in enhancing data collection, work analysis, and problem-solving skills among group members, as well as alerting them to common inhibitors to group decision-making. Work groups need information—specifics about business plans and goals, performance results, technical capabilities, and competitive insights—if they are to develop recommendations that win approval from their superiors. Sometimes work groups gather this information up front in the operating procedure development process; other times it comes as a result of discussion and analysis in meetings with superiors to review recommendations. At the retailer, resource specialists offered their assistance to any work team needing an extra set of hands to procure information, collect data, interview technical experts, or simply serve as a sounding board to test propositions. The regular process of reviewing recommendations with superiors facilitates enhanced information exchange.

When all employees understand that their contributions on the job are aligned with the greater vision and mission of their workplace, they begin to move beyond a recovery mentality and start developing a self-reinforcing capacity for creativity and enhancement on the job. This is living the vision at its fullest. Like a human being who pursues continual improvement, the organization living a vision does not content itself with hitting a target or reaching a threshold of improvement, rather it sets forth on a journey toward ever-increasing improvements in competitiveness and work life quality.

In many organizations today, fine statements of vision and values have been conceived but never brought to life—that is, appropriate words were chosen to indicate a desired future state for the organization, but they never influenced on-the-job behaviors in any significant way. In this circumstance it is possible to build upon the investment that went into the formulation of the vision statement. With the twin objectives of engaging more people in the development of the vision and attempting to understand what interfered with bringing the vision to life, focus group interviews can be conducted with employees to assess their feelings about the vision. Questions asked in these sessions typically center on the direction of the organization and how ready people are to contribute to its achievement:

- Is a new vision for the organization emerging?
- To what extent do you understand and support this vision?
- How you can contribute to this vision through your own work?
- How well equipped are you to contribute to the vision?
- How is success defined in the new organization?
- What is interfering with your ability to succeed on your job?

Findings from the interviews are fed back to senior management to determine if the current vision statement suffices as the starting point for guiding employee behavior in line with the new organizational order, or if the statement must be revised.

Living the Vision at DisCo

In the highly competitive electronic products distribution business, slim margins are a fact of life. Profitability rests on even the slightest savings that can be garnered through efficiency, volume, and technology utilization. The "big four" players in the industry each commanded about 20 percent of market share until, in a surprise move, the second- and third-largest ranked companies agreed to merge. The combined entity became the new industry leader and now had the clout to negotiate better prices with wholesalers and offer more comprehensive service to customers, large retail stores and value-added resellers of high-end products.

Joseph Bamber, CEO of WestCo Products, number one in size prior to the merger, knew he had to take dramatic action to regain the leadership position in the industry (the company and executive names in this section have been fictionalized). He approached his counterpart at EastCo, the remaining "big four" firm, with discussions of an acquisition. EastCo's CEO, who founded the company by distributing equipment stocked in the trunk of his car, was not fond of the notion of giving up his "baby." Yet he knew the merger of two strong competitors swayed the balance of price-setting power in the industry strongly in their favor. Rather than stay at the helm of an also-ran, he convinced his stockholders to accept an acquisition offer from WestCo. When the deal closed, Bamber again was at the top of the firm with the largest market share in the industry.

Bamber was genuinely excited about the acquisition. He envisioned a "meritocracy" in which the best people and policies would be selected to build the best new company without regard for from which side they came. He also looked forward to using the merger as an opportunity to alter some behaviors in the company that had persevered despite his efforts at changing them. Most important to Bamber was improving standards of customer service in the company, for years the brunt of industry criticism. To symbolize the themes of meritocracy and change, Bamber selected a new name for the combined distribution company, DisCo. Bamber commissioned several transition task forces to study integration options and set off to communicate his vision of a customer-driven organization to the work force.

Despite the merger's friendly beginnings and Bamber's good intentions, the integration planning process got bogged down by key executives' personal posturing and by the culture clash prevalent in all combinations. Although they were of about the same size, the merger brought together two firms with strikingly different cultures. The lead company operated in an entrepreneurial mode with decision-making authority pushed down the hierarchy as far as was reasonable, and it offered employees opportunities for fast career growth and professional development in exchange for low base salaries and miserly benefits. The target company's CEO had centralized leadership and held tightly onto decision-making authority but treated the work force benevolently through a strongly paternalistic culture and generous base pay and benefits. And while CEO Bamber was looking ahead to a bright new future, others below him were still clinging to the behaviors that had prevailed in their old organizational orders. Rather than advance a new and better company, merger planning sessions became a battleground for determining which side's ways would win out. Executives on the losing end of decisions suffered bruised egos, and middle managers became cynical about the highly political basis upon which the decisions were being made. Meanwhile, the overall work force steadily grew angry at what seemed like one decision after another resulting in "takeaways" of pay and benefits. Two waves of postmerger downsizing, essential for meeting the cost-cutting goals upon which the merger was predicated, further eroded morale.

Bamber was concerned about the unintended effects of the merger and continued to be frustrated in his efforts to realize higher standards of customer service in the company. Three months after final transition plans were implemented and the merger dust began to settle, Bamber called in a consultant to assess the situation and help him determine a course of action. In diagnostic interviews, managers expressed their anger at how the merger was handled and their pessimism about the company's failure to realize the competitive advantages touted in early merger communications. Managers also reported lingering we/they distinctions between the two sides and several hindrances to effective team performance, including role ambiguity, the absence of shared goals, and a lack of cooperation across work areas. To avail a larger number of managers to the benefits of the venting and to strengthen team leadership, a "Building Postmerger Teams" workshop was presented to all managers. The workshops were effective in helping several managers let off steam and let go of their need to beat up on the merger process but, as expected, only realized moderate success in getting managers to focus on postmerger team-building tasks. About one-third of the attendees worked diligently at team-building back in their work groups, another third gave it a lukewarm effort, and the remaining third did not bother at all.

Concurrent with the planning and implementation of the workshop, the consultant conducted one-on-one interviews with Bamber and each member of his top team to determine their views about where they should be steering the company. Bamber convened a meeting of the senior executive team. Using the information from the interviews as a base, the executives developed a consensus on a shared vision of where DisCo was headed: "Being the industry leader in customer service, technological advancement, employee respect, and profitability." The vision statement integrated the CEO's two pet interests—industry leadership and customer service—with other executives' attention to the critical need for a massive technological overhaul in the company's systems and en-hanced financial performance. In addition, the statement acknowl-edged the human pain of the merger and signaled to employees the importance placed on restoring morale and supporting innovation on the job.

The executives also discussed how to make the vision statement worth more than the paper on which it was printed. The executives warmed to the idea of having employees generate ideas for aligning their work with the vision rather than mandating change from above. Drawing from their own disappointing experiences with companywide organizational change efforts at DisCo and else-where, they readily understood the need to avoid topdown pro-grammatic change and instead create a context to support local change efforts. Much debate followed, however, about the priority of living the vision relative to pressing business demands. Following the merger and downsizing, managers and employees were tired from long, hard hours of transition planning meetings and stretched by trying to get more work done with fewer people. Moreover, DisCo ran a lean operation, and no human resources or other staff specialists were available to serve as internal resources. Bamber made clear his expectations for function heads to guide the process through their areas and offered to provide support in the form of external consultation and the temporary reassignment of two communication specialists from the marketing area who could be trained to assist function heads. In the end, the group agreed to a general plan and timetable for living the vision in each of their business areas.

The rollout of the vision statement came in a special issue of the company newsletter and was reiterated in a specially made video, large group meetings convened by Bamber, and a series of small group meetings conducted by the top team members in their work areas. Each time the vision was presented, a case was made for the urgency and importance of attaining it. "If we are to survive in an increasingly competitive industry," proclaimed Bamber in the video, "we have no choice but to dedicate ourselves to being the best at providing customer service that goes beyond the expecta-tions of the retailers and resellers who receive their product from us, becoming innovators in taking current technological capabilities beyond standard applications, providing a work environment and relationship with our employees that goes beyond merely having a job, and generating a return on investment to shareholders that goes beyond what they have received in the past." And every communication rang out the caveat that the vision statement was nothing more than the starting point for preparing a blueprint to guide employee efforts on their jobs: the vision would be realized only in concert with employee efforts.

First, though, each member of the top team—the leaders of the operations, marketing, sales, finance and administration, and international functions—convened his or her own group of direct subordinates to develop a mission statement for each business area consistent with the vision statement. The operations group, for example, declared its mission to be to "contribute to the attainment of organizational goals through the efficient and innovative organization and execution of product ordering, storing, and distribution." A vapid statement to be sure, yet it reflected the no-nonsense style of the vice president of operations and, according to the results of some focus group testing with employees, succeeded at capturing the operations area's reason for being.

Guidelines to help employees align their work with the vision and mission statements came next. In the operations area, each department head was charged with developing operating principles to clarify the philosophy underlying that department's approach to getting the job done. The head of warehouse operations chose to work independently on this task and came up with several principles to link work activity in the distribution centers with the company vision and operations area mission. One operating principle in particular caught the fancy of his managers and employees: "Be the easiest company to do business with in our industry." It was simple, relevant, and clearly associated with the vision of enhanced customer service. After reviewing the operating principle with the vice president, the head of warehouse operations directed his cadre of warehouse supervisors to work as a group to determine operating policies that would go further in establishing guidelines for their work activities. The supervisors were wary of overwhelming employees with what might be perceived as conflicting policies and chose to present just one operating policy to the head of warehouse operations. Although singular, it was keenly important to enhancing customer service, highly practical as a guide for aligning work, and truly challenging to employees: "Any order placed by 5:00 P.M. will be shipped out the same day."

The warehouse head approved the policy and instructed supervisors to make time and other resources available to employees to develop operating procedures to align their work with it. Each employee was invited to a one-day training program where they reviewed the living-the-vision process, learned creative problem-solving techniques, and importantly, gained insight into common pitfalls to small group decision-making. The program leaders (an outside consultant and one of the internal communication specialists), carefully took employees through the process to be followed for approving suggested revisions in operating procedures. Once a month, a panel of supervisors would be convened to hear operating procedures proposed by work teams, individuals, or ad hoc groups representing multiple work teams. After some discussion, the panel would either accept the proposal and move it through regular management channels with decision-making authority or return it to the proposing individual or group for refinement. In the event that managers rejected a proposed operating procedure accepted by the panel of supervisors, clear reasons for the decision would be communicated to the employee sponsors. Operating procedures accepted by management would be assigned to appropriate personnel for implementation, with an understanding that the assignment would be pushed as low as possible in the hierarchy.

Employees began meeting weekly in their work groups to consider how to operate in a way that would provide for orders placed by 5:00 P.M. to be shipped out that day. Some groups took advantage of coaching and facilitation services provided by the in-house communication specialists, while others worked on their own. Those utilizing the resources requested assistance ranging from meeting facilitation to data gathering. Frequently work groups needed additional business information, such as projections for new business development, to make educated decisions. Managers and supervisors responded by sharing information historically withheld from employees at DisCo.

Before too long, proposals for new operating procedures came forth. These ranged from minor revisions in work shift scheduling to major overhauls in the stockkeeping unit numbering scheme used. Suggestions also cut across traditional boundaries in the company. One work team from the warehouse proposed that telephone order takers volunteer to customers the standard of same-day shipping for orders placed by 5:00 P.M. and also inquire if the products indeed were needed in that time frame; orders for customers who did not need them sent out that day would be given a lower priority. An ad hoc team of warehouse and telemarketing employees refined the proposal, which was presented to a joint panel of supervisors from the two departments.

As living the vision took hold and success stories of successful implementation of enhanced operating procedures circulated throughout the company, all levels of DisCo people became comfortable with the process. Over time, managers and supervisors in the warehouse area generated additional operating principles and policies to guide employee groups in their efforts to suggest new ways of operating on the job. Some work teams continued meeting weekly to develop proposals aligning their work with these guidelines; others reduced their frequency to semiweekly or even monthly.

Did the living-the-vision effort at DisCo succeed at revitalizing employee spirit in the company? While no objective and systematical efforts to measure of levels of employee faith in their leadership, hope for the future, or motivation to act were undertaken, some anecdotal signs of renewed employee spirit emerged. First, several employees met on their own time to advance the work of preparing and refining proposals for new operating procedures. Second, many employees integrated attention to looking for new ways of operating into their day-to-day activity on the job rather than relegate that responsibility to the confines of formal work group meetings. Third, DisCo people subjectively reported positive changes in their workplace. Noted one warehouse employee, "We all seem to be marching in the same direction." Added a supervisor, "I can't really put it in words, but everybody is more in sync or something. It's like we are on the same team for the first time in quite a while." Finally, praise for DisCo and its people from outside the company confirmed internal impressions. The most cherished acknowledgment came when a prominent industry newsletter awarded DisCo its "customer service provider of the year" honor the year following the introduction of the living-the-vision process. This external validation of internal feelings reinforced employee pride for their part in changing the organization and nurtured optimism for the company's future. People saw DisCo truly on its way to realizing its vision of "being the industry leader in customer service, technological advancement, employee respect, and profitability."

Variations on Living the Vision

Living the vision is not the only way to revitalize individual spirit after a transition. What is important is not the method's name or intricacies, but that it succeeds at meeting employees' needs for understanding how their contributions on the job are aligned with the greater vision and mission of their workplace. Two successful efforts offer particularly interesting variations of the core living-the-vision approach. The first, at Los Angeles-based First Interstate Bank, shows the power of modeling new behaviors at the top of the organization. The other, in PepsiCo's soft drink division, exemplifies the clarity of vision and guidelines in aligning work activities with the new organizational order.

Facilitating Cross-Unit Activity at First Interstate

When Ed Carson took over in 1990 as chairman and chief executive officer of First Interstate Bank, the twelfth largest commercial bank in the United States, he inherited a work force shellshocked from the battles for corporate control fought in the preceding decade. For most of the 1980s Joseph Pinola, Carson's predecessor, had rallied executives and employees around a vision of a broad-based financial services institution competing with the likes of Citicorp and Merrill Lynch, with an interstate retail branch network as its crown jewel. In addition to conquering banks throughout the western United States, Pinola led forays into international banking and trading. By 1986 Pinola and his executive team were the darlings of Wall Street and the business press. They glowed amid speculation that First Interstate was poised to make a takeover bid on its gargantuan competitor Bank of America. Soon, however, the upward climb turned into a free-fall. A crisis in loans to developing countries in 1986 wrecked First Interstate's balance sheet; within less than a year, real estate problems in Texas and Arizona added to the bank's financial problems. As California headed into the depths of recession shortly thereafter, betting money put First Interstate, once the aggressive acquirer, at the mercy of now-high-flying rival Wells Fargo.

First Interstate employees were dazed by the series of events. "We were riding high, on top of the world, and we could do no wrong," recalled a senior vice president, "The press had nothing but good things to say to us, and we thought we were invincible. It was exciting being led by Joe Pinola; he was going to take us to the top by buying Bank of America. Then the bottom fell out. And it wasn't just a sense of concern—we were scared to death and running for our lives. Being acquired by Wells Fargo was everyone's worst-case scenario: we saw how they butchered people from [acquisition target] Crocker Bank, and we wanted nothing to do with them." A series of restructurings and other defensive moves aimed at protecting independence were small consolation, however, as employees became obsessed with worrying about their future.

Carson knew he had problems both in financial performance and, in his words, "employee relations." He figured that shoring up the business would help on both accounts. He liquidated nonbanking subsidiaries, took steps to fend off any unwanted suitor, and returned First Interstate to acceptable levels of capitalization, expenses, and nonperforming/performing assets ratio: "The street started telling us we were doing okay. We had hit bottom and were turning up, but it took some time for those feelings to be reflected internally." Carson crafted a vision for where he wanted to take the company, a sharp contrast to Pinola's jump-at-any-opportunity aggressiveness in making acquisitions, and used that vision as the basis for articulating a new organizational order (see Exhibit 8.3). To begin with, First Interstate would stick to its knitting and be one retail bank rather than a bank holding company. This meant increased coordination throughout the corporation, a sharp contrast to the highly autonomous fiefdoms granted to regional heads under the old organizational order. Where it made sense, services previously run separately across the regions would be combined into corporate centers; the eleven data processing centers across the regions, for example, eventually were consolidated into one operation.

Yet Carson did not cherish centralization as a characteristic of his new organizational order. Rather, he wanted authority and accountability to reside in the regions, close to the customer. Comfortable with his vision, and himself empowered by positive finan-

The Old and New Organizational Orders at First Interstate Bank

Old Organizational Order	New Organizational Order
Lack of vision	A clear vision
Global bank holding company	Local retail bank
Regional autonomy	Corporate coordination
Empower staff	Empower line
Fix it	Grow it

EXHIBIT 8.3

cial results and external praise, Carson took on the job of spreading the good news internally to employees. He decreed the "fix it" mentality that dominated during his first years at the helm to be replaced by one of "grow it." Recalled Carson, "I knew we were good and I wanted our people to feel that way. I talked positively: we had moved beyond rebuilding the machine, and now were at a point of revving it up."

Of course, forces for maintaining the status quo were strong at First Interstate. Regional executives tested the threat to their accustomed autonomy. Carson's vision of empowering line managers was a direct threat also to the historical power of First Interstate's staff groups at headquarters. As dramatically as the number of staff personnel dropped (from 500 to 200 employees), so did their morale. Carson was revved up for the future, but his troops were stalling out.

To "bring people into the strategy," Carson established councils to translate his vision and guidelines into key areas of bank management: cash management, corporate banking, corporate compliance, credit, human resources management, information and operating services, retail banking, and trust and private banking. Initially the councils were the focal points for generating recommendations for the elimination of more than a quarter of First Interstate's 35,000 employees. Then the councils took on the job of making recommendations for ongoing standards, including becoming a preferred employer. "It's tough to talk about being a 'preferred employer' when you are slashing 8,000 jobs. So we had to space out the responsibility of the councils," recalled Carson.

Carson challenged the councils to develop implementation standards that were best for the bank and, at the same time, were acceptable to each regional operating unit. The regions pressured the councils to keep centralization by Carson in check. A wide range of managers were invited to give input to the councils, including known critics of emerging proposals. Consensus was required before a council could bring a recommendation to Carson and his team of regional CEOs. To counteract forces for autonomy within business regions, membership on the councils cut across business units. A regional CEO chaired each council, with other members drawn from the executive ranks of each of the regions and corporate headquarters.

The strength of individual pride in the decision process drove Carson's concept of councils. Rather than mandate programmatic change, Carson created a context for recovery by establishing—and nurturing with resources—a forum for translating his vision and guidelines into operating principles and procedures. "We didn't look for fads," summarized Carson. "If we implemented a program, it was grown from within." To push the process further into the organization, a bank mission statement was developed by the regional CEOs, who then took on the responsibility of engaging employees in their units to bring the statement to life on their jobs (see Exhibit 8.4). In communicating the mission statement to employees, Carson announced:

> We are going to focus our energy in the areas where we have the potential to differentiate ourselves from other banks. These are the strengths that will make us winners in an ever-changing environment. And although each region will continue to pursue activities to meet the needs of its markets, the corporate mission will help them direct their efforts. It gives us both flexibility and unity. By implementing the mission successfully, our regions will enable the corporation to reach its goals.

First Interstate is building a new organizational order by translating the mission statement into on-the-job behaviors that cross traditional boundaries. These actions, which would have been unheard

---

First Interstate Bank
Mission Statement

At First Interstate Bank, our mission is to provide superior value and exceptional service to our customers.

To accomplish this:
We believe in being a preferred employer.
We believe in the importance of maintaining superior asset quality.
We believe in actively supporting the communities we serve.
We believe in maintaining the highest levels of professional integrity and personal ethics.
We believe in rewarding our shareholders with returns that consistently meet their expectations.

As a result, we will be recognized as a leader in the financial services industry.

EXHIBIT 8.4

of in the old organizational order, range in scale from broad human resources initiatives to establish consistency across regions in compensation and other policies to individual behaviors such as a corporate support specialist who made her graphic design skills available to revamp one region's out-of-date forms, even though she was not a regional employee. In what the *New York Times* labeled "one of the most remarkable transformations in banking," Carson has delivered on a promise to shareholders to cut First Interstate's bad loans to 1 percent of assets in 1993 (from 5 percent when he took over in 1990), and earnings have consistently improved during his tenure. He also has led a transformation of the bank's human assets, revitalizing a moribund work force that not only had been through the MADness of the 1980s and early 1990s but also was reeling from the effects of California's debilitated economy and being in a quickly consolidating industry offering fewer and fewer employment alternatives. He did this by clarifying the direction of where he wanted to take the bank, embracing change at the top of the organization, and inviting people to participate in the process. Along the way, he resuscitated the life and spirit of employees throughout First Interstate's ranks, a work force that went from feeling like shellshocked losers to energetic winners with a can-do attitude ready for the next challenge.

Giving Guidelines for Behavior at PepsiCo

As soft drink sales turned flat in the early 1990s, senior executives at PepsiCo's soft drink division set out to make over the unit into a "complete beverage company." They added new products, like designer drinking water, and used the transformation as an opportunity to reinvent the corporate culture. An inverted organization chart, tagged the "right-side-up organization," symbolized the vision of the new organizational order: the customer on top, followed by employees, and then management at the bottom. Several guidelines defining the behaviors that would achieve this vision accompanied the chart. One, "customer focus," counseled that activities that did not add value to the customer should be eliminated; another, "empowered organization," directed that it was all right to take risks. Further clarifying their intentions for the new organizational order, Pepsi leaders publicized shared values of diversity, integrity, teamwork, and balance between work and life outside of work.

To help create a mind-set for change in the organization, Pepsi brought together the full management team from the business unit to attend "Right Side Up" training programs about implementation of the vision. That left employees home alone to run the business, a dramatic way to walk the talk of empowerment. At the training, managers learned of expectations for their role in leading work teams through a process of reengineering work processes. One exercise asked managers to apply the guidelines to their own work activities by preparing two lists: "behaviors I am going to *stop* doing," and "behaviors I am going to *start* doing." As a first step in bringing the guidelines alive back home, managers shared their lists with subordinates, peers, and supervisors.

Reviving the Motivation to Act

DisCo, First Interstate Bank, and Pepsi are just some of the many organizations making efforts to revitalize their work force. These examples show the great potential inherent in rebuilding the human spirit of the organization, getting people to produce their best effort to succeed personally and to help the organization move toward its goals. When accomplished in a genuine manner that lets people from all ranks in the organization know where things are headed, what is expected of them in getting there, and what they can expect to be in it for them, faith is restored, hopefulness about the future becomes bountiful, and people feel empowered by their internal motivation to act. For revitalized employee spirit to make a difference in an organization's business results, however, it must be supported by teamwork and organizational systems that reinforce positive change.

————————————— **9** —————————————
–

Revitalizing Team Performance

The work team is receiving extraordinary attention as a leverage point for organizational renewal. Prescriptions for "self-managed work units," "autonomous work groups," and "empowered work teams" abound in business journals and magazines for good reason: most of the work in organizations is done in small groups or teams. Work teams permit flexibility in dealing with everything from changing work loads to day-to-day fluctuations in available staff. When managers seek faster and better ways to meet customer needs or other competitive challenges, the critical building block is increasingly at the team, and not the individual, level. Teams have, in addition, the potential to satisfy today's workers' demands for greater participation, autonomy, and influence over results. Increasingly, new organizational orders will call for team-based performance and evaluation and sport architectures described as containing "networks," "alliances," "clusters," or "self-directed teams."

The Importance of Teams During Recovery and Revitalization

The work team also is a focal point for recovery and revitalization after a transition. First, teams are the link between the individual and the organization. It is the team level at which employees assess whether the new organizational order truly works or is nothing more than just another round of executive lip service. Either people see that their work team is embracing experimentation, adopting new and improved work methods, and as a result achieving short- and long-term goals, or they see that time for learning is not allowed, new and better ways are not emerging, and goals are not being met. While success elsewhere in the organization helps influence employees' sentiments about life after a transition, evidence from their own work teams matters most. People are more firmly and mutually committed to team goals, and are more readily able to influence their attainment, than widespread company goals beyond their reach. They are much more likely to be able to make a difference—and receive relatively immediate feedback as to success or failure during recovery—in local team performance than in overall organizational results.

A second way in which the work team operates during revitalization is similar to the way a family responds when a loved one goes through a difficult time: the team amplifies the small victories and offers support during the setbacks. The tone set within the work team influences the extent to which successes are celebrated and built upon, experimentation and innovation are nurtured and parlayed into even greater earnings and returns, and ultimately, faith and hope come to replace cynicism and distrust. It also forms the foundation for social support by both reducing levels of occupational stress and buffering individuals from the physical or psychological consequences of what stress there is.[1] A work team with a high level of social support is not as susceptible to dynamics such as increased interpersonal conflict that tend to accompany life during and after a transition. Moreover, being able to share the experience with others and to have a group with which to discuss and process signals about the posttransition organization helps alleviate potential consequences in a group that remains composed of somewhat fragile and vulnerable individuals.

Finally, teams are important to organizational recovery and revitalization because of their potential to produce results far greater than the sum of individual contributions or, conversely, to stifle the contributions of even the most talented individuals. Depending on how well members develop shared goals and operating procedures, team dynamics can stimulate creativity and enhance productivity or restrict innovation and hinder performance. In turn, the extent to which members of a team work well together and with other teams in the organization will determine, to a substantial degree, the overall success of the organization.

The classic decision-making simulation "Lost in the Arctic" (or similar ill-fated excursions to the desert or the moon) provides one of the most straightforward and quantifiable ways to demonstrate the power of the team to build upon or detract from individual performance. Participants, working on their own, rank a list of ten items salvaged from their disabled airplane in order of their importance to survival. They then work together as a group to consider and rank order the items. In well-performing groups, one member will offer a piece of information—perhaps that a compass is useless so close to the magnetic pull of the North Pole—that is combined and leveraged with the contributions of others. In poorly performing groups, a lack of communication or a preponderance of conflict between members interferes with problem solving. Scores are calculated to determine the degree of discrepancy first between the individuals' rankings and those of survival experts, then between the group's rankings and that of the experts. If group interaction has added value, the team garners a score better than the mean average of the individual rankings and exceeds the results of even the highest-performing individual. Conversely, the group has been dysfunctional if, by working together, the members do no better than they could have by themselves on average or if any one member was able to do better than the group's combined performance.

What does it take to build a new, unifying work culture within a team whose members may have come from different companies or departments prior to a transition, or have remained intact yet find themselves in a new work context? Top-level managers can announce a vision and new values and norms that, when reinforced by other signs of togetherness, guide culture building through the ranks. But sometimes senior executives do not send the right signals or simply go their own ways. Either way, a team leader must be prepared to take responsibility for building his or her team. Understanding what makes a team effective helps, but so does being aware of the enduring impact of transition on employee mind-sets.

Establishing Team Performance Following Transition

How teams form during the transition influences how they perform afterward. Team leaders do not work with blank slates when attempting to mold a group of individuals into a team after a transition. Rather, their team-building tasks are complicated by the experiences, perceptions, and mental models that linger beyond the transition. Any unsavory dynamics that prevailed during transition, such as a staffing process contaminated by favoritism, haunt the team-building process afterward. Even when adaptation to transition has been accelerated by interventions like venting meetings, there always remain within individuals and teams counterforces to accepting the new order.

Effective teams—that is, those that achieve their objectives and sustain member commitment and motivation—share key characteristics. Team success is based on open communication, mutual trust, mutual support, identification with the task, and management of human differences.[2] The transition process interferes with the development of some of these critical characteristics of effective teams. These qualities are apt to deteriorate during the looking-out-for-number-one days of organizational transition. Their languid nature following the transition, if unchecked, will hinder team-building and ultimately, team performance as the organization attempts to recover.

Team Membership. New organizational orders that value teamwork benefit from selecting people who possess (or are capable of acquiring) the competencies, skills, and values necessary for successful performance in teams. A recent study produced a list of team member dimensions, including teamwork, problem identification and solution, the ability to learn, communication, initiative, work standards, coaching and training, job motivation, technical ability, and work tempo (the ability to work at a relatively fast and constant speed).[3] Yet staffing decisions during transition typically are made without the care and foresight to consider needs during recovery. Instead, politics predominate as individuals seek to exert some control in protecting and promoting themselves. In a reduction in force, people who possess or are capable of acquiring team-oriented skills may get so turned off by the prevailing dynamics that they jump ship and set sail for calmer seas elsewhere. In a merger, staffing decisions often are plagued by insufficient time to consider fully the merits of competing candidates for positions or may be mandated from the top. A team's leader may be instructed by senior management to add to his or her staff a person from the other side to achieve cosmetic balance, rather than select the best person for the job.

Mutual Choice. This leads to another characteristic of effective teams that erodes during transition—mutual choice. Highly effective work teams are a lot like top-ranked college sports teams: talent is scouted as coaching staffs carefully identify what positions need to be filled on their teams. Sought-after recruits weigh competing alternatives and think through a number of variables in coming to the decision of which team to join, like the team's history, the coach's reputation and style, and the role on the team being promised. Invitations go out, and based on mutual choice, players sign up to be part of what both sides regard as a very special team.

Business team leaders have little time to go through this careful selection process during the hectic transition period. Instead, they take what they can get (and/or have been given) and struggle well into the recovery period trying to shape a team out of a bunch of individuals. From most individuals' perspective, few alternatives from which to choose are seen. During transitions, people feel financially locked into unappealing situations rather than psychologically committed to or excited about their team membership.

History and Culture. Educators Lee Bolman and Terrence Deal call the power of a shared and cohesive culture an "invisible force" that gives a team its drive.[4] In particular, they note how specialized language, history, and values foster cohesion and commitment and how history and values reinforce team identity. Every team develops words, phrases, and metaphors unique to its circumstances that both reflect and shape its culture. At a consumer products firm, for example, the language "let me tee this up with you" preceding the expression of an idea or issue means that an immediate decision is not necessarily sought. This language lets team members communicate easily with minimal misunderstanding. Additionally, in most high-performing teams, stories keep traditions alive and provide real-life examples to guide daily behavior. The team's history and the values that underlie past behaviors reinforce the subtle and powerful influence of the group's identity on current and future behaviors.

Common culture, language, and history are lost when a work team is formed by a merger or reorganization. In fact, shared language and histories set groups apart and raise up differences rather than similarities in values and experiences. This afflicted a newly formed team following the merger of two international banking groups. The dinner scheduled after a venting meeting attended by the merged bank's North American and British executives coincided with the retirement of a senior vice president from the lead company. After cocktails, wine with dinner, and a fine port to accompany cigars, stories rolled out about the executive's notoriously outrageous behavior at social functions and business meetings over the years. The dinner—and in particular the telling of stories—was an excellent way for people from one side to deal with the loss of a respected and loved colleague: they roared with laughter as one hysterical tale after another was recounted, lamented how his antics would be missed, acknowledged his many contributions to business results, and expressed genuine regret for the moving on of a friend. While it was a necessary ceremony to help former coworkers come to terms with their loss, the evening had the inadvertent consequence of setting back overall team development. Attendees from the acquired side, outnumbered by about two to one relative to those from the lead company, sat passively and unengaged as they listened to the stories. In an impromptu debriefing session a few days later, acquired executives noted how the recounting of someone else's past temporarily reinforced barriers between the groups. They also acknowledged, however, that they garnered rich insights into the lead team's history and values by listening to the stories at the dinner.

Over time, teams will develop their own cultures, languages, and histories, either by building upon those from the past or by beginning anew. Nonetheless, these attributes of mature teams cannot be utilized early in the recovery period.

Shared Purpose and Process. Effective teams have a clear and shared sense of their purpose (their reason for being) and their process (how they will achieve that purpose). Near-term goals must relate directly to overall purpose, otherwise, the team members become confused, pull apart, and revert to mediocre performance behaviors. Consultants Jon Katzenbach and Douglas Smith have noted several reasons for this in their work with companies.[5] First, shaping and sharing a meaningful purpose sets the tone and aspiration by which teams develop direction, momentum, and commitment. Building among members a sense of ownership of a team's purpose, however, is not incompatible with taking initial direction from outside the team in the form of a vision, mission, or operating philosophy. It is in fact enhanced by the knowledge that local efforts are aligned with overall company goals. Second, specific performance goals are an integral part of a team's purpose. Transforming broad guidelines into measurable performance goals is the best way to define a team's purpose to its members. These goals should be clearly distinguished from both the organizationwide purpose and the summation of individual job objectives.

An effort at doing this took place in a large consulting firm that downsized following three years of disappointing financial results and reorganized by combining offices and practice areas. The corporatewide purpose shifted from a historical aim of being "the thought leader" in its consulting arena to one of producing significant increases in margins and returns on investments. Office heads called in each individual consultant to clarify personal financial objectives—billable-hour targets and new revenue generation goals—that would contribute to overall financial goals. One office head, however, wanted to create more than "a bunch of individuals chasing after their targets." Working closely with his team of consultants, he clarified a purpose for the office of "becoming the company leader in cross-selling across consulting practice areas." He established specific performance goals for the number of cross-selling sales calls expected to be made by senior consultants and for the percentage of office revenues to come from clients using two or more of the company's consulting services.

Third, commitment is enhanced by crafting a common approach to how people will work together to accomplish their purpose.

Everyone must agree on who will do what tasks, how work will be divided, how schedules will be set and adhered to, which skills need to be developed, how continuing membership will be earned, and how the group will make and modify decisions. Note that teams may "agree to disagree" and provide for special treatment of certain members. At the consulting firm, for example, it was recognized that newly hired professionals in emerging practice areas should not be expected to meet the same targets as senior consultants in mature businesses. Team members in the office agreed that new hires would be exempt from the cross-selling goals and would not be chastised by colleagues for not carrying their weight in contributing to office performance results. In contrast, consultants in the emerging practice areas were seen as laying an important foundation for the office's longer-term success and balancing the short-term focus that controlled the attention of the firm's national leadership. (As we will see in the next chapter, however, eventual actions did not back up these words.)

The transition process typically obscures the purpose and process of teams that are formed by merging, rightsizing, reorganizing, or realigning with new cultural or strategic realities. Shared perspectives are offset when individuals are preoccupied with looking out for themselves. Certainly efforts to articulate the new organizational order and to clarify the organization's vision and bring it to life establish a foundation upon which a clear and shared work team purpose and process can be developed. The extent to which the team is successful in contributing to overall organizational aspirations, however, will be determined by the extent to which its members feel they are pulling together rather than being left to fend for themselves.

Experimentation and Learning. Effective teams explore opportunities and options for enhanced ways of doing things. They can only do this if they have the freedom to experiment even if the consequences of experimentation may be failure. During a transition, exploration and risk taking give way to reliance on the tried and tested. Experimentation and learning may not have been characteristics of the old organizational order, or more conservative ways of acting may have been frozen into team members' behavioral repertoire as a result of transition mismanagement. Either way, the experience of living through a transition offsets this vital component of effective team performance.

Aspiration. Members of effective teams have high aspirations for the future and ambition beyond the limited horizon of the immediate task. Living through a transition, however, diminishes this spirit. People regress to very basic expectations and behavior; the goal of keeping one's job through the end of the day supersedes lofty hopes of creating something special over the long haul. Success is redefined as survival, not as achieving dreams.

Fun. Finally, effective teams have fun on the job. They balance seriousness with play and humor. As Bolman and Deal note, surgical teams, cockpit crews, and other groups learn that joking and playful banter are an essential source of invention and group spirit.[6] Humor releases tension and resolves issues that arise from a day-to-day routine or in a prevailing emergency.

Life during a merger or downsizing, though, is anything but fun. This is a key complaint of many people moving through transition. Their work teams have lost the ability to laugh and relax. Humor is ribald and risqué, poking fun at the ineptness of leadership or merger partners. It primarily serves a denigrating function, rather than one of tension reduction.

Sources of Conflict in Building New Teams

Team building after a transition is complicated when there are changes in leadership and membership of a team. Any one of the following factors enhances the likelihood of tension in newly formed teams.

A New Boss. The appointment of a new boss creates tension as subordinates naturally jockey for influence and visibility. Conflict is especially high whenever a subordinate expected to have the new boss's job, when former peers are placed into a superior-subordinate relationship due to a reorganization, or when the new boss comes from the other side in a merger.

New Peers. When transitions mix people from the previously separate groups, either across companies in a merger or across teams in an internal reorganization, they naturally divide into coalitions and exchange confidences with former peers. This can continue the we/they feelings and force managers to take sides in resolving conflicts.

New Methods. Members of acquired teams not only have to adapt to job-related changes, they also have to learn the politics and protocol of operating within a new parent company. Similarly, members of teams in organizations engaged in reengineering or transformational culture changes are confronted with new systems, duties, and expectations. Predictably, there is a tendency to stick with what (and who) you know. This means that people may have trouble gaining access to the informal social and communication networks of the new organization and will likely encounter untold problems in simply getting the job done through normal channels.

New Power Bases. Team leaders have to establish or reestablish their authority and clout with their team. It is difficult for a new executive to win over people when he or she comes from the dominant company in the merger or perceived "winning" group in an internal reorganization, but it can also be difficult for a manager from the acquired or losing side to retain people's loyalty when he or she is seen to be weaker as a result of the transition. People are looking for leaders who are well connected to new power bases, and this may or may not include their current boss.

New Relationships. Diversity can enhance team creativity and performance, but it takes time to turn what initially is likely to be a source of conflict into an enhancement. The feel and flow of relatively homogeneous work teams is disrupted by people from different organizations, cultures, or countries. This raises tension levels, especially when the differences interfere with work quality or quantity.

Understanding Posttransition Mind-sets

In rebuilding after a transition, team leaders have to work with employees with very different attitudes (see Exhibit 9.1). Some team members willingly let go of the old organizational order, adapt to new realities, and are ready to get on with the work at hand. Others want more support and more reasons to be part of a team. Still others feel shut out and resist efforts to move forward.

Employees who get the job they wanted or expected in the posttransition organization are usually ready to enlist in the new team. They may even be "charged up" by new challenges and opportunities. After their acquisition by Delta Airlines, for example, data processing people at Western Airlines were genuinely excited about the prospects of using Delta's sophisticated computer systems. These employees are often the mainstays of a new team; their positive at-

---

Recognizing People's Posttransition Emotional States

THE READY

Their situation:	Have been promoted or retained the job they want
	See greater opportunity to produce and advance
What to hope for:	Energy and excitement; charged up
What to watch for:	Overly aggressive; acting superior

THE WANTING

Their situation:	Did not receive the job they wanted or were demoted
	Miss former mentors, projects, and status
What to hope for:	Working through loss; adjusting to new realities
What to watch for:	Depression; anger and vindictiveness

THE WRUNG OUT

Their situation:	Have the same job, but things have changed
	More distant from leadership
	More competition for advancement
	Feel jerked around by the process
What to hope for:	Working through frustration; regaining footing
What to watch for:	Demotivation; lack of direction and purpose

EXHIBIT 9.1

titudes can be infectious. An overly gung-ho outlook, however, can alienate less-spirited employees who still need time to adapt. Hence team leaders are well advised not to single these employees out for special treatment. Sometimes it may even be necessary to urge them to "cool it" for a time.

By contrast, other employees are found wanting. They did not get their desired job title or responsibilities, their mentors or friends have departed, or their budgets or pet projects have been slashed. These employees may remain preoccupied with their lower-than-expected status and wonder if it is a harbinger of a dead-end career. Their self-esteem continues to suffer as it did during the transition period. Plainly, they need more time to sort things out.

Finally, there are employees who are simply wrung out by the transition. Contrary to their fears, most people retain the same or somewhat similar positions and responsibilities following a transition. Still, they are listless and weary from the ordeal they have survived. These people often hold onto the pessimism that was bred during the transition, believing the situation around them has changed for the worse. For example, some workers may complain that a merged organization adds layers between them and the highest levels of management. Those previously housed close to the action at headquarters fret when they find themselves far removed from the center of power in a new order that decentralizes authority. And upwardly mobile employees bemoan increased competition and decreased opportunity for advancement in delayered organizations.

There are also employees who, for one reason or another, feel they have been "jerked around" by the transition process. Cynicism remains rife among those who believe that appointed managers are incompetent or insensitive, or that something is going on behind closed doors. But some others may not latch onto a new direction or purpose, simply going through the motions of their jobs. It is imperative for managers to reenlist them as members of a new team and help them rededicate themselves to their jobs.

Understanding people's current emotional state is more difficult than it may at first seem. Team members who are not close to the boss may put on a poker face and hide their true feelings. Some simply cannot verbalize their reasons for persisting discontent. And still others seem ready for the new organizational order but turn out to be resistant. Straightforward one-on-one talks between leader and team member can uncover hidden emotional states. Involving a human resources professional, trained counselor, or even a trusted peer can also help open up discussion and assist a superior with hard-to-read employees.

Building the Team—One Member at a Time

Successful teams are built one person at a time. The team leader must recognize that each individual has had his or her own unique transition experience and can be motivated toward team performance in different ways. Three common factors frame the team leader's tasks in taking individuals and making them into team members:[7]

- *Psychological enlistment.* People need to feel wanted and have an emotional stake in their team's mission.
- *Role development.* People need to be excited about their new jobs and about their team's potential.
- *Trust and confidence.* People need to develop trust and confidence in their colleagues and supervisors.

Although these needs are part of any employment situation, they become especially prominent in the context of posttransition mindsets and dynamics (see Exhibit 9.2).

Psychological Enlistment: Forming the Team

Managers begin by forming teams and setting expectations. Meanwhile employees reporting to new bosses, working with new peers, or contending with new team charters or procedures go through some self-examination. They must ask themselves, "Do I really want to be part of this team?" Several factors influence their decision. First, employees need to know the team's purpose and how it contributes to the overall organizational scheme. Second, employees want to know if they have to prove themselves. If so, there may be heated competition or, alternatively, withdrawal and apathy. Egos can easily be bruised. Finally, some people exhibit passive or active aggression as posttransition trauma lingers, alienating the

Stages in Building A New Team

STAGES:	I SIGNING UP	II SORTING OUT	III SETTLING DOWN
Leader's Role			
	Form the team	Establish norms	Motivate performance
	Set expectations	Set ground rules	Set objectives
Member's Issues			
	Inclusion— am I a member of this team or not?	Control— who is in charge?	Openness— are we achieving?
Sources of Resistance			
	Unclear sense of purpose, mission, role	Holding onto old allegiances; moves to gain advantage	Holding onto ways of doing business
	People on trial	Internal conflict	Clash of cultures
	Personal distress	Gamesmanship	Foot dragging
How to Counter Resistance			
	Rally people	Negotiate roles/ responsibilities	Performance management
	Personalize the sign-up	Develop role agreements	Incentives to perform
	Massage egos	Clarify reporting relationships	Model desired behaviors
	Lay it on the line	Establish ground rules	Team building

EXHIBIT 9.2

boss and peers. Leaders can take several steps to lessen these sources of resistance to psychological enlistment in a team:

Re-recruit Employees. It is not too late for team leaders to act like college recruiters courting top athletes: they have to sell employees on the near-term merits and long-term advantages of being part of *this* team. This involves thoughtfully assessing people's goals and aspirations within the context of the new organizational order, carefully considering what might motivate people or turn them off, and then formally signing them up for the team. Needs for inclusion are met by reminding people of their importance and by showing them their value to the team.

Massage Egos. Many employees need extra reassurance of their worth, especially when they have not gained what they hoped for following a transition or when they sense they are being tested at a point in their career when their accomplishments and capabilities should be recognized. The team leader may need to do some stroking and ego massaging. For employees who feel on trial because of job or group changes, as well as for the many who want to experience a quick win, there is a need to clarify performance standards and establish some short-term targets. Creating opportunities for even small successes and acknowledging their achievement helps here. It is, of course, important to acknowledge people's past contributions and to remind them that they are still needed and appreciated.

Lay It On the Line. Over time, however, individuals and the team have got to get on with the work at hand. Employees who continue to mope around the office, bad-mouth the new organizational order, or perform well below expected levels may need a "shape up or ship out" message from the boss. The leader's objective is to lay things on the line, but this can be best accomplished with a private conversation rather than public finger pointing.

Role Development: Team Organization

After team members are in place, team leaders and members often test one another in a new way—struggling to determine relative degrees of influence and control. Group dynamics experts refer to this as the "storming" phase of group development. Leaders have to help their teams weather this storm by clarifying people's roles and setting ground rules. Here, the group's modus operandi and pecking order are established and recognized.

Again, three factors can interfere with team leaders' efforts to manage these dynamics. First, managers leading well-established groups often find people still holding on to their old allegiances and ways of doing things. This, for example, hampered team-building between two merged sales forces. Despite being reassigned to new teams at new locations, sales representatives would travel back to their old offices to use demo equipment and their former secretaries. Some even teamed up with former service technicians who, although no longer part of their team, were bribed with six-packs of beer to join in customer calls.

Second, internal conflict can wrack team development. Some employees will brownnose the boss and backstab their peers in an effort to gain power. Others may gain command of their peers and orchestrate a revolt against the new boss—a classic dynamic as small groups develop. The storming phase can put leaders in a no-win situation. If they assert their authority preemptively, conflict goes underground. But if they let conflict get out of control, the bad feelings developed may not be assuaged by later intervention.

Finally, work groups have their own informal rules and norms—and woe to the boss who does not respect them. One group of engineers in a high-tech company had a traditional casual-dress day where employees wore jeans or slacks and sportswear. When a new boss first suggested that they abandon this practice, he was ostracized. Everything turned around, however, when he began to wear a cowboy hat on the appointed day.

At stake in these situations is the degree to which the team leader is able to develop esprit de corps rather than mindless obedience. At this stage, team leaders should do the following:

Negotiate Roles. Positions and players may be set, but new job duties and responsibilities require clarification. Role negotiation, a technique devised by management consultant Roger Harrison, has a team leader and subordinates discuss expectations of roles, identify areas of conflict or ambiguity, and engage in the give-and-take of negotiating a realistic role definition acceptable to both parties.[8]

To formalize these negotiations, a "contract" between the boss and team specifies role expectations and importantly, commits them to evaluate and revise the agreement at a future date. Formal agreements like this are resisted by some managers who regard them as too legalistic. But this distorts their intent and spirit: role contracts are living documents that outline common understandings and set a working relationship off on a mutually agreed course.

Establish Reporting Relationships. Employees regularly complain about ambiguous reporting relationships following a transition. To counter this, managers have to bring organizational charts to life and delineate who reports to whom and with what authority and responsibilities. This may seem foreign to companies accustomed to fluid structures and hesitant to put on to paper the extant chain of command. It is useful, however, to overstructure in the early stages of team-building, when areas of responsibility are contested and everything seems up for grabs. When possible, it helps to keep reporting relationships in place for at least a while. This adds to the sense of stability and offsets wariness that management is coming up with another round of change.

Set Group Ground Rules. Finally, there is a need to establish both formal procedures (regarding budgetary authority, communication formats, and so on) as well as informal norms (concerning dress, timeliness, protocol, and so forth) in a team. To the extent practical, these ground rules should be congruent with any guidelines for behavior that come forth from the organizational vision, business unit mission, and department operating philosophy. When operations have to change, effective team builders provide a clear and straightforward reason why policies and procedures are changing, even when the reason is because "headquarters says we have to." The rule "sell people on change, just don't tell them about it" remains valid here.

Trust and Confidence: Getting Down to Work

Before the team is finally ready to get down to work, members must have trust and confidence in each other. Until now, team members have had to make individual accommodations to change; now the group must function as a whole. In a chicken-and-egg predicament, team members require trust and confidence to operate in a fully productive mode, yet they require some evidence in the form of achieving results and identifying new and better ways of doing things to become trusting and confident of their fellow team members.

There are several reasons why teams have trouble moving into a fully productive mode. First, posttransition teams need time to sort out new methods and procedures and to learn how to work new systems. In the case of two merged manufacturing groups, for example, one team formerly used Deming's methods of quality improvement and the other used the Crosby model. This led to "religious wars" that took months to resolve until a hybrid approach, drawing from features of both models, was thrashed out.

Second, there may be different performance expectations in work teams formed during transition. Consider the case of a manager who was historically the first to work and the last to leave and expected his employees to demonstrate an equally strong work ethic. When his work area was integrated with that of another manager who had a more laid-back style, trouble ensued. By all accounts the easygoing manager's group was every bit as successful as his hard-driving counterpart's, but there was no way to divide their responsibilities. The hard driver secured the top post and forced his ways onto the laid-back manager and employees, who thereupon left in droves.

This speaks to a final problem in achieving high performance: how to handle diversity. Naturally it is difficult to reconcile differences among team members who are used to different ways of doing things. Can a team accommodate members who like to plan out their work in detail as well as those who take a more spontaneous approach? How about team members who yell and swear at meetings versus those who are accustomed to sober discussion and polite disagreement?

Differences become even more sensitive when they involve gender, language, race, national origin, and sexual orientation. In one case a male manager, taking over the accounts receivable department in a firm that had delayered, never established the rapport or performance level achieved by the female manager he replaced. In another instance, African-American employees relocated into a largely white production department never felt part of the combined team. Female executives in a merged media company encountered a "glass ceiling" far thicker than their previous one. Organizations and units within them have different philosophies and approaches to responding to diversity. It takes time for managers and employees to figure out the rules in each group, and more time still to try to change them. Team leaders can speed the development of trust and confidence in various ways:

Model New Behaviors. The most subtle tactic a new team leader has in influencing people is to model desired behaviors. In one case, a senior vice president publicly heralded how much top management of an acquired firm "brought to the party" but regularly ridiculed them in closed door sessions. His team picked up the cue and began to disparage subsidiary management. The result was the gradual exodus of acquired managers, sales representatives, and technical experts, coupled with a 30 percent drop in revenues in one year.

In another case, a general manager drew on the ideas and talents of both sides through regular meetings and technical exchanges. He was committed to experimenting and finding best practices in building the service philosophy and systems of a combined function. Team leaders down the ranks emulated their superiors' evenhanded behavior, and a newly developed suggestion system yielded five hundred recommendations for improvements in service delivery.

Manage Performance. Directly rewarding desired performance is the most effective technique team leaders have for clarifying what they expect from members. Basic principles of effective incentive programs apply here: find out what rewards (financial and otherwise) people want, and clearly link them with desired behaviors. Often it helps to reward people's contributions to team-building and to a climate of experimentation and learning in addition to their operations-oriented results. To encourage the cross-fertilization of personnel following the merger of two engineering firms, for example, project managers were rewarded for staffing task forces with talent from both companies.

Incentives can also be applied to people management tasks. After a painful reduction in force, team leaders in a financial services firm were given the objective of raising employee morale in their departments and were measured through employee attitude surveys and records of absenteeism and turnover in their departments. To be effective, superiors and subordinates need to meet to determine performance objectives, how they will be measured, when they will be evaluated, and what rewards can be attained. This kind of performance discussion is especially important when new performance criteria are established and when a new type of appraisal system is introduced.

Manage Diversity. One U.S.-based firm volunteered its own "valuing diversity" program to its Japanese owners in anticipation of difficulties in managing a diverse work force. The training program focused on prejudice and stereotypes and had participants roleplay situations of managing majority/minority relationships in work teams. According to one participant, the session was "an eye-opener" and revealed considerable discontent within the lead company over its inattention to diversity in the age of globalization. The training session was heated, but many said it helped to build trust and understanding among members of merged teams.

Managing Teams in the New Organizational Order

Team leaders are essential links in the adoption of new ways of thinking and acting during recovery. Senior executives may provide the direction of a new order and contribute to developing a context for recovery, but it is those in the middle that make the move from the old organizational order to the new order by taking ideas from all quarters and putting them to work in daily operations. Team leaders set the climate in work groups by exuding confidence and excitement about the team's and the organization's future, or by sustaining pessimism and cynicism; by focusing people on the future, or by languishing with them in the past.

Today's Challenges

Despite their important role in making change happen in organizations, these are difficult times for middle managers and supervisors who lead teams. Their ranks are being thinned by downsizings and delayerings. Middle managers are squeezed between senior executives who understand where they want things to be and see no reason why their vision cannot be implemented and employees who lack the motivation and confidence to make the vision a reality. And they constantly are having to do more with less—less support staff, less training, less money, and less cooperation from equally stretched peers. Managers in organizations that have delayered may have taken on the responsibilities of those who had been above them, without receiving their title or pay. Meanwhile they are coping with the loss of friends and trusted associates who have been laid off or have taken early retirements, as well as the loss of their own status, perks, and upward mobility.

Of particular concern to many team leaders are popular programs for employee empowerment and self-directed teams that they see as a threat to their authority. The switch to high employee involvement requires a sharing of power and information with the lowest levels of the organization, and operating employees may start making decisions and solving problems that previously had been handled by supervisors and managers. In many organizations, team leaders feel out of the loop of the transformation process *even when their organizations profess to be moving toward a new order characterized by involvement*. A study of thirty firms that attempted to implement employee involvement programs revealed that just eighteen companies involved supervisors in the effort from the beginning, and five failed to involve supervisors at all.[9] Interviews with managers in these last five firms revealed that the key proponents of the change process simply overlooked involving the first-line supervisors in the change. They also acknowledged that they had made a big mistake in failing to involve the supervisors; they now had to deal with team leaders who were sabotaging the employee involvement effort, doing little to promote it among employees, and feeling threatened or abandoned.

As a result of perceived and real threats to their position, many team leaders retreat to primitive behaviors even as a new order is being built around them. They dig in to protect their domain and focus on looking out for number one. Short-term results are sought not to lift the spirits of the team members but to relieve their own survival panic. Long-term efforts to experiment, learn, and align work with the new order give way to activities that will ensure a profitable quarter or year at most. When short-term thinking sets in and the survival instinct becomes dominant, relationships between the team leader and team members deteriorate. Alienation and diffidence increase, and an antagonistic climate often develops. With the team and its leader out of sync with the new order, neither the team nor the organization can meet its goals.

Team Leadership

There is no question that managers and supervisors heading work teams in posttransition organizations are in a precarious situation. They are asked to produce results and to contribute to positive organizational change, but they may be given little support and few resources. In situations in which senior executives have articulated a new order and laid the foundation for recovery, the team leader must contend with major disruption to expectations and modes of operation. In cases in which senior executives have *not* provided a vision and guidelines for the future or created a context for recovery, the team leader must think long and hard about how he or she can exert control to rebuild team performance after a transition.

In either circumstance, the manager or supervisor has to come to terms with changing characteristics of teams and team leadership in contemporary organizations. First, the people who make up teams, all in all, are more educated today than in the past. Knowledgeable employees can contribute to refining and improving the planning and implementation of organizational recovery. Moreover, their awareness of and participation in the recovery process can clarify and motivate performance toward team and organizational objectives. People want meaningful and challenging work, but they also want to be active participants in change and not just passive recipients of it.

Second, team membership in organizations increasingly will vacillate, with full- and part-time members moving in and out. Dynamic market conditions, competitive pressures, and technological advances push and pull at team composition. Ad hoc teams, cutting across traditional boundaries, create new groupings of people. All of these pressures contribute to an even greater need to clarify team charters, deliverables, roles, behavioral norms, and working relationships.

Third is the pronounced distinction between team *management* and team *leadership*. A team manager coordinates and supervises work tasks in pursuit of the group's objectives. A team leader basically does for the team members what senior executives should be doing on the organizational level to create a context for recovery: articulate a vision where the team is headed, clarify its mission, provide guidelines for desired behaviors, and develop the opportunities, resources, and mind-sets required to have team members align their work with the vision, mission, and guidelines. If this has been done on an organizational level, then the team leader acts to coordinate local efforts with the new order in general and with other teams in particular. If this has not occurred on a broader level, then the team leader has an opportunity to step up and provide the leadership that is sorely missing but essential for recovery, at least, on a local level.

The fact is that most teams in organizational America have been overmanaged but underled. Tight control and oversight breed passivity and hinder innovation and, at best, result in a group of people "doing things right." Revitalizing team members to participate actively in recovery by establishing vision and guidelines, sharing information, and building well-functioning teams cultivates a shared sense of responsibility among people who want to contribute in creative and important ways to "doing the right things."

The requirement, then, is to replace managing business as usual with leading teams through recovery. Team leaders must learn how to change the direction of their groups even if senior executives do not help. Research conducted by business professors Chester Borucki and Philippe Byosiere suggests four ways in which team leaders must transform or expand their traditional roles to effect the continuous changes necessary to make their firms more globally competitive:[10]

- *The visionary role*—Developing a mental picture of the possible future of their unit as well as roles for subordinates that support the overall vision of the organization.
- *The strategist role*—Moving above and beyond traditional responsibilities for strategy implementation by thinking and acting strategically and running their units as if they were their own businesses, and by sharing strategic formulation and implementation processes with team members
- *The architect role*—Recognizing the advantages and disadvantages of various design and system configurations and being able to effect change
- *The knowledge creation role*—Wielding influence upward and downward based on access to data, increasing abilities to inte-

grate a wide range of information and ideas, and developing the capacity to learn

Team Building with Vision and Values

Concurrent with the tasks of psychological enlistment, role development, and trust and confidence building, leaders need to infuse their teams with a sense of purpose and with values. To establish shared levels of commitment, the leader must help the team members find goals and values that all can believe in and put into practice. When senior executives articulate a new order, team leaders through the ranks have a blueprint from which they can build this collective sense of purpose and values. Frequently, however, the head of a group of people will be confronted with the job of developing them into a team without the benefit of visionary guidance from above.

This was the case following the merger of Chemical Bank and Manufacturers Hanover. Former Manufacturers Hanover CEO John McGuillicuddy and his counterpart Walter Shipley from Chemical Bank agreed to work in tandem in the postmerger organization. To their credit, it is quite exceptional for two premerger CEOs to bond and work together productively following a combination. Still, their situation prevented the clear articulation of a new organizational order. McGuillicuddy, who retained the CEO title after the merger, was just two years away from retirement. His attention was focused on relatively immediate issues of integrating operations rather than on using the merger as an opportunity to develop new assumptions, expectations, and behaviors to build a new and better organization. Shipley, who would become CEO upon McGuillicuddy's retirement, recognized the opportunity to cast a new mold but did not interfere with McGuillicuddy's leadership.

Eschewing the cultural dimensions of the merger was subdued by the positive reaction the combination received from outsiders. The business press greeted the merger of what had been two pedestrian institutions as a bold move and an opportunity to build a leading financial institution. Externally, people felt very good about the Chemical Bank/Manufacturers Hanover merger: Wall Street bid up the stock price, and Chemical executives were sought after like never before to speak in front of important industry groups or provide quotes for important magazine or newspaper articles. Internally, however, Chemical people did not see a new and better way emerging and grew cynical of the merger and its opportunity for positive change. "The outside world is very high on this merger, but inside the bank we are very disappointed," noted one executive who echoed the sentiment of many managers and employees. Said another, "We really haven't done too much wrong in this merger, but we sure have missed some opportunities to do things in a great way." Chemical people were ready to let go of their old organizational order and grasp onto a new one, but none was placed within their reach.

Bill Harrison, the executive in charge of Chemical's Global Bank, saw the effect the lack of a new order was having on his efforts to form a team. There had been some progress in adapting to transition: most of Harrison's direct reports, and those a level down, had let go of most of the negative feelings that developed during the merger integration process. For example, the upset and cynicism generated toward a merger staffing formula perceived by many employees as giving a higher priority to balance between the sides than to competence had dissipated. Yet, there was nothing pulling managers together into a well-functioning and coordinated team. Traditional barriers and conflicts between groups like relationship and product managers carried over unaltered from before to after the merger. In surveying the situation, Harrison concluded that aspects of the merger had been well managed but that people were not being led toward the development of a new team.

Not content with this, Harrison took action to build his team in a way that would instill a sense of pride, excellence, and cross-functional cooperation in pursuit of desired financial results. He commissioned interviews with individual managers to identify deterrents to Global Bank success. They revealed a strong yearning for guidance on how to behave in the postmerger organization. Harrison responded by defining his vision of a new order and engaging his team in delineating the behaviors and values that would contribute to its attainment. Primary to this effort was taking a dozen key executives, including those reporting directly to him, offsite to develop a Global Bank mission statement (see Exhibit 9.3).

The mission statement communicated a desired end state to the

---

Global Bank Mission Statement

Our mission is to be the best broad-based global bank, a leader in our chosen markets.

We are committed to significant, mutually profitable relationships with clients as their banker, advisor, and trading and investment partner.

We will optimize our risk profile, emphasizing underwriting, distribution, trading, and proprietary risk-taking skills.

Success depends upon the effectiveness of our people, we will develop and empower top-quality professionals. We value integrity, partnership, initiative, and discipline.

We are action oriented and dedicated to excellence in everything we do.

EXHIBIT 9.3

Global Bank's 6,000 employees. As part of the process of rolling out the statement, Harrison capitalized on an opportunity to engage his own team in bringing the statement to life and, simultaneously, to bond the members together with a shared vision and values. A second offsite meeting was held, this time with the attendance list expanded to include all direct reports of each member of Harrison's own team, a total of seventy executives. Harrison kicked off the meeting by presenting the mission statement, seen for the first time by his team's reports, and soliciting questions. As expected, a skeptical silence predominated during the question-and-answer portion of the presentation. Then the meeting facilitator introduced the process through which the attendees would determine exactly what the mission statement meant for doing business in the Global Bank. The process was built around, first, debate and clarification of the intent and practicality of the mission statement and second, the use of force field analysis (identifying enablers and inhibitors of a desired end state and then determining ways to weaken the inhibiting forces and strengthen enabling forces) to determine how to bring the mission statement to life on the job.

Each of Harrison's direct reports led a breakout group—composed of members from various teams—responsible for clarifying one passage from the mission statement and determining its implications for business strategy, operational tactics, and team development. The phrase "We are committed to significant, mutually profitable relationships with clients," for example, was confronted through several questions that moved the "motherhood" statement into the realm of agreed-upon operating principles: What is a relationship? What does it mean to be "committed to significant, mutually profitable relationships"? To what extent is this definition changing or staying the same? How do we define "significant, mutually profitable relationships"? What systems do we use to quantify these relationships? Does the bank's approach to relationships reinforce this commitment? How do we take "relationships" and make them "mutually profitable"?

The group addressing the sentence "Success depends upon the effectiveness of our people; we will develop and empower top quality professionals," also considered several questions: How effective are our people? What do we mean by "develop and empower"? Do we currently develop and empower our professionals? What tools can we use to make our people more effective, develop them, and empower them (in terms of systems, information, or compensation)? Are there any externally imposed constraints or aids to this process?

Each breakout group reported the clarifications and implications of its assigned passage. Lively discussion and debate ensued among the full group. Then individuals regrouped with members of their natural teams to take each set of implications and conduct a force field analysis to determine the forces for and against successful implementation in their work areas. This set out a course of tactical action within each team to realize the mission. Combined across all teams, the output formed the basis for the development of a new strategic plan for the Global Bank. Additionally, the process of this work brought individuals together to determine collectively the vision and values that would guide work activities in their teams. It focused people on a shared vision of the future and a shared sense of the desired values underlying the attainment of business success, both of which were essential components of Global Bank managers coming together as a team.

Harrison's work in building a team with vision and values, coupled with co-vice chairman's Edward Miller's leadership in Chemical's Retail Bank, have contributed to excellent operational results. The new Chemical Bank is the leader in corporate loan syndications, a strong force in trading and selling currency and derivative products, the dominant player in New York in the middle-market lending business, and a powerful retail presence in the greater New York area. Solid increases in revenues and a dramatic drop in nonperforming assets lifted the company's stock price from $18 a share as merger implementation began in earnest in early 1992 to over $40 a share in late 1993. These results have played to excellent reviews by critics who questioned whether Chemical and Manufacturers Hanover could successfully merge their banks and corporate cultures. The *Wall Street Journal* labeled the combination "one of the best mergers of equals," yielding "superb operating figures," and *Business Week* offered "a model for other banks that are looking to merge as the banking industry consolidates."

To be sure, what occurs in the broader organizational context influences a leader's and members' ability to maximize team performance. For example, old systems that rewarded individualism may have to be revised because they fail to measure commitment to the team. These are built-in organizational mechanisms that discourage identification with and pursuit of team goals. Instead new reward systems are necessary that encourage individual effort, provided it is collectively employed. As the next chapter shows, reward systems—along with other organizational forces like communication norms and training priorities—can act powerfully to facilitate or inhibit revitalization.

Revitalizing Organizational Systems

Actions taken to revitalize individual spirit and team performance must be reinforced by efforts to rebuild overall organizational effectiveness. This is the refreezing component of the recovery process, in which new attitudes and behaviors become ingrained in the organizational order. Refreezing may occur on purpose or by accident, but it will happen. The trick to reinforcing mental models congruent with the desired organizational order is consistency of message. Every manifestation of the organization—every system, procedure, policy, and decision—has meaning. Unless care is taken to think through what messages are being sent, they are likely to be in conflict and result in a new organizational order by default rather than by design. Alternatively, deliberately aligning systems, procedures, and decisions with desired mental models will result in a posttransition organization headed in its chosen direction and meeting its key goals.

The notion of "refreezing" desired attitudes and behaviors perhaps is the oddest aspect of organizational recovery. How can any prescription for enhancing organizational effectiveness suggest locking in certain activities or mind sets in an era of persistent change? The answer is to conceive of organizational revitalization as a dynamic state created by the forces for and against the development of a new organizational order. There is an inevitable give-and-take between, on the one hand, the need to experiment and create new and better ways of doing things and, on the other, the desire to establish standard ways of doing things with predictable outcomes. Executives, managers, and all workers must realize that their organizations should not refreeze to the extent of rigid routines, but must stabilize some broad guidelines.

The result is that the term *refreezing* must be recalibrated away from its traditional meaning of immovability or solidification and toward a more relative definition. Part of refreezing new mental models is keeping expectations set that unfreezing and remolding may—and likely will—be needed at any time. Put in popular parlance, the only constant these days is change.

Part of the new organizational order is a recognition that it is constantly being redefined as the organization and its people move ahead with new knowledge and new challenges. What should be solidified are enduring values that underlie specific actions in building the new order. With ongoing change and transition in organizations, values, beliefs, and guidelines for behavior (rather than rules and regulations) will furnish the cohesion and direction and achieve coordination in the new organizational order. For example, the value of teamwork may be refrozen as part of the new organizational order rather than the structure delineating teams at a certain point in time. Similarly, the value of accountability may be reinforced, while the specific results or responsibilities for which one is accountable may change.

This chapter looks at some of the systems organizations can use to refreeze employee attitudes and behaviors congruent with the new order. While almost any aspect or characteristic of an organization can influence employee beliefs and actions, four major points of leverage in rebuilding organizational effectiveness after transition are examined: compensation, benefits, communication, and training and development.

Compensation

Each organizational member wants to know, "What is in it for me to play by the rules of the new order?" Nonspecific gains like "building long-term organizational capability and enhancing competitiveness" will not cut it for employees who are rebounding from a transition. "What's my incentive for reengineering my job?" asked a manager when he learned of his appointment to a task force charged with implementing a consulting firm's recommendations for redesigning work processes.

Any hope for using the compensation system to reinforce the new order must be based on the understanding that people behave in ways that get them the rewards they want. Employees look around and draw conclusions about which behaviors are rewarded in the new order. Eventually these observations become refrozen in new mental models of life after the transition. If any inadvertent messages are received about the link between behavior and rewards, then the only hope for reinforcing the desired way of doing things is to repeat the full process of unfreezing, changing, and refreezing.

Reward systems are highly symbolic. How rewards are distributed sends a powerful message to employees about what the organization values. Early in the posttransition period, cause-effect relationships are molded in employees' minds regarding the attractiveness of available rewards and the probability of receiving those rewards in the new order. Unfortunately, it is easy to err in rewarding employee activity after a transition. Job rating schemes and compensation policies that base rewards on the number of direct subordinates run counter to the intentions of reorganizations aimed at eliminating hierarchical levels. Companywide profit sharing programs, implemented with the hope of encouraging people to eliminate waste and cut costs on their jobs, are bound to fail if people feel their contribution cannot make a difference in overall results, or if they do not trust that the company will pay out. Conversely, well-timed and smartly conceived changes in reward systems can strengthen and reinforce desired behaviors and rebuild trust in and commitment to the organization.

Traditional Reward Systems

Traditional reward systems often work at cross-purposes with efforts to revitalize teams or individuals. They reward the wrong behavior or fail to reward behaviors desired in the new order. Most organizations' reward systems were designed and implemented during a less competitive and less volatile era. These systems emphasized base pay (a holdover from days when fixed increases in the cost of doing business could be passed onto the customer) and rewarded individual achievement (often promoting competitiveness among coworkers). Traditional job-based reward systems, built upon a hierarchy of pay levels that are tied to the purported importance of a job, did not provide incentives to support teamwork. The emphasis on hierarchy and specific job descriptions associated with job-based pay undermined the sharing of responsibility within the team. Also typical of traditional compensation systems was restricting incentives to the upper levels of organizations. With a strong base salary mentality, most managers viewed incentives as add-ons rather than as a truly significant portion of compensation at risk. Importantly, the link between pay and performance was obscured. Double-digit merit increase budgets during times of high inflation and seemingly limitless revenue growth meant that everyone, even the most mediocre of performers, could expect a decent, if not sizable, pay raise. And money was seen as the key motivator in finding, holding onto, and motivating employees, a view that ignored such factors as life-style, interesting work, and challenging opportunities.

Traditional pay systems also tended to support hierarchical relationships and slow, incremental change in both jobs and performance. If these are characteristics of the new order, then the traditional reward system should do just fine; given the host of environmental factors that require fast-paced change, however, it is likely that they are not. As a result, traditional reward programs are under strain. Nearly half of two hundred senior executives surveyed believed that performance measurement and reward programs in their companies actually encourage counterproductive or narrowly focused behaviors. Ninety percent of the executives said their employees spend much of their time engaged in cross-functional tasks, but that this work is not recognized by their companies' compensation programs. In another survey, 70 percent of employees said they see little or no relationship between what they do on the job and what they take home in their paycheck.[1]

Reward Systems for the New Order

Companies and other organizations must design a fair reward system that reinforces values and behaviors congruent with the new order and is sufficiently flexible to respond to rapid changes in the competitive environment and in organizational priorities. The rewards offered also should be consistent with business strategy, management philosophy, employee needs, and (of course) financial realities. Ultimately, a reward system should attract, motivate, and retain good employees at all levels. Doing this while solidifying the new order requires the following:

- Recognizing and rewarding behaviors that contribute to the new order
- Understanding what rewards are attractive to employees
- Clarifying the system's advantages for employees
- Linking rewards with performance
- Building a performance management system that supports the new order

Some basic questions need to be addressed in designing reward systems to reinforce the new order. Can new values and behaviors be rewarded and recognized adequately through existing compensation practices? If not, what kind of changes are needed in incentives, rewards, or recognition? How can the desired values and behaviors be quantified and measured? If they cannot, would recognition programs be a better alternative than financial incentives? What if any distinction is to be made between producing desired results at any cost and getting the job done in line with the new order? And what respective weightings will individual, team, and organizational performance receive in compensation equations?

Answers to these questions clarify what really matters in the new order. First, they redefine what "performance" and "results" mean in the organization. A software publisher who wished to increase risk-taking behaviors after a series of downsizings and restructurings earmarked a certain percentage of both merit increases and bonus pay to be based on suggestions for new products, even if they did not come to market. Contrast this with the major consulting firm described in the previous chapter that espoused the importance of cross-selling as part of its quest to expand into new business areas. Consultants who met their revenue targets despite not introducing colleagues from other practice areas continued to receive pay increases and bonuses in line with those from the past.

Despite platitudes for cross-selling, office heads were afraid to unsettle senior consultants who maintained relationships with large clients and thus took no sanctions against those who continued to play by the old rules. People learned that what mattered was *what* results they produced, and not *how* they were accomplished.

Second, the answers to these questions elucidate changing emphases in performance management and reward systems. There may be movement toward role definition and away from job definition, with attention to outcomes such as customer service rather than tasks like order processing. Or there may be changes from the old to the new order related to the role of teams vis-à-vis individual contributors. Finally, they yield a menu of reward vehicles. Existing plans may be modified by altering the balance between base salary and at-risk pay or by changing weightings for individual, team, and organizational results. Or it may be advantageous to establish new systems like short- or long-term cash incentive awards based on individual or team performance, profit sharing programs that pay to all employees a flat dollar amount or a percentage of base pay at certain milestones, or stock awards that recognize individual or team performance based on the long-term success of the company. There are also nontraditional (and sometimes nonfinancial) rewards, such as allowing employees to buy an occasional day off or qualify for a six-month or one-year community service or personal development sabbatical.

Thought also needs to be given to what events or behaviors the organization wants to celebrate. New orders with flatter structures and fewer promotional opportunities have to find alternatives to replace the traditional rewards of promotion up the hierarchy. The celebration and hoopla that went with a move up the organizational chart could be used to acknowledge such horizontal moves as transferring to new departments, learning new skills, or working across boundaries.

In short, the design of a reward system comes down to what the organization values, what it wants to pay for, and what it wants to celebrate. Ensuring that the reward system reinforces what the organization intends, however, requires asking people what kind of rewards they find *attractive*, making sure that people feel they can influence their *ability* to receive the rewards, making the rewards *timely* so people feel the connection between the reward and their efforts, and issuing the rewards *consistently* across various individuals and groups.

Attractiveness of Rewards. The best way to find out which rewards are most attractive to employees is to ask them. When looking to broaden the reward mix, it takes some prompting to get employees to weigh nontraditional rewards they had not considered to be within the realm of possibility. To heighten overall reward attractiveness, some organizations allow employees to tailor their incentives. In one service organization that promoted employee "self-sufficiency" in career planning as part of its new order, an administrative assistant who wanted to move into the human resources function proposed a tuition reimbursement amount double the company limit in lieu of an annual merit increase so she could complete her college certificate program on an accelerated schedule.

Following a transition, people are concerned with how they are going to succeed on the job (now that they know they have one), and they refocus their concentration on what is in it for them personally to be part of the new order. This is especially a concern for top talent, who may be demotivated by a perceived reduction in advancement opportunities and by the allure of greener grass on the other side of the fence. This issue was addressed head-on by Bank of America following a massive restructuring in the mid-1980s—involving divestitures, downsizing, and a new strategic concentration on business markets where it had a competitive edge—that shrank head count from 87,000 to 53,000 employees. To avoid losing the people they wanted to keep, Bank of America executives met with key employees to discuss future opportunities and understand how they wanted to be recognized for significant contributions. The company responded with compensation tactics ranging from cash bonuses to stock options for the people who were leading the way in turning around the company and contributing to the new order. Additionally, Bank of America executives never lost sight of the fact that their competitors had money, too, and so they gave star performers something else they really wanted: assurances that the company had a bright future, and if they hung in, equally shining personal opportunities.

Ability to Influence Outcomes. No matter how attractive the reward is, if people feel it is beyond their reach they will not make a wholehearted effort to gain it. This is why it is important to give individuals and teams attainable goals soon after transition, to promote quick wins and rebuild confidence in the self, the work group, and the organization. It is also important to structure pay increases and incentive and reward programs to pay out on the basis of individual and team performance. Companywide gain sharing or profit sharing programs may be too distant from the individual's sphere of influence to rebuild or sustain motivation. As one employee stated after the electronic products firm he worked at was acquired by and integrated into a much larger company, "I know and trust the people I work with; give us a reasonable goal and we will get the job done."

Rewards should reflect the ways in which employees are asked to operate in the new order. If breadth in skills and competencies are valued—and if horizontal moves in the organization are expected to pick up the allure previously held by hierarchical advancements—then there needs to be some element of skill- or competency-based pay in the overall scheme that rewards people for what they can do for the company and for progressing to the next competency level. And if teamwork, either within or across groups or both, is encouraged in the new order, then people had better be given a chance to demonstrate it and be rewarded for doing it.

Pratt & Whitney, the designer and manufacturer of jet engines, embarked on a major transformation in the 1980s built around four strategic goals: lowered costs, improved marketing and customer support, more help for customers in managing existing and emerging fleets, and the development of new technology needed for the future. Culturally, management wanted a new organizational order that stressed cooperation, continuous improvement, and sound customer and supplier relationships. It was clear, however, that the incumbent performance management system did not support these qualities of the new order. In response, Pratt & Whitney's overall vision and mission statement were developed and communicated throughout the work force. Each work group in the organization established its own mission statement. Then each dyad of employee and supervisor, with the counsel of company compensation professionals, clarified the individual's role in supporting the mission and established measurement standards for key job requirements. The purpose was to put into writing the major duties of a job during the next year or other performance cycle, encompassing such traditional standards as quality and quantity of work and the behavioral competencies describing the knowledge and skills that employees must have as well as the tasks and activities they must perform to meet the group and company mission.

A coordinating task force of ten people from various parts of the organization established universal competencies and provided measurement standards for all employees. New cultural initiatives and business requirements translated on an individual level into customer satisfaction, technical expertise, initiative, quality, commitment and contribution, teamwork, and effective relationships and communication. At the managerial level, succeeding in the new order also meant creating a shared vision, empowering others, developing people, recognizing merit, and achieving results. On a local level, employees and their supervisors refined and mutually agreed upon key job requirements and competencies and designed a self-assessment process to be integrated into the performance appraisal at the end of the evaluation period (usually one year). The task force linked the measurable performance with appropriate recognition and rewards, which ranged from appreciation memos to group awards and special cash bonuses for individuals or teams. Meanwhile, a second task force set out to examine current job grading and evaluation practices in the company. A point factor system, backed by thousands of job descriptions, had been in place for years. It soon became clear that the existing system clashed with emerging values of participative involvement and teamwork. Combining salary ranges—and generally rebracketing the existing structure into broader bands of pay ranges—presented an obvious solution. Along the way, Pratt & Whitney reduced its number of salary levels from eleven to six and cut the number of job descriptions by more than half, from three thousand to several hundred.

Timeliness of Rewards. To succeed at reinforcing desired values and behaviors in the new order, rewards must be paid out on a timely basis. Many compensation consultants suggest setting easy targets for the first year of profit sharing and other newly instituted reward programs to ensure that employees see that they receive some gain from it. Similarly, a special three- or six-month performance review may be established rather than have employees wait for the more typical twelve-month review (or, as is the case in a growing number of organizations, an eighteen-month review), to begin rewards for contributing to the new order. A medical center, moving to limit merit pay increases severely in its new order, structured one-time-only incentives to occur in a relatively brief cycle to begin reinforcing the link between performance and reward.

Consistency and Fairness. At the consulting firm that preached but did not reinforce the gospel of cross-selling, junior partners initially were confused by the inconsistency between leaders' words and their actions. Despite what seemed like a lot of energy being put into memos and pep talks to extol the virtues of cross-selling, they saw how senior consultants managing the largest accounts defied the office head and shielded their clients from penetration from other practice areas, yet still continued to receive excellent bonuses and perks. This inconsistency not only shut down any hopes of cross-selling in the office, it created a level of cynicism that hindered the introduction of other initiatives. Within a year, a total quality management program fell flat on its face despite being introduced amidst much hoopla and fanfare.

The link between performance and reward must be established as early and as firmly as possible in the new order. While there may be exceptions to every rule, they send inadvertent messages to people who read between the lines to draw conclusions about who gets treated "more fairly" than others or about what behaviors are most valued. Moreover, people make judgments about their own compensation in part based on how they perceive others to be treated. The fat payouts of golden parachutes and silver handcuffs during the 1980s, as well as of the enormous compensation packages awarded to senior executives in even the poorest-performing companies in the 1990s, have led to a demand for more equity in the workplace. People are willing to make a sacrifice if they see that all around them are doing the same. If funds are available for bonuses and other rewards, people want a piece of the action, too. At PepsiCo, a stock option plan called SharePower includes virtually all full-time employees and some who work part-time, from senior managers to Frito-Lay truck drivers. The company stock has more than doubled since the program began, and people are starting to realize significant value from the program.

Issues of attractiveness, influentialness, timeliness, and fairness are not novel concepts in the design of reward systems. They are, however, especially instrumental in clarifying and reinforcing desired behaviors following transition.

Benefits

Employee benefits programs are being stretched in many ways, even outside the context of organizational transition. Wholesale changes in national health care policy, shifting responsibilities for individuals to provide for their own retirement funding and planning, and changing demographic and social pressures are among the factors straining the ability of benefits programs to cull a balance between cost containment and responsiveness to employee needs and desires. Yet benefits programs also have a role to play in contributing to organizational recovery after transition. Together with compensation, benefits contribute to the total remuneration that employees receive in exchange for their contributions to the workplace; thus they can exert leverage on employee perceptions and behaviors in the new organizational order.

Evidence for the increasing significance of employee benefits programs come from a survey of executives in three hundred U.S. companies. As Exhibit 10.1 displays, over two-thirds of the companies expect that retirement programs will be important or extremely important to retaining employees in the year 2000, up from about one-half of the companies reporting so today. Dramatic increases are also predicted for the future significance of some nontraditional objectives of retirement plans: offering employees more choices, shifting financial responsibility to employees, accommodating work force mobility, and encouraging phased retirement.

The 1980s witnessed major changes in employee benefits planning and administration. Some were proactive efforts to contain costs and remain competitive relative to other firms, such as adoptions of flexible group benefits plans (sometimes called "cafeteria plans" for their feature of letting employees choose the type and amount of benefits they desire) and shifts from defined benefit to

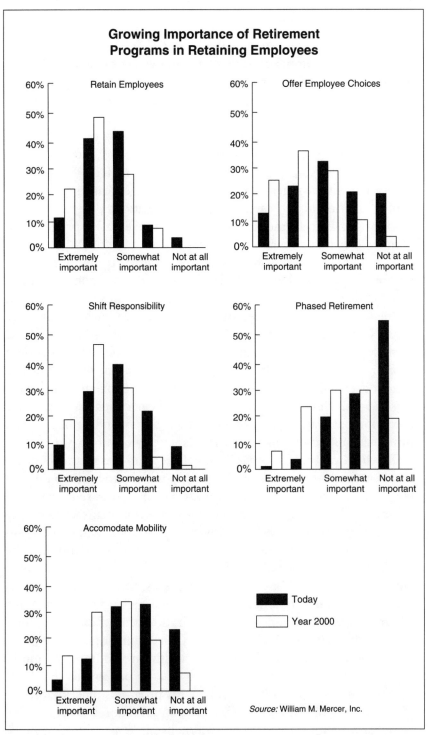

Growing Importance of Retirement Programs in Retaining Employees

Retain Employees

Offer Employee Choices

Shift Responsibility

Phased Retirement

Accomodate Mobility

■ Today

□ Year 2000

Source: William M. Mercer, Inc.

EXHIBIT 10.1

defined contribution retirement plans. Other changes were reactions to organizational MADness, including the calculation of voluntary severance and early retirement programs to facilitate headcount reductions in downsizings and restructurings and the move from paternalism to partnership in making decisions about benefits options to mirror the changing psychological work contract and to handle the increased mobility of employees across companies. Already, the 1990s are contributing their own roster of major employee benefits changes. These include managed care programs to contain soaring health care costs, retiree relations programs to extend assistance to former employees, and preventative programs to curtail worker's compensation claims.

The changing work force also is contributing to the tumultuous nature of employee benefits today. Some of these changes are measured in demographic terms. For example, more than 60 percent of women with children under six years of age are in the labor force today, compared to just over 10 percent in 1950—this is but one factor contributing to the growing need for affordable dependent care programs. Other changes are gauged in social terms, like the greater acceptance of nonmarried couples living together, including gay and lesbian couples. Employers like Levi Strauss, MCA, Lotus Development, and the city of Santa Cruz are extending health care insurance and other benefits to domestic partners of employees.

The implications for organizational recovery are relatively clearcut. Benefits programs are one more opportunity to back up the language of the new order with action. If the new order reflects broader social changes in the psychological work contract and the mobility of people across employers, then modifications or additions to benefits plans introduced after a transition should give the employee more responsibility for choice and management and provide for more portability across workplaces. Offering more choice and customization in benefits packages is a highly salient tactic for documenting a new and better organization after transition. Building on the practice of flexible benefits plans, some firms are allowing employees covered by their partner's health care insurance at another employer to choose another benefit or even opt for a cash rebate.

Providing increased choice in benefits programs places more responsibility in the hands of employees, an act that reinforces cultural transformations away from paternalism. As part of its culture change effort, J. P. Morgan & Company made some clear changes in its benefits package reflecting both a need to keep its own costs in check and a recognition that people are more frequently changing employers and want a "portable" retirement fund through which they can take an active role in determining their financial future. Specifically, in the retirement area, Morgan decided to stop being a sole provider of benefits and asked people to start sharing responsibility. A recently introduced 401(k) plan, for example, allows employees to add their own money to supplement what the company provides through its pension plan. In its profit sharing program, the company is becoming more of a facilitator in ways like lessening the amount of time employees have to wait between switching investments among funds from quarterly to monthly, and adding two additional investment funds, bringing the total to eight.

A few organizations are starting to treat benefits like compensation and link company payments to employee performance. NACCO Industries, a Cleveland-based holding company for a conglomerate of operations ranging from fork-lift truck production to kitchenware retailing, has adopted a "benefits-for-performance" concept. A portion of the firm's contributions to 401(k) retirement plans varies based on business results.

What exacerbates the difficulty of modifying employee benefits plans during organizational recovery are the many and varied pressures that, in relative terms, are shrinking the size of the pie from which employers serve up their benefits. Rising health care costs, exorbitant worker's compensation claims, the increasing longevity of retiree populations, and underestimated costs of early retirement programs are among the factors constraining what can be provided to today's work force. Employers may justifiably feel they are giving their people a fair, perhaps even generous, slice of the pie, yet employees only see it as less filling and less appetizing compared to what they have been fed. Years of paternalistic protection from their employers have resulted in an employee mind-set that views benefits as entitlements rather than earned rewards. With changes in the relationship between employer and employee and increasing pressures for cost containment in organizations, part of building a new order is to recast the role of employee benefits programs and remold employees' perceptions and expectations accordingly. As with any organizational change, the rationale underlying any additions to, eliminations from, and modifications to the employee benefits program must be communicated in a complete and timely manner. Employees are especially impressionable after a transition, and are prone to overinterpret events. In cases when incomplete information is provided about the benefits program changes, it is inevitable that the conclusions employees draw will be less favorable than organization's intentions.

Benefits Strategy at Bank of America

Bank of America is facing up to the reality of being in an industry that is expected to consolidate from more than 12,000 banks in the U.S. in the 1990s to around 7,000 in the first decade of the twenty-first century. Its regulatory environment continues to change, enhancing its product base and blurring distinctions between banks and other financial services institutions like insurance companies and stock brokerage firms. Moreover, like firms in any industry, it is grappling with soaring employee benefits costs. Norm Snell, senior vice president of benefits at Bank of America, used the period immediately after the bank's acquisition of Security Pacific to develop a benefits strategy that balanced a set of competing objectives:

- *Reinforce business strategies* by focusing on the customer (employees), minimizing benefits expense and its future growth, and anticipating changes in the work force.
- *Create value* by listening to the diversity of employees, monitoring changing demographics, managing employee expectations, and creating greater awareness of the value provided.
- *Provide flexibility* through greater employee responsibility and participation, added communication, recognizing life-style differences and emerging shifts, and enhanced visibility and portability.
- *Enhance cost-effectiveness* by realizing economies of scale, standardizing systems and plan administration, evaluating health care hot spots and emerging abuses, and establishing partnerships and performance expectations with vendors.

This benefits strategy has proven successful by providing a constant philosophical orientation amid much turbulence, translating into meaningful business and benefits objectives, and managing employee expectations about the future role of benefits in their total remuneration. It also has produced a series of tactical steps that have reinforced the message of greater employee responsibility in benefits decisions. One featured a series of publications addressing matters ranging from determining financial goals and estate planning to projecting net worth and insurance needs.

"We swept away the rules," recalled Snell. "The transition is subtle, but it's there. We told people, `Here is the job that needs to get done, you figure out how to do it best'." Among the enhancements implemented by employees were flex time in scheduling work hours and self-directed training. Other changes reinforcing employee responsibility in benefits choices included broad-based financial planning and widened selection of flexible benefits options.

Flexible Work Schedules

Many firms, in addition to Bank of America, are extending more flexibility in scheduling work as a way of reinforcing new orders while contending with both employee needs and competitive pressures. Hit by the recession and squeezed margins in its worldwide computer market, the French subsidiary of the American computer manufacturer Hewlett-Packard faced the alternatives of additional layoffs or a sweeping redesign of working schedules. The choice put to employees at Hewlett-Packard's microcomputer components plant was simple: either change working habits or the company would relocate to Singapore and all jobs would be lost. The result was an entirely revised work structure that has tripled production at the plant. Instead of the previous five days, no employee works more than four days a week; but the plant runs twenty-four hours a day. Employees gain more options in scheduling their work shifts and enjoy three days a week off, while the increased number of shifts means more employment and heightened efficiency in operating the plant.

The four-day workweek has sparked a national debate in France regarding proponents' claims that it would slash unemployment, improve life outside of work, and bring new hope to a disenchanted society. Increased flexibility in work scheduling has already taken hold in Germany and other western European countries. Automakers Volkswagen and BMW have introduced four-day workweeks to keep more employees on the payroll in a manner that allows individuals to work less but more flexibly, and that enables machinery to operate for longer periods. Although wages are unchanged in the shift from a five- to a four-day workweek, productivity gains more than offset the cost of keeping more people employed in the new order.

Communication

A new order—and with it, new and better ways of approaching work—cannot be built without the exchange of accurate, timely, and complete information. Employees will not know how to align their tasks with where leadership wants to take the organization unless they understand what that vision is and what the guidelines are for their expected behavior on the job. Teams will not be able to coordinate and convey knowledge within and across their boundaries unless information flows freely in multiple directions. And organizations will not receive valid and reliable feedback about critical internal and external matters unless a climate is established that invites input in a relatively uninhibited and uncensored manner.

Communicating to revitalize after transition, however, is much more than conveying information. It is a yardstick by which the predominating values and behaviors of the truly emerging organizational order—as opposed to what is being espoused—are measured. The content and frequency of communication vehicles, for example, indicate the degree of trust and concern between parties that prevails in the new order. The accuracy and genuineness of communications measure the extent to which spirit, teamwork, and effectiveness have developed. And the proactiveness and multidirectional nature of communications gauge commitment and consideration to and from employees in the organization. The impact of communication on revitalizing an organization cannot be overstated: open communication topped the list of reasons given by a national sample of 3,000 wage and salaried workers for deciding to take their current job.

As is clear from earlier sections of this book, communications is important at all times in organizational life. There are, however, some particular benefits of effective communication during post-transition recovery and revitalization:

- Giving people the information they need to do their job well, to contribute to both personal and organizational success
- Providing the information needed to unleash the creativity of individuals and teams as they devise new and better ways to approach work
- Accelerating learning by disseminating the results of experimentation in various parts of the organization
- Helping team leaders establish their positions and coordinate their teams' activities with organizational vision and business unit mission
- Bringing issues out into the open and to the attention of those who can respond to them before they mushroom into major problems and contribute to a downward spiral in effectiveness and morale
- Providing feedback up the organization
- Signaling respect for all individuals in the organization, no matter where they are in the hierarchy
- Celebrating small and large successes

General rules of effective organizational communication apply during recovery: explain the rationale underlying decisions, repeat the same or similar messages through multiple media, recognize that people prefer face-to-face communication from their immediate superiors, check to ensure that the message sent was the message heard, and accept that not communicating has negative rather than neutral effects. Communicating to revitalize, however, does pose some special needs and opportunities.

Reactive Versus Proactive Communication

Sharing information has traditionally followed the need-to-know philosophy in most organizations. Management shares only enough information with employees to enable them to do a specific job, and then only at a time when it is "safe" to reveal the information. The messages being sent by managers who communicate in this way are that employees would not understand more information, that employees cannot be trusted with sensitive data, and that people are not being productive when time is spent on communication, so why bother?

If these messages are congruent with the values underlying the new order, then managers need not bother to bolster their communication efforts. But if the new order calls for a more respectful, trusting, and open relationship across levels, then managers at all levels must become aware of the inadvertent messages that standard communication practices send. Moreover, what managers continually fail to consider is how much time is being wasted in their organizations on second-guessing other people's intentions because they have not built effective lines of communication or how much time and effort is lost because of gamesmanship, politics, and maneuvering.

Trust is rebuilt following transition by communicating honestly the facts about the organization, its actions, and its points of view. This must include problems and controversies as well as attributes and achievements. Open and honest communication helps people gain a feeling of personal control—something they have sorely missed during transition. One major multinational corporation installed a toll-free telephone number so the media could have daily recorded update of company news. Much to their surprise, company executives discovered that most of the calls were from their own managers, who wanted to know what was going on in the corporation.

Revitalizing communication during recovery takes more than simply committing to telling the same story in more and different ways. Rather, it requires a commitment to assessing and understanding the fundamental role of communication within an organization. This, in turn requires an understanding of the communication needs of the intended audience. Researcher Michael Cooper, working with several years of survey data, concluded that if management is going to address the communication needs of the employee audience, it can only understand those needs by understanding the values that shape them.[2] Then it must identify and talk about the organizational issues that most closely match employers' needs. And in the process it must identify, define, and articulate those issues that are the product of management's own perspective from the top of the organization. But for successful communication to happen, such issues must be tempered with and couched in terms that are important to the employee audience.

Typically, organizational communication has worked in the opposite direction: what Roger D'Aprix, while manager of employee communication at Xerox Corporation, tagged the "reactive communication process." Organizational communicators—staff specialists or line managers—react to events inside or outside the company and report the facts with little or no attempt to shape them to address employees' needs. Perhaps slick publications are produced or visual media are used, but as D'Aprix notes, they report positions and responses in reactions to events. They represent the apologies for what went wrong, or are the elaborated defenses for what a company had or had not done. With employees this kind of reactive communication has led to an assumption that all an organization needed was a good media program so management could tell its side of the story. That's a telling phrase—"its side of the story"—clearly suggesting an adversary relationship and a defense of management actions.[3]

There are several limitations of reactive communication. It focuses on *what* happened, not the *why* underlying it. Consider a fairly typical communication to employees describing a reorganization of top management in an organization following a period of disappointing financial results:

To: Acme Corporation Northeast U.S. Region employees
Fr: Luke Tobias, Region Head
Re: New Management Structure

As you know, weak economies in many of the countries in which we conduct business have placed downward pressure on the demand for our services. While your management continues to believe that our reputation and services are among the best in our industry, our company's operating results have failed to achieve levels consistent with our budgeted expectations.

As a result, Acme's Board of Directors met last Friday and has announced the following changes in management structure, effective immediately:

1. To enhance efficiency and ensure greater responsiveness to our customers, we will consolidate from our current structure of eight regional operating groups to five. The new regional operating

groups are: Eastern U.S., Western U.S., Canada/Mexico/Latin America, Europe, and Asia/Pacific.

2. Arie Bernard will move from his current position of Chief Operating Officer of Worldwide Operations to the newly created position of Executive Vice President, Client Relations for the Europe region.

3. Jessie Burns, our CEO, will assume the former responsibilities of Mr. Bernard. He will become directly responsible for Acme's worldwide operations. The five Regional Directors (to be announced shortly) will report directly to Mr. Burns. Together they will constitute the Management Committee for our company.

I know this has been an extremely difficult time for all of our employees. The Board of Directors joins me is the belief that these changes should help our company return to expected levels of performance. Your continued hard work and contribution to Acme are appreciated.

In most organizations it is not difficult to find out what happened, but it is difficult to find out why something happened. This leaves people to speculate on the event's cause and significance. Acme Corporation's reactive communication reported what was happening but made no mention of why these particular courses of action were selected. Nor did it consider employees' issues related to major transition, such as needing to know how they might be affected by change, wanting to feel part of the team, and caring about the plight of coworkers. This reactive communication resulted in more questions than answers for employees: What is really underlying Acme's poor financial performance? Was the problem Mr. Bernard's fault? Is his transfer a punishment? What does an executive vice president of client relations do, anyway? Why are we going from eight to five operating regions? Wouldn't a larger number of regions mean we could stay closer to our customers? What is going to happen to people whose jobs are affected by the reorganization—will three region heads be out of a job now? What about their secretaries and other regional support staff like controllers and human resources professionals?

The reactive communication process depends on people's ability to figure out reasons and management motivations by starting at the event itself and reasoning back from that event. This is difficult to do because employees do not have access to all the facts and because business events generally have complex causes. The grapevine, however, spreads an overly simplistic explanation that may fit the incomplete data at hand but is likely to be inconsistent with true underlying causes or management's intentions. At Acme, the top management team actually had considered many alternatives to the restructuring and was moving ahead in a careful manner rather than adopting a crisis mode. Employees had no insight into these actions, though, as all they heard through the grapevine was how Pierre Bernard was being put out to pasture and being paid a handsome salary to jet around the Continent and take customers out to lunch at fancy restaurants. Ironically, Acme's management was proactive in thinking about how to handle changing business fortunes, but not in its communication with employees. It could have alerted employees early on to the looming financial situation and addressed employees' needs to know that leadership had a handle on the situation and to feel involved. Instead, Acme's reactive communication style contributed to the growth of cynicism, anger, and worry within its work force.

Finally, the reactive process makes communication an organizational stepchild. Management do the best they can with an air of cynical resignation, believing that people will believe the worst anyway; worse yet, they wash their hands of the process and delegate the responsibility to a staff specialist or an external consultant. This never works, because the communicator cannot be a proxy for the management. The result is an impression created among employees that organizational life is chaotic, unplanned, and unmanaged. That may have been true during the transition, but to maintain this approach to communicating during recovery reinforces a climate of uncertainty, distrust, and despair—which are unlikely to be desired qualities of the new order.

The antidote to the reactive communication process, according to D'Aprix, is a proactive process of *issues communication*: identifying, defining, and articulating the major issues that the organization must address if it is to be successful. D'Aprix defines an issue as "any major concern that is likely to have a significant effect on the organization's ability to achieve its goals and whose outcome is in doubt."[4] Employees want to know early in the life of the issue, not when it has fixed its grip on the organization and is threatening to do it serious harm.

Exhibit 10.2 outlines the proactive communication process. It begins by honestly and thoroughly assessing where the organization is today, developing assumptions about the probable effects of good communication practice in the organization (understanding why time and resources are being invested in the communications process and what returns are expected), developing program and content strategies, and evaluating the effectiveness of the process.

The proactive communication process offers some important advantages over the reactive process during recovery. First, it tends to identify the organization's concerns and priorities and to indicate what management intends to do about them. This is reassuring to employees, who otherwise will become anxious if they do not hear

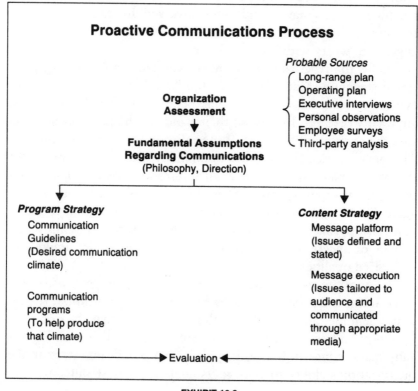

EXHIBIT 10.2

the organization's problems—which they experience on a day-to-day basis—discussed and possible solutions considered. Second, it focuses on the significance of events rather than their mere occurrence. Third, the proactive communication process provides a frame of reference within which particular events may be placed and explained ("Yes, this may be a setback, but it is no disaster. Remember we told you that we anticipated one of the toughest issues confronting us this year would be . . ."). A fourth advantage of the process is that it can be used to foreshadow subsequent change and provide justification for the change. Organizations in recovery may have to take actions that look poorly conceived when viewed in isolation. But when explained in the broader context of where the organization is headed and why, they can begin to make very good sense. Fifth, proactive communication pressures leaders to match their words with actions, as changes made are linked to previously discussed issues. Finally, proactive communication encourages hope and optimism among employees who understand and see more fully where their organization is headed, why it is going in that direction, and how it will get there.

Leadership must set the tone of communications during recovery. Their hands-on involvement demonstrates that keeping employees in the know and keeping in touch with employees' issues are important components of the new order. Managers and supervisors must play an active role in the communication process also, to ensure that messages are heard and to reinforce the role of communications in the new order. To reinforce its stated values of "honesty and integrity in the way we communicate," "properly motivating professionally minded people," and "respect for each other," one organization committed to the most comprehensive employee communications program ever attempted in the company as part of reinforcing its new order. As Exhibit 10.3 shows, the program spreads the communication responsibility across all levels of the organization.

What to Communicate During Recovery

The proactive communication process highlights particular issues that the organization must address if it is to be successful. In addition to these issues are a set of content areas that must be commu-

---

Key Components of Communication Plan

CEO	Periodic videos and newsletters
	Quarterly business result reports to employees
Management committee	Quarterly vision implementation reports
Division/department leaders	Quarterly business results reports to employees
	Periodic videos and newsletters
All managers and supervisors	Attendance in communication skills workshops
	Regularly scheduled staff meetings
	Impromptu one-on-one meetings and management by walking around
Corporate communications	Monthly employee magazine
	Monthly question-and-answer packets and other materials to help managers and supervisors communicate
All employees	Participation in selected upward communications opportunities

EXHIBIT 10.3

---

nicated in revitalizing after transition. Exhibit 10.4 lists general areas of information that people want to know during recovery. Many of these areas, like communication of vision and mission, have already been discussed, but some warrant fuller attention.

Make People Aware of the Organization's Goals. An important step in helping employees understand what is happening around them is to make them fully aware of what the new organization expects to accomplish.[5] This includes not only the reasons for an action, but also the specific results the organization expects. For example: "We eliminated layers to push decision making closer to the customer. Account representatives now have authority to grant discounts of up to 20 percent on customer orders without needing management approval. Here is how criteria for granting a discount should be set. . ."

Additionally, people are more willing to accept what they perceive as immediate injustices in the building of the new order if

What People Want to Know During Recovery

What is our organization's vision?

What is our business area's mission?

What factors are most important to our future success?

What are our major initiatives this year?

What do we expect to accomplish?

What changes are planned or being considered and why?

How do I best align my behavior on the job with organizational and area objectives?

What personal opportunities exist today?

What are the new realities about career advancement and development?

How does someone get ahead here?

What is going on in other parts of the organization that matters to my job?

How will our industry change over the next five years, and how will our company respond to those changes?

Who are our competitors, and how do we differ from them?

What are our performance results?

EXHIBIT 10.4

they can see an action will contribute to long-term benefits for themselves and others. The communication goal is to provide employees with a sense of how the organization's vision and guidelines eventually will lead to a more equitable situation for themselves and their coworkers. Moreover, knowing the organization's plan helps restore levels of personal security.

Make Certain That People Recognize New Opportunities. Paths toward success as demarcated in the old organizational order are gone, and many transition survivors falsely conclude that there are no new opportunities at hand.[6] In reality, the new order may provide many opportunities (along with other positive changes), but these may be quite different from those that existed previously. Therefore the organization's responsibility is to make explicit the opportunities in the posttransition organization. They may range from improvements in getting work accomplished on a day-to-day basis to methods for enhancing one's career prospects over the long haul. And the rewards provided to people for adopting desired new behaviors must be publicized. People learn a lot simply by watching the outcome of others' behavior; if they know that others have been rewarded for taking the steps necessary to live the vision or otherwise contributing to the new order, they are encouraged to do so themselves.

Make Clear What Is and Is Not Known. Even as the new organizational order is being built, employees often assume that leadership really knows more than it is saying. As a result, managers should communicate what they know and be clear about what they do not know. Acknowledging areas of uncertain or incomplete information staves off employee suspicions that important matters are being withheld from them. Obviously there will be some information that is too sensitive to communicate on a general basis through the organization; having established a norm of communicating on a full and timely basis, however, will enhance employee tolerance for these situations.

Communicating the New Organizational Order

Beyond merely imparting information, communication patterns and norms powerfully establish and reinforce the essence of the new organizational order. The act of communicating sends a series of messages over and above the content of what is being conveyed.

Changing Employee Expectations. Employees' perspectives of organizational life must be recalibrated during recovery. This ranges from standards of what defines right and wrong in the organization to expectations of fair and equitable treatment. Explanations of new realities within the organization help here, but so do comparisons with other organizations in similar or even less positive situations.

Communicating Bad News. Communication consultant Dennis Ackley notes that organizations show their real values when they communicate bad news.[7] Not communicating is not a choice; if there is bad news it will find its way into the work force, generally in a form worse than reality. Think that communicating takes too much time? Add up all the hours employees spend standing around the water cooler or coffee machine, gossiping on the phone, and stopping in the hallway to pass on the latest rumor. Executives and managers have a choice: control the formal communication channel, or rely on the inevitably more dubious informal channels.

Proper planning prevents poor performance when communicating during recovery. Good planning cannot occur at the last minute. Organizations that are good at communicating even the worst of news have contingency plans ready if they are needed. These plans include prototypes for direct communication with employees, along with timelines and materials to ensure that supervisors and managers have the information they need to reinforce the proper messages to be sent to the work force.

Facilitating Multidirectional Communication. Calls for better communication between levels or teams in the new order need to be backed up with some actions that break traditional barriers. Some organizations get key middle managers talking to one another at periodic meetings that create opportunities for peers to exchange information on business challenges, operational results, and successful adoptions of new operating procedures. In addition to helping managers learn what is happening in other parts of the organization, these meetings raise opportunities for coordination and cooperation across previously entrenched teams.

Many organizations work hard to enhance upward communication during recovery. In some cases, executives rely on informal ways of keeping in touch with people's feelings. They spend unstructured time with employees, individually or in groups, to hear their views on the new order and the extent to which it is being realized. At first the executive may have to reveal his or her own feelings to encourage employees to do the same. A sincere concern for the employee point of view will be reciprocated with an increased regard for the welfare of the organization.

Other organizations use more formal methods for upward communication. Employee attitude surveys are excellent vehicles for involving most or all employees in two-way communication. Nucor Steel conducts an all-employee survey every two years, asking workers what they think of newly emerging programs and policies. Chemical Bank surveys a sample of employees every quarter, with a focus on employees' feelings and needs regarding what they need at that point in time to best contribute to organizational results. The survey findings are reviewed by Chemical's top-level management committee, and then managers receive specific results for their work areas to use for action planning.

It may take some time for communication behaviors to catch up with the vision of the new order. Barriers built up through years of constrictive communication in the old organizational order do not come tumbling down overnight. Employees may be shy about revealing their true feelings, and managers may be cautious about exposing to peers what is really happening in their work areas. And poor communication during transition mismanagement may have residual effects on the sharing of information in the posttransition organization. To revitalize communication effectiveness in their organization, leaders in recovering organizations must offer more than just lip service. They must model open, timely, and complete communication, and they must reward it when they see others doing the same.

Clarifying the New Psychological Work Contract. When the psychological work contract between employer and employee is revised as part of building a new organization order, careful and comprehensive communications are required to ensure that employees hear how the relationship is changing and why. This makes a big difference between realizing a new organizational order by design rather than by default, and contributes to values and operating principles that are lived up to rather than merely spoken about.

Concurrent with its change in business strategy, J. P. Morgan & Company is acting in both explicit and implicit ways to signal to employees the inevitability of changing from a paternalistic culture to one in which more obligation is entrusted to employees. One of the most direct ways in which Morgan is reinforcing new mental models is through a comprehensive program to inform employees about not only what changes are happening but also to let people know *why* these changes are necessary given current and emerging business conditions and *how* they are contributing to a new psychological relationship between the firm and its employees. One especially straight forward and comprehensive communications piece, entitled "Mutual Commitment: Guiding Principles of the Relationship Between Morgan and You," describes business changes in the company and relates them to the employer/employee relationship. The brochure states not only the firm's obligation in upholding the new psychological work contract but also the employee's (see Exhibit 10.5). Importantly, it also states what has not changed in the relationship between Morgan and its people.

Sample Pages from J.P. Morgan's Booklet Clarifying the New Psychological Work Contract

Development Helping all our people realize their full potential is critical to our success.

The firm expects you to:

Take the initiative in your own professional development.

Make learning a part of your job.

Take more responsibility for developing other people as your level of experience increases.

You can expect the firm to:

Provide opportunities for training and development.

Promote from within the firm when possible.

Encourage and reward coaching and mentoring.

Require managers to provide constructive feedback and development plans for their staff.

Seek to stretch the abilities of a diverse range of people in filling challenging assignments.

Merit We believe in a meritocracy where the best people and ideas are recognized and rewarded.

The firm expects you to:

Improve and expend your professional skills to keep pace with the demands of the business.

Meet higher standards of performance as your career progresses.

Contribute more to the firm as your level of experience increases.

You can expect the firm to:

Provide frequent, objective performance measurement and feedback.

Develop and communicate criteria for advancement.

Recognize that time alone does not equal value, and that qualilty and efficiency are the best measures of achievement.

Reward excellence with development opportunities, advancement, and compensation in ways that clearly reflect accomplishment.

Treat fairly those who do not keep pace with the demands of the firm, helping whenever possible with training or transition to employment elsewhere.

EXHIBIT 10.5

Training and Development

Training and development budgets and opportunities have been ravaged during the years of organizational MADness. While Japanese and European firms spend 4 percent to 6 percent of expenses on training their workers, U.S. companies are investing only 1.5 percent of payroll costs on improving employee skills, according to the American Society for Training and Development.[8] As a result, just one out of every fourteen employees has received any formal training from his or her employer. One manager put it in these terms: "We haven't had a training course other than CPR in three years."

Training

A revitalized organization requires a work force that has the training to do their jobs well. In addition to overcoming the bumps and bruises of years of transition, organizations are contending with demographic and social dynamics that exacerbate the need for effective training. For example, aging baby boomers, who are likely to dominate the labor force well into the next century (nearly two-thirds of the workers who will be in the labor force in the year 2005 already are on the job), need to update their knowledge and skills. And an increasing number of entry-level employees do not have even the most rudimentary skills. Nearly four in ten members of the National Association of Manufacturers say that deficiencies in math, reading, and technical skills are causing serious problems in upgrading factories and increasing productivity.

Many organizations are learning from the MADness and realizing that recovery cannot occur solely—or even primarily—on the basis of cutting away at head count and other expenses; rather, they must build their productive capacity. Says Labor Secretary Robert Reich, "American companies have got to be urged to treat their workers as assets to be developed, rather than as costs to be cut."[9] As competitive pressures and customer demands increase, new orders are likely to recognize the need for flexible, responsive delivery of products and services in the global economy, and only highly skilled and well-trained employees can quickly master these challenging new processes.

Training during recovery provides some essential benefits for both organizations and their members. First, it helps the organization bolster prevailing perceptions of the link between effort and performance. An organization may have identified attractive rewards and have every intention of paying off for a job well done, but employees who feel they do not have the information or skills necessary to get the job done will only grow increasingly demotivated. Second, skills training provides knowledge and tools to help people align their work with the new order and organizational objectives. Third, awareness training conditions people for ongoing change and disruption in their work settings; organizations need to develop a work force that can change several times, not just once. Like never before, individuals today share the responsibility—and the rewards—for acquiring new skills and capabilities. Lifelong learning increasingly will be the rule, not the exception for employees. People who have training and experience in a variety of areas will be all the more valuable to current or alternative employers. And those who can document transition management skills, team building behaviors, and other process skills acquired during recovery will distinguish themselves from competing job candidates with similar technical or professional backgrounds. Finally, training regenerates a quality hit hard by years of organizational MADness: it raises people's self-esteem and self-confidence by equipping them with the skills and ideas to contend with new organizational realities.

Training for Results. Of course, training will only help the organization or employees if it is effective. There is not enough time, money, or energy in organizations to go around to support unproductive training programs. Four questions to be asked when designing a training program help produce desired results.

1. What business problems are we trying to solve? All training efforts should be rooted in the needs and strategy of the organization. If training is not linked to the challenges confronting the organization or to its goals, participants will see it as virtually useless. The starting point is to conduct a needs assessment, integrating both senior management and employee input regarding training needs and requirements. The executive perspective ensures that organizational needs are being met, while the employee perspective ensures that training offerings address their specific needs. If training participants sense a disjunction between course content and life in the new order, they will become cynical about the course.

2. What specific changes do we want to see? The purpose of training is to support revitalization, and revitalization requires focus. Training programs that try to accomplish too many changes typically fall short. Thinking through desired outcomes raises the question of what can be realistically expected from classroom training.

3. How will classroom learning be continued on the job? Classroom activities are valuable in understanding the need for new behaviors, and in teaching a modicum of skills, but true behavior change (whether attitude- or skill-related) requires on-the-job practice and support. Integrating real time applications into program design and planning follow-up activities are the keys to transferring classroom learning. In one organization, implementation of knowledge learned in a training program was linked to established milestones for the yearly budget planning cycle.

4. How will senior management support the effort? To be successful, training programs must have the clear support of senior management. They must play a role every step of the way. Up front, senior managers have to promote the value of the programs and make clear that attendance is expected. During the session, their delivery of a module or availability for an informal question and answer session demonstrates their commitment to achieving the objective at hand. Afterward, senior managers can request updates on implementation of skills and concepts learned, as well as ongoing documentation of results. Senior managers who make training an important personal priority will generate the same regard for it through the ranks.

Training content. While the training curricula must be grounded in the organization's business needs and strategy and derived from needs assessments conducted with executives and employees, some oversight is required by training professionals to ensure that training courses continually prepare people for their roles in the new order. Employees' job skills must be expanded to include not only the basic work tasks but also the analyzing and problem-solving skills necessary to change the way in which organizational work is performed. This contributes to an ongoing learning capacity that enables the organization and its people to respond to changing demands.

Exhibit 10.6 shows the results of a needs analysis conducted by training professionals in a large telecommunications firm. The company had made several acquisitions and went through a series of restructurings before the chairman articulated his vision for a revitalized organization. Most prominent in the new order was enhanced communication and cooperation within and across work teams in anticipating key business problems and generating creative solutions. Through interviews, focus groups, and assessment center–type simulations, training professional derived the core list of training subjects and integrated them into course offerings. These programs were complemented by courses addressing specific technical needs in the firm.

Training Subjects in Large Telecommunications Firm

Team building/team dynamics

Problem-solving skills

Total quality/continuous improvement

Interpersonal skills

Leadership skills

Adjustment to new role

Communication skills

Company culture

Facilitation skills

Self-managed work teams

Values

Giving and receiving feedback

Coaching skills

EXHIBIT 10.6

Another firm used training in quite a different way to reinforce its new order. Following the adoption of a new vision and values statement, the CEO asked internal training specialists and an external consultant to design a training program that would help people understand how to put the values into action. The workshop was built around a series of vignettes describing common decision-making situations confronting middle managers and supervisors in the organization. One vignette centered around a potential conflict between work and family life; another raised the issue of ethics and integrity. Groups of managers and supervisors attending the workshop offered their personal reactions to the cases and then discussed similarities and differences among each other's approaches to handling the difficult situation. Using the statement of company values as a template, a final discussion centered on what the "company way" was for handling managerial and supervisory issues in the workplace. Evaluations from workshop attendees noted how the session helped "the words of the values statement jump off the pages and into action" and "let me know where my behavior and style fits with what is expected of a manager here and where it doesn't."

Leadership Development

Organizational revitalization is aided by a far-reaching review of the way in which executives and managers are selected, promoted, rewarded, and developed. The management development systems of most organizations created managers who fit well with the old organizational order. Factors that contributed to managerial success in the past, though, are likely not do so in the future. Thus the skills and capabilities needed to manage and lead through recovery and beyond need to be determined. Then people having such competence must be recruited or people capable of developing along those lines must be reoriented. Training and other educational interventions contribute here, but the most potent factor in the development of effective leaders is the nature of their job experiences. Preparing people to lead a recovery may mean rethinking the type of experience needed; that is, considering situations and problems faced by managers in the past rather than just the functions and disciplines they have managed.

The best way to develop the kind of leaders a recovering organization needs is to make leadership—as distinct from management—an important criterion for promotion, then manage people's careers to develop it. This will take time and may not immediately benefit organizational recovery, but it will contribute to longer-term adaptability during ensuing cycles of transition. Moreover, it is another way in which people observe the development of a new and better organization. Michael Beer reports that best-practice companies move managers from job to job and from area to area based on their learning needs, not their position in the hierarchy. Successful leaders are assigned to units that are targeted for change. People who need to develop their leadership skills are moved into model units where those skills are demanded and therefore learned.[10]

Leaders capable of succeeding in recovering organizations must have greater awareness of their own strengths and development needs, as well as of their career aspirations and how these can be fulfilled. One multinational firm launched a process of "personal development plans" to support a new order moving toward partnership and away from paternalism. The process, which was made available to all managers and launched initially with a "high-potential" group, began with a workshop consisting of two modules. The first was designed to increase self-awareness through 360-degree feedback from superior, peers, and subordinates and from the Myers-Briggs personality type assessment. The second module placed the individual's development needs in the context of the company's leadership development systems. The outcome of the workshop was a personal development plan that was checked by senior executives and used as a key document in the company's leadership development system.

Organization Development

Rebuilding organizational effectiveness requires that barriers to performance be identified and removed and that work groups develop self-sufficiency in managing future hurdles. This performance-related development relies on a group diagnosis and unifying goals. The assistance of an internal organization development (OD) specialist or an external organization development professional helps a group first to assess, analyze, prioritize, and confront the truly important issues affecting its performance, and second to develop and integrate the capacity for doing so on its own. Work units, especially those led by managers with little or no experience in the organizational development process, need assistance in identifying proficient practitioners and thinking through the appropriate chemistry between consultant and client. The client determines whether he or she can relate well with the consultant, whether the consultant's previous experience is applicable to the current situation, and whether the consultant is competent and can be trusted. Concurrently, the consultant assesses whether he or she can relate well to the client, whether the motivation and values of the client are likely to contribute to a positive working relationship, and whether the client has the readiness and resources necessary for change.

If both parties are satisfied, they make a "contract" establishing mutual expectations for the relationship. In practically all cases, the consultant's work will begin with some form of diagnosis to understand the situation and players more fully. The collection and analysis of information necessary for the diagnosis may be facilitated by other revitalization efforts, such as data from employee attitude surveys or findings from team building sessions. Still, the OD specialist must collect valid information, feed it back to the client, and proceed in planning, implementing, and evaluating change.

In addition to helping a work unit improve its performance, organization development tactics can be useful for addressing a particularly sensitive aspect of organizational life after transition: intergroup relations. Transition puts tremendous strain on interdepartmental relations in organizations. Teams reacting to reduced head count, new operating procedures and systems, or changing mandates typically put a higher priority on their internal needs than on providing assistance to other units. Delivering less timely or lower quality work, or not performing those duties at all, adds to the posttransition strain experienced in other departments. And the lack of support comes at a time when they are least able to recoup due to their own internal limitations. A chain reaction of negative reciprocity may begin interdepartmental war.

Organizational development practitioners Kimberly Buch and Jack Aldridge have adapted the role negotiation technique, originally designed to help clarify individual group member's roles, to aid in enhancing intergroup relations.[11] The technique begins with a meeting attended by managers from all affected departments. The manager of the focal department begins the session by sharing his or her interpretation of the department's revised role, focusing on how it has changed in the new order, its rationale for existence, and its redefined functions and responsibilities. The OD consultant lists these on a flipchart and encourages the group to amend and clarify the list until a consensus is reached. The next step examines the focal department's expectations of other departments present. Next, managers from these departments describe what the focal department can do to facilitate their performance. The consensual results of these steps are added to the flipchart notes, which are used after the meeting by managers in the focal department to develop a focal role profile. This role profile is reviewed at a second intergroup meeting before beginning the entire process again with another department assuming the focal role. Meetings continue until each participating department has an opportunity to serve as focal role.

The Human Resources Department in the New Organizational Order

In most organizations, responsibility for compensation, benefits, communication, and training and development is "owned" by the human resources department. This provides a front stage position for the HR team to show its stuff in rebuilding after transition, but it also puts pressure on the department (which may be struggling with its own need to revitalize) to respond to broader organizational needs in a manner that is simultaneously creative and practical.

With some notable exceptions, HR managers historically have played out their role by reacting to operating managers' requests rather than generating new ideas and working with others to solve organizational problems. HR managers traditionally have been trained to listen and respond; as such, they have avoided proactive, innovative behavior. Their deftness in dealing with organizational issues is restricted by being in a function fraught with such administrative paperwork as maintaining personnel records, coordinating performance appraisals, and conducting job analyses—paperwork that increases during and after transition as transfers, early retirees, and the like have to be processed while budgets and staffing decrease. Many HR professionals fixate on their non-revenue-producing status. In most organizations, they are not seen by operations managers as adding much value; even in times of recovery, HR professionals are paralyzed by the fear that their position may be cut. Their response is to lay low and hope that "out of sight" means "out of mind." Rather than display and promote their value, HR managers have for the most part stepped to the back of the stage during times of transition and recovery.

The new organizational order brings with it the possibility of a rebirth for the HR function and in particular, how it is marketed to and perceived by operating managers. Because HR managers are involved with virtually every organizational unit, they bring a broad perspective to building the new order and can serve as catalysts for positive change across traditional boundaries. And because the potential customers of their services—line managers—have such a tremendous need for advice and assistance in revitalizing their operations, HR managers have an opportunity to add important value to organizational recovery and concurrently to enhance their own function's capabilities and status.

In reality the HR function is likely to have made a positive contribution during the transition process in such ways as accomplishing downsizing objectives while minimizing the company's exposure to litigation. But because of their traditionally reactive posture, HR professionals have waited for their customers (management) to request their involvement before responding to the situation. In the new order, the HR function has the opportunity to market itself and what it can do proactively. This is accomplished best by meeting with managers, understanding their needs, and proposing appropriate interventions. The HR function may have a job to do in raising awareness among managers about how human resources programs and processes can be used to find or develop employees that fit managers' needs in the new order. In either case, it implies the development of a new partnership between human resources and line management.

This partnership, according to consultant Peter Block, develops by focusing on an educational role and giving line managers the right to define their own ground rules for operating and the responsibility to assess their needs and control their relationships with

HR.[12] This is in direct contrast to the controlling style of many staff groups in organizations. Often during transition and recovery, HR managers place their needs above those of their customers, such as when they block access to external consultants in hopes of generating more dependence on internal resources. The outcome, however, usually is counterproductive: the exclusion of the HR department from issue identification and problem solving, meaning that either the human resources perspective is totally eliminated up front or sought by line managers from anywhere but the internal HR function. If instead the HR professional acts in a way that places the managers' needs ahead of his or her own agenda, that professional is likely to be brought into the inner circle of decision making.

HR practitioners must also become more proactive in suggesting innovative ways to revitalize their organization after transition. This occurred in the U.S. Department of Education where, after four years of budget and staff cuts mandated to trim the federal bureaucracy, a conscious effort was made to add new blood at entry levels in the organization. Terry Newell and Ron Redfoot of the department's training office raised three issues: encouraging talented people to pursue a career in an organization known to be cutting back, inspiring new employees to be creative and take initiative in their jobs when so many around them suffered from low morale, and running a strong orientation program when the training staff had been cut in half over the past four years.

Training managers conceived a two-part strategy to address these impediments to organizational revitalization. First, the training office decided to provide a support system for the new hires. The "welcome aboard" one-day orientation approach simply was not enough to keep the morale and enthusiasm of the new employees high, given the frustrations they would run into in a large bureaucracy under stress. Second, the training managers realized they had to get others to do a lot of the work of the orientation program; their own staff were already too small and too overloaded.

The support system strategy integrated each new hire into a web of people networks. First, each new hire's supervisor was a key support person. The supervisors came to a training session before the new hires arrived where they were asked to recall their own entry into the agency, what helped, and what was frustrating. Each supervisor developed a written action plan covering the new employee's first thirty days, addressing the physical environment (furniture, supplies, and the like), social environment (getting to know coworkers and integrating into the work team), and work environment (explaining office goals and giving the new hire something substantive and meaningful to do on his or her first day of employment). Second, a personnel team (composed of a training specialist, a personnel staffing specialist who hired the new employee, and a career counselor) met with the new hire on a regular basis to help solve problems and keep morale up. Third, a key person from each unit into which a new hire was placed met to review program progress and get the attention of senior managers to unblock organizationwide hindrances to frustrations that may have been building on the job. Fourth, new hires attended monthly training sessions to learn more about the agency.

Lacking the bodies to pull off the project, the training staff turned to the only logical choice left—the new hires themselves. They were told it was up to them to identify the topics and sponsor most of their monthly training sessions and that they would have to create any special programs. Training staff would provide logistical support to clear channels for higher-level approvals, and offer technical support to enhance program presentation. Having local ownership over the project, new employees generated a wealth of ideas and training opportunities, including a visit to Capitol Hill to learn about congress' view of the department, the preparation of a catalogue of the various software applications throughout the department, and a tutoring program in local schools to learn firsthand about today's educational challenges.

While these efforts helped the training office accomplish its goals without weighing it down with additional workload, the most profound benefits were for the new employees themselves. They built networks with each other and within their work teams, gained visibility in the department and learned techniques normally taught at the middle-management level in the agency. And the new hires were seen—and saw themselves—as highly professional and involved in meaningful work. For the Department of Education, the results included lower turnover (the turnover rate for the first "class" to participate in this program was 9.4 percent, well below the department's historical rate of 13 percent, and not a single new hire from the second "class" left the agency), lower training costs (with interns doing much of the work themselves, their salaries were lower than those of staff trainers), increased quantity of training, and the development and frequent use of new training products (such as orientation manuals and the software catalogue).

Of course, there was some downside to the program, too. Many veteran employees demanded to know why they could not have their own orientation sessions as well. They argued that orientation is an ongoing need, not just one for new hires; they were right, but the training office simply did not have the staff. And there were substantial time pressures put on new hires, who still had to meet the needs of their full-time jobs in addition to contributing to the orientation program. Still, the orientation program succeeded beyond anyone's expectations in meeting its twin strategic objectives: developing a strong support system, and involving new employees in designing their own training. Moreover, the program contributed further to revitalization by increasing the training staffs' own energy levels and belief that they could make a difference in the new order.

Refreezing Desired Change

Articulating and building a new order is no easy task. Especially in 1990s environment of ongoing change and multiple waves of transition, it is common for inadvertent messages to be sent to a work force starved for clues about their evolving work situation. Organizations must go out of their way to ensure that systems like compensation, benefits, communication, and training and development reinforce efforts to revitalize employee spirit and team performance. This means understanding employees' needs and issues, thinking through the organization's intended messages, and carefully anticipating and contending with any gaps between the two.

Tremendous patience is needed to recover from transition and revitalize human spirit and team performance. People will not accept the new until they let go of the old. This means they need time not only to pass through denial, anger, and other reactions to loss, but also to move along phases of trying to keep a grip on and letting go of the old order. It is here that the organization can clarify the direction and guidelines for the new order, create a context for recovery within which employees can experiment with new approaches to work and learn new mental models of what breeds success, and revitalize individuals, teams, and systems to sustain desired change. This presents a rare opportunity, after people have been unfrozen by the turmoil of transition, to cast a new mold and refreeze attitudes and behaviors congruent with a new way of doing things. Either leaders will invest the time, energy, and other resources to reinforce their desired organizational order or they will resign themselves to take whatever may come their way as a result of inadvertently reinforced messages (or, perhaps worse, they will continue to be burdened by the perceptions and actions that predominated in the old order and are unlikely to help the organization respond to new challenges).

Building a new order is a lot to ask of a senior executive cadre who themselves have lived through the turmoil of transition—anxious times bred on worst-case fears and apocalyptic rumors; the lessened capacity to act; the loss of identity with the old organization and the loss of connection with mentors, colleagues, and friends; not being able to depend on peers or subordinates; and persisting questions of "What am I doing here?" and "Is it worth it to stay?" If they themselves have triumphed over the turmoil, senior executives still have to work at enlisting the hearts and minds of their employees to take advantage of emerging opportunities as the economy strengthens. They must help people recover from the turmoil of transition, then revitalize their troops' self-confidence and motivation to triumph in their charge up the hill to capture the prize that awaits.

Conclusion

The rapid pace and massive scope of transitions in contemporary organizations—often coming in overlapping, multiple waves—along with the enduring impact of organizational MADness preclude prescriptions for when recovery and revitalization should be initiated. In some organizations, the best timing comes following a major transition that stands out from others in terms of its pervasiveness or intensity. In others, recovery may be indicated when the saturation effect has resulted in a listless work force, unable or unwilling to garner the physical or psychological energy necessary to make a run at business opportunities. In still others, there simply comes a time when the CEO, business unit leader, or other senior executives become so frustrated with the lack of employee responsiveness to renewed business opportunities that they throw up their arms and accept that recovery is essential to meet current or future organizational goals. One point is certain, though: recovery, revitalization, and the building of a new organizational order are most likely to succeed when people remain at least somewhat unfrozen following the turmoil of transition. Employees' mental models, aligned with the old organizational order, have been confronted and begun to break down, but they have yet to be replaced by new ones built upon the perceptions and experiences of life after transitions.

The Critical Period for Organizational Recovery

This relatively unfrozen state provides a tremendous opportunity for impression management with employees, comparable to the critical period for the imprinting of baby ducklings in psychologist

Conrad Lorenz's famous studies. Lorenz found that at a certain time in their development, ducklings would psychologically attach themselves to and follow whatever large figure was in their midst. If no impression was made during the critical period, the ducklings wandered aimlessly, never able to make a psychological connection in their later years.

Mature employees are substantially more cognitive than baby ducklings. Yet they have their own critical period after a transition when their attitudes and behaviors are unfrozen and subject to change. This is a finite interval in which people will settle down into and rely upon new assumptions, perceptions, and behaviors that are reinforced by design or by default during and after the transition. Once this critical period for psychological attachment to the new organizational order passes, then the only hope for recapturing employment commitment and directing their behavior in line with new business objectives is to repeat the whole process of unfreezing, changing, and refreezing. Inevitably, breaking down the old diverts much more time, energy, and resources away from core business operations than do recovery and revitalization.

The implications of this critical period for winning over employee commitment following a transition became clear in a manufacturing firm that was acquired, reorganized, and assigned new leadership within a two-year time frame. Before and after the transition events, the company's management placed a high priority on combining a genuine regard for employee work life quality with the pursuit of business results. During the two years of transition, however, senior management turned its attention toward managing relations with the new owners. In their hearts and minds, the manufacturing firm's leaders still had a strong regard for and concern about their work force. Their actions, however, sent quite a different message to employees.

One manifestation of the company's concern about employee relations was the sponsorship of an all-employee attitude survey every two years—a practice continued during and after the flurry of transition activity. Survey results following the transition period revealed significant drops in employee perceptions of their working life. The findings made a dramatic impact on senior leaders, who owned up to the fact that their efforts to manage upward had detracted from their ability to manage downward. They set out to re-build relations with employees and reestablish their commitment to providing an excellent work environment.

Subsequent survey measures showed that these efforts paid off; employee perceptions of work life rebounded. But while overall employee satisfaction levels rose significantly, they failed to reach the peaks experienced prior to the transition period. Deeper analysis showed that veteran employees who were socialized in the company prior to the transition madness actually returned to their pretransition levels of satisfaction. Those who entered the company during the two years of transition turbulence, however, consistently expressed lower ratings of satisfaction than employees who joined the organization before or after them. This trend continued into the next survey period: the critical period for winning over these people's psychological attachment to their work place had been lost.

On a broader level, the critical period for recovering from the organizational MADness of the late 1980s and 1990s is upon us. There is no doubt that the old order characterized by paternalistic cultures, womb-to-tomb employment relationships, and pre-dictable upward mobility and base pay increases is over. Senior executives let go of these assumptions some time ago. Only more recently have employees at middle and lower levels begun to loosen their grip on these old expectations. And while senior executives have had a nice vantage point to see transitions coming and a position from which to exert control over them, employees at other levels learned about the changing psychological work contract the hard way. Employees had few if any ways to control these changes.

What has especially hurt workers during the years of MADness is that their leaders did not warn them that this powerful locomotive of change was speeding down the tracks and heading their way. Many saw former coworkers who did not have the deftness to jump out of the way become casualties; and others who managed to survive but received the fright of their lives. No one argues against the essentiality of the train coming down the tracks, yet the angst and anger remains over why people were not prepared for what came their way.

Commitment to Recovery

Programs do not change people, the psychological commitment to making things better does. A person who decides to overcome an addiction may take some course of action like checking into a hospital-based recovery program. The truly significant factor here is the decision to change and not the program itself. Individuals do not let go of their addictions and accept new patterns of thinking and behaving because of being exposed to some technique or activity; rather, they psychologically commit to changing their life situation and stick to it.

The same holds true for the organization attempting to recover from the transition MADness. Recovery will succeed only when people, usually at the senior levels initially, accept the unintended consequences of organizational transition and commit to the need to revitalize individual spirit, team performance, and organizational systems. Certain steps help along the way—facilitating letting go, articulating a new organizational order, creating a context for change, living the vision, team building, and reinforcing desired behaviors prominent among them—but it is the recognition of the need to rebound from the crippling effects of transition and of the opportunity to build a new and better organization that make recovery possible.

This implies a recognition that people saturated with the unintended consequences of transition are not able to capture current or imminent opportunities. Programs such as total quality management, reengineering, or empowerment, no matter how well conceived and implemented, will continue to be rejected by employees who are unable to accept a new way of doing things before letting go of the old. Nor can quick fixes be layered over the experiences of individuals who have been through round after round of wrenching change.

The commitment to building a new organizational order must be deep and strong enough to withstand tremendous counterforces from within the organization (such as lingering distrust, prevailing politics, and scrambling work teams reeling from the effects of reduced head counts), as well as from outside the organization (like ever-increasing global competition and changing social and demographic realities). Just like the addict who does not make a real commitment to kick his or her habit, organizations making only halfhearted efforts at rebuilding after transition invariably will fall short.

Recovery cannot be rushed. It took years for the old organizational order to be established, and it will take time to break down antiquated mental models, facilitate letting go, contend with hang time, convey the new organizational order, prepare a context for recovery, live the vision, and validate new mental models. Only a persistent emphasis on desired attitudes and behaviors will ensure rebounds in employee well-being and organizational performance in a recovering and revitalized organization.

Recovery cannot underestimate the consequences of transition. The years of organizational MADness fostered a dramatic and crippling impact on the American work force. People are pessimistic about their personal ability to act and control their fate. They are suspicious of leadership's motives and cynical about the efficacy of organizational endeavors, and they are more cautious and risk averse than ever. These qualities and the detrimental attitudes, maladaptive behaviors, disappointing performances, and other unintended consequences of transition run directly counter to organizational needs to contend with increasingly complex and rapidly changing competitive challenges. The starting point for a recovery effort is to dissipate and recoup from the negative forces; any effort that ignores the need to let go of the old before building the new is doomed to failure.

Recovery is not a one-dimensional answer to organizational woes. Recovery is one step in an effort to revitalize after transition. It must be coupled with a genuine effort to build a new organizational order. The contours of the new order may draw from concepts and practices like fast cycle time, business process reengineering, or self-managed work teams. The *content* of the new organizational order must be articulated along with the *process* of building it.

Recovery is not linear. The work of building a new organizational order may be interrupted by a necessary wave of downsizing, an unexpected acquisition opportunity, or the discovery and application of a new technological breakthrough. In any of these situations, the natural tendency is to regress to primitive and counterproductive behaviors. Confusion, stress, politics, and the many other unintended consequences of organizational MADness will rev up the forces against positive change. People must be prepared for these occasional steps backward and come to accept them as part of the "new status quo" rather than as signs of failure. Indeed, when they occur after being predicted by a leader, they contribute to rebuilding trust and faith in the organization.

Alternatively, the commitment to recovery and revitalization can pay off through a number of important outcomes that simultaneously contribute to rebuilding after transition and preparing for future competitive challenges. These outcomes include the following:

Establishing a new working relationship. The new organizational order is an opportunity to make a fundamental change in the way in which the organization relates to its human resources. This means listening to, and empathizing with the employee perspective on change and transition rather than denying or ignoring it. It is an acknowledgment that the past was painful and sometimes mismanaged, but that the time has come to establish a new relationship between employer and employee based on mutual respect and trust. Even though that partnership may be more temporary and tenuous than in years gone by, it nonetheless remains the basis for the joining together of the brass and the troops in pursuit of mutual objectives.

Letting go of the old. Freeing people to look ahead and get ready to charge up the hill requires that one leave behind the psychological baggage still being carried from the days of transition. Organizational recovery facilitates the letting go of outdated expectations, maladaptive behaviors, and the many other impediments to personal and organizational success. It breaks down mental models associated with the old organizational order so that new ones can be developed. And it contributes to a healing of the emotional wounds inflicted during transition, eventually leading to a revitalized work force.

Clarifying the new psychological work contract. Part of establishing a new working relationship is to own up to and clearly present the changing psychological work contract between employer and employee. Organizational recovery does not and cannot mean a return to the good old days of job security, regular raises in base pay or advances up the corporate ladder, and employer responsibility for training and development. The best that can be done is to convene a dialogue on how and why the work contract is changing, and what is expected from both parties going forward. Clarifying the new psychological work contract acknowledges change, establishes mutual expectations between employer and employee, and prepares people for the future ride.

Joining people together in a common pursuit for success. While norms of womb-to-tomb employment relationships may be waning, many people still will spend several years with one employer. And the basic concept of organization implies bringing people together and coordinating their efforts toward the pursuit of a shared goal. The organizational recovery process bonds together people who have gone through a painful and unsettling experience and aligns their vision and work behaviors toward a common end.

Inspiring excitement at the workplace. Recovery also rebuilds excitement in the organization and develops a can-do attitude in meeting short-term objectives and long-term challenges. Employee spirit may have been knocked down during years of MADness, but it has not been knocked out. People still want to be on a winning team, to know their efforts are making a difference, and to be part of something special. Today's workers are not lazy, but they have been lulled into a semicomatose state of not being able to control their work life. Organizational recovery is a rallying point to revive and restore what is inherent in the employee population.

Restoring the individual capacity to act. Building a new organizational order goes beyond slogans and plaques to put actions and commitments behind promises of a new and better organization. Revitalization produces true empowerment of employees by giving them the information they need to align their work behaviors with overall organizational objectives and by providing them with the skills and resources needed to get their jobs done in a way that is congruent with the new organizational order. It also provides empathy and emotional support for a group of people who have survived painful transitions. Both the "hard" information and skills and the "soft" empathy and social support are essential ingredients for rebuilding self-esteem and a sense of self-control, precursors to restoring individual capacity to act.

Enhancing organizational competitiveness. Enhanced individual capacity to act in turn results in an organization better able to sense and respond to intensifying competitive challenges. Increased experimentation and learning, abandoned obsolete ways of doing things in favor of new and better methods, heightened sharing of business information, and other fruits of recovery and revitalization contribute to an organization that, in addition to having shed the unintended consequences of transition, emerges as a stronger competitor.

In addition to rebuilding one organization at a time, recovery and revitalization provide an opportunity to reformulate the norms and expectations of what it means to work in a large organization in the coming century. Layoffs, increased use of temporary or contract employees, reductions in benefits, and a host of other actions have eroded the psychological bond between employer and employee. A work force with one eye watching out for the next swoop of the layoff ax or looking back in anger for past injustices is not going to be focused on enhancing organizational performance and achieving organizational goals. A new meaning of what the organization and the worker are willing to commit to one another needs to be specified and mutually accepted if the potential opportunities in an economic recovery are to be realized. Organizational leaders cannot expect to charge up the hill and capture business opportunities with a bunch of out-for-themselves mercenaries or with a raggedly equipped, poorly trained, and undermotivated outfit. Sustained success will depend on developing a ready-to-act core of committed troops.

This implies a tremendous opportunity for corporate executives—along with work team leaders, human resources professionals, and others who have or create the ability to act—to become social engineers by designing new molds for the mental models that contribute to new perceptions and expectations of what it means to be an employee. We all know what the MADness of the 1980s and 1990s has done to people, organizations, and the relationship between them. We know better than to let the pain and other unintended consequences linger and become, by default, the template for behavior in organizations. We can do better than this and must do better if we are going to raise productivity, improve quality, boost customer satisfaction, and do all the other things required to keep up with and pull ahead of increasing global competition. A new human spirit and sense of organizational achievement are possible, however, only through the acknowledgment and working through of where we have been.

Once the economic recovery is in full swing, it will be too late to begin thinking about recovery after transition. By the time it takes to let go of the old, articulate the new, and get people to live that vision, a competitor will have charged up the hill and grabbed whatever prize was in sight. This will not only result in an immediate setback, it will also contribute to recurring patterns of disappointment in both human and economic terms. In contrast, the organization that is thinking today about what it needs to be building to gain a competitive advantage for the future will be ready with a committed, excited, and motivated work force ready to charge up hill after hill in pursuit of mutually rewarding victories.

Notes

Chapter 1

1. Survey released by Robert Half International, New York, September 9, 1991.
2. Mitchell Lee Marks, "Downsizing and Restructuring," in Philip H. Mirvis (ed.), *Building a Competitive Workforce*, New York: John Wiley & Sons, 1993. The study, sponsored by the Commonwealth Fund, assessed the priorities and practices of U.S. companies in keeping pace with changes in the marketplace, work force, and society.
3. "1992 AMA Survey on Downsizing and Assistance to Displaced Workers," New York: American Management Association, 1992.
4. Robert Reich, *The Next American Frontier*, New York: Penguin, 1983, p. 241.
5. "Morale Crisis," *Fortune*, November 18, 1991, pp. 70–80.

Chapter 2

1. Kurt Lewin, "Frontiers in Group Dynamics," *Human Relations* 1 (1947), pp. 5–41.
2. David A. Nadler Marc S. Gerstein. Robert B. Shaw, and Associates, *Organizational Architecture*. San Francisco: Jossey-Bass Publishers, 1992.
3. Quoted in Walter Kiechel III, "When Management Regresses," *Fortune*, March 9, 1992, p. 157.
4. In general, empirical support for expectancy theory is quite strong. It is highly predictive of behavior of groups in general but does have limitations in terms of applicability to different types of people. Individuals for whom the theory is most predictive have an internal, as opposed to external, locus of control. For individuals who are motivated more by unconscious motives than conscious processes, the theory does not work well. Despite these problems, expectancy theory is one of the dominant motivation theories in industrial/organizational psychology today. Probably no other theory has received the consistent support or has the generalizability of expectancy theory. For a full discussion, see L. W. Porter and E. E. Lawler, *Managerial Attitudes and Performance*, Homewood, IL: Richard D. Irwin, 1968.

5. Edward E. Lawler III, "Strategic Choices for Changing Organizations," in Allan M. Mohrman et al. (eds.), *Large-Scale Organizational Change*, San Francisco: Jossey-Bass, 1989.

Chapter 3

1. See Joel Brockner, "The effects of work layoff on survivors: Research, theory, and practice, in B. M. Staw and L. L. Cummings (Eds.), *Research in Organizational Behavior* (Vol. 10, pp. 213–256), Greenwich, CT: JAI Press, 1989; and Leonard Greenhalph, "Maintaining Organizational Effectiveness During Organizational Retrenchment," *Journal of Applied Behavioral Science* 19 (1989), pp. 155–170.
2. Gantz-Wiley Research Consulting Group national survey of 2,500 households, 1991.
3. Don A. Kanter and Philip H. Mirvis, *The Cynical Americans,* San Francisco: Jossey-Bass, 1989.
4. Anne B. Fisher, "CEOs Think That Morale Is Dandy," *Fortune*, November 18, 1991, pp. 83-84.
5. Brockner, op. cit.
6. Mitchell Lee Marks, "The Disappearing Company Man," *Psychology Today,* September 1988, pp. 34–39.
7. Susan Dentzer, Why Workers Have Little to Cheer," *U. S. News & World Report*, August 17, 1992, p. 26.
8. Quoted in Larry Reynolds, "America's Work Ethic: Lost in Turbulent Times?" *Management Review*, October 1992, pp. 20–25.
9. "Economy Creates More Stress," *Fortune*, October 5, 1992, pp. 11–12.
10. See M. Lubatkin, "Mergers and the Performance of the Acquiring Firm," *Academy of Management Review* 8 (1983), pp. 218–225; and "Merger Strategies and Stockholder Value," *Strategic Management Journal* 8 (1987), pp. 39–53; C.C. Mueller, "Mergers and Market Share," *Review of Economics and Statistics* 67 (1985), 250–257, pp.; A. Michel and I. Shaked, "Evaluating Merger Performance," *California Management Review* 27 (no. 3; 1985), pp. 109–118.
11. Cited in Harry Gaines, "Put High Priority on Job Satisfaction," *Executive Excellence*, January 1993, pp. 8–9.
12. "A Study of Worker Compensation Costs in Companies following Downsizing," New York: William M. Mercer, Inc., 1992.
13. "Industry Report 1992," *Training*, October, 1992, pp. 25–28.
14. Marc J. Wallace, "Rewards and Renewal: Competitive Advantage Through Work Force Effectiveness," presentation to American Compensation Association, August 24, 1992, Boston.
15. R. D. Laing, *The Divided Self,* London: Pelican Books, 1965, pp. 78–79.

Chapter 4

1. Study by the American Quality Foundation and Ernst & Young, 1992.
2. See, for example, Philip H. Mirvis and Mitchell Lee Marks, *Managing the Merger: Making it Work*, Englewood Cliffs, NJ: Prentice Hall, 1992; and Robert M. Tomasko, *Downsizing*, New York: Amacom, 1987.
3. Philip Mirvis and I presented this research at the 91st annual convention of the American Psychological Association in Anaheim, 1983, in a talk on "Situational and Personal Factors Influencing Employee Response to Corporate Merger." It was reported in Mitchell Lee Marks, "Organizational and Individual Response to Corporate Acquisition Impact," *Dissertation Abstracts International*, 42:9B (University Microfilms No. 82-4708).
4. Joel Brockner, "Managing the Effects of Layoffs on Survivors," *California Management Review* 34 (no. 2, Winter 1992), pp. 9–28.
5. Ibid., p. 12.
6. Irving L. Janis, *Psychological Stress*, New York: John Wiley & Sons, 1958.

Chapter 5

1. Elisabeth Kubler-Ross, *On Death and Dying*, New York: Macmillan, 1969.
2. Philip H. Mirvis and Mitchell Lee Marks, "Merger Syndrome: Management by Crisis." *Mergers & Acquisitions*, January/February 1986, pp. 65–84.
3. Robert Tannenbaum and Robert W. Hanna, "Holding On, Letting Go, and Moving On: Understanding a Neglected Perspective on Change," *Human Systems Development*, 1985, p. 99.
4. Ibid., p. 117.

Chapter 6

1. William Bridges, *Managing Transitions,* Reading, MA: Addison Wesley, 1991.
2. Anthony F. Buono and Aaron J. Nurick, "Intervening in the Middle: Coping Strategies in Mergers and Acquisitions," *Human Resources Planning*, 15 (2), pp. 19–27.

Chapter 7

1. Michael Beer, Russell A. Eisenstat, and Bert Spector, "Why Change Programs Don't Produce Change," *Harvard Business Review*, November–December 1990, pp. 158–166.
2. M. A. Carre and P. M. Bouvard, "The Courtship and Honeymoon of Successful Mergers," *European Business*, 25 (1970), pp. 36–43.
3. See, for example, Warren Bennis and Burt Nanus, *Leaders: Strategies for Taking Charge*, New York: Harper & Row, 1985; Noel Tichy and Maryanne Devanna, *The Transformational Leader*, New York: Wiley, 1986; and David

Nadler and Michael Tushman, "Beyond the Charismatic Leader: Leadership and Organizational Change," *California Management Review*, Winter 1990, pp. 77–97.

4. W. Steven Brown, "Cutting the strings," *Executive Excellence*, March 1993, pp. 8–9.
5. Beer, Eisenstat, and Spector, op. cit., p. 159.
6. Nadler and Tushman, op. cit., p. 90.
7. Carol Berrey, Amy Klausner, and Darlene Russ-Eft, *Highly Responsive Teams: The Key to Competitive Advantage*, San Jose, CA: Zenger Miller, 1992.

Chapter 8

1. Douglas Lavin, "Robert Eaton Thinks "Vision" Is Overrated and He's Not Alone," *Wall Street Journal*, October 4, 1993.
2. Quoted in Charles Baden-Fuller and John M. Stopford, *Rejuvenating the Mature Business*, London: Routledge, 1992, p. 169.
3. Research conducted by Scott Myers at Texas Instruments forms the basis for these needs, as reported in "Who Are You Motivated Workers?", *Harvard Business Review*, 42 (no. 1, January–February 1964), pp. 73–88.
4. These interviews were conducted between 1990 and 1993 as part of ongoing interventions to assist in the organizational recovery process after transition. The ten organizations varied widely in size—from 100 to 45,000 employees—but tended to be skewed toward large organizations. Three of the organizations were from the financial services industry, two were in computer or computer peripheral manufacturing, and one each were in the health care, entertainment, consumer products, low-technology manufacturing, software publishing, and government industry sectors. The large majority of interviews were conducted with middle- and upper-level managers, although non-managerial employees were interviewed at four of the sites. Eight of the organizations were U.S. based, with one based in Europe and the other in Japan.
5. Dennis Ackley, "The Secret of Communicating Bad News to Employees, *Communication World*, August 1992, pp. 27–29.

Chapter 9

1. James S. House, *Work Stress and Social Support*, Reading, MA: Addison-Wesley, 1981.
2. See, for example, Douglas McGregor, *The Professional Manager*, New York: McGraw-Hill, 1967.
3. Richard S. Wellins, "Building a Self-Directed Work Team," *Training & Development*, December 1992, pp. 24–28.
4. Lee G. Bolman and Terrence E. Deal, "What Makes a Team Work?" *Organizational Dynamics*, pp. 34–44.

5. Jon R. Katzenbach and Douglas K. Smith, *The Wisdom of Teams,* Cambridge, MA: Harvard Business School Press, 1992.

6. Bolman and Deal, op. cit., p. 41.

7. The concepts in this section were developed in collaboration with Philip Mirvis and are reported in Mitchell Lee Marks and Philip H. Mirvis, "Rebuilding After the Merger: Dealing with Survivor Sickness," *Organizational Dynamics*, pp. 18–32; and Philip H. Mirvis and Mitchell Lee Marks, *Managing the Merger*, New York: Prentice Hall, 1992.

8. Roger Harrison, "Role Negotiation: A Tough-Minded Approach to Team Development," in W. Warner Burke and Harvey A. Hornstein (eds.), *The Social Technology of Organizational Development*, La Jolla, CA: University Associates, 1972.

9. Edward L. Harrison, "The Impact of Employee Involvement on Supervisors," *National Productivity Review*, Autumn 1992, pp. 447–452.

10. Chester C. Borucki and Philippe Byosiere, "Transforming U. S. Corporations to Enhance Global Competitiveness: Implications for Middle Management Roles and Responsibilities," paper presented at the 12th Annual International Conference of the Strategic Management Society, London, October 1992.

Chapter 10

1. Robert P. Gandossy, "It's the Process, Not the Design: The Move to Nontraditional Rewards," *HR Horizons*, Autumn 1992, pp. 49–53.

2. M. R. Cooper, B. S. Morgan, P. M. Foley, and L. B. Kaplan, "Changing Employee Values: Deepening Discontent?" *Harvard Business Review*, January–February 1979, pp. 124–125.

3. Roger D'Aprix, *Communicating for Productivity*, New York: Harper Collins, 1982, p. 43.

4. Ibid. p. 51.

5. Dan Rice and Craig Dreilinger, "After the Downsizing," *Training & Development*, May 1991, pp. 41–44.

6. Joel Brockner, "Managing the Effects of Layoffs on Survivors," *California Management Review* 34 (no. 2, Winter 1992), pp. 9–28.

7. Dennis Ackley, "The Secret of Communicating Bad News to Employees," *Communication World*, August 1992, pp. 27–29.

8. Janice Castro, "Where Did the Gung-Ho Go?" *Time*, September 11, 1989.

9. Quoted in Ronald Henkoff, "Companies That Train Best," *Fortune*, March 22, 1993, p. 62.

10. Michael Beer, Russell A. Eisenstat, and Bert Spector, "Why Change Programs Don't Produce Change," *Harvard Business Review*, November–December, 1990.

11. Kimberly Buch and Jack Aldridge, "O.D. Under Conditions of Organizational Decline," *Organization Development Journal*, Spring 1991, pp. 1–5.

12. Peter Block, "Empowerment Means Reform," *Executive Excellence*, March 1993, p. 11.

Index